Couscous
and Other Good Food from
Morocco

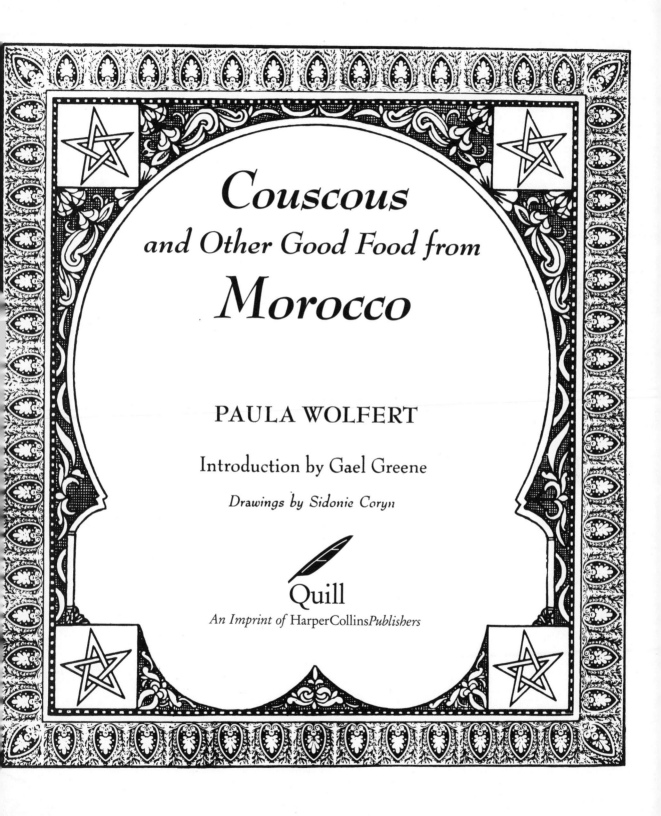

Couscous
and Other Good Food from
Morocco

PAULA WOLFERT

Introduction by Gael Greene

Drawings by Sidonie Coryn

Quill
An Imprint of HarperCollinsPublishers

To Bill Bayer

Black-and-white photographs facing page 1 and on pages 16, 48, 56, 64, 130, 166, 184, 230 and 324 by Andrée Abecassis.

Photo page 290 by Charlotte Thorp.

Map by Jean Paul Tremblay

A hardcover edition of this book was published in 1973 by Harper & Row, Publishers, Inc.

COUSCOUS AND OTHER GOOD FOOD FROM MOROCCO. Copyright © 1973 by Paula Wolfert. All rights reserved. Printed in the United States of America. No part of this book may be used or reproduced in any manner whatsoever without written permission except in the case of brief quotations embodied in critical articles and reviews. For information address HarperCollins Publishers Inc., 10 East 53rd Street, New York, NY 10022.

HarperCollins books may be purchased for educational, business, or sales promotional use. For information please write: Special Markets Department, HarperCollins Publishers Inc., 10 East 53rd Street, New York, NY 10022.

First PERENNIAL LIBRARY edition published 1987.

Reprinted in Quill 2001.

Designed by Gloria Adelson

Library of Congress Cataloging-in-Publication Data

Wolfert, Paula
   Couscous and other good food from Morocco.

   "Perennial Library."
   Bibliography: p.
   Includes index.
   1. Cookery—Moroccan.   I. Title.
TX725.M8W64   1987   641.5'964   72-9165
ISBN 0-06-091396-7 (pbk.)

10 11 12 FOLIO/RRD 30 29 28 27

Contents

Illustrations

Introduction

The Paula Wolfert I know is an adventuress, a sensualist, a perfectionist cook, a highwire kitchen improvisationalist. And this book is the story of her love affair with Morocco. Her passion is contagious. All the senses come alive, intoxicated by her evocations of cinnamon, garlic and mint . . . stirred by the promised taste of herb butter and saffron-sparked broth and by blurred fantasies of ritual Moorish feasts and the turmoil of the walled *medina*.

There are not too many otherwise sane and civilized humans capable of tears for a too salty green sauce, rage at a soggy noodle, ecstasy in a chocolate truffle. But Paula Wolfert is. And I am. We are soul sisters.

We met, of course . . . where else? . . . in Tangier. Two wandering American provincials meeting inevitably in the 007, pitch-dark, deserted discotheque on a narrow Moroccan street. We spoke only briefly. In those few minutes I learned we were both students of the late great kitchen genie, Dione Lucas. Paula had been Dione's apprentice for a year and made the ultimate sacrifice . . . her gall bladder.

Two years later Paula Wolfert was in New York. One heard reports of her extraordinary couscous. And rumors about her Moroccan cookbook-in-work. We shopped together. Now . . . Paula Wolfert in action is not gentle. She moves through the greengrocer's like an avenging demon. To Paula, an overage string bean is an outrage. A mushy tomato is a personal attack. The merchant of such shabby provisions gets withering scorn and muttered insults. Before her contempt, even tyrant greengrocers cringed.

I am invited to taste. Do I bring flowers? Wine? Bonbons? No, I bring *cilantro* (green coriander) because fresh *cilantro* is the badge of our friendship. (She can't buy it in her neighborhood. I can. A friend would not cross town without *cilantro*.) Paula opens the door, a chicken nestled in one hand. Toasting almonds perfume the air. The apartment is cluttered with the gleanings of her Moroccan adventures: rugs and hassocks and samovar and earthenware *tagines*. And books, a shelf of classics, five of gastronomic texts. The kitchen is tiny, cramped, a treasury of mysterious herbs and powders and lemons pickling in their brine. And there is Paula cursing her recalcitrant oven thermometer, ripping chickens apart with bare hands, smearing and sprinkling and jabbing . . . trying by sheer force of will to coax a cloak of egg to hug the back of a baked bird.

And now proud bird to table . . . or cumin-scented stew . . . or sweet and savory couscous. Fingers tear at the steaming limbs. Paula shows us how to roll fluffy broth-moist grains into crumbling spheres. One night it is an experimental *bisteeya*. The next, an exaltation of quince. One evening I arrived after dinner, too late for shad stuffed with almond paste. The leftover fish was sitting on the counter. I tasted. Oh almond-perfumed glory! I couldn't stop eating. "Don't eat it," Paula cried. "It's too rich. Stop."

"I can't stop."

She smiled. "You like it." And she grabbed the plate away. I hated her. But an almond-paste crisis had been averted.

Good Food from Morocco says the title of this book, pointedly. Paula flatly refused to succumb to the fetish for quantity. She would not include a recipe unless she loved it. She would watch our faces as we ate. "What do you think?"

"Good," I would venture.

She would taste. "Ecchh. Don't eat it. It's terrible."

"No really, Paula, it's quite edible. It's just . . . not great." But she would snatch the offending viand away and toss it into the garbage, leaving us to chew hungrily on our anise-scented bread.

"What did you do wrong, Paula?" asked Bill, her champion-hero-protector-writer-companion, one evening as we tasted a rather bland vegetable stew.

"Nothing," she said. "I did everything right. The dish tastes exactly the way it should. I don't like it. I'm not going to put it in the book."

One day Paula telephoned in sheer euphoria. "The most absolutely fantastic thing happened today," she began. Visions of great fortune tumbled through my head: legacies, lottery wins, emeralds, income tax refunds. "I discovered today that spring-roll skins are positively related to warka," Paula went on. Oh . . .

When the testing and winnowing and retesting were done, there was a wondrous and numbing feast. The ultimate *bisteeya* was so enchanting that when Paula started to remove it from the table, one guest simply would not permit it. "If you touch that plate, Paula," she said, "I'll bite your arm."

Well, Paula is back in Morocco now, terrorizing the merchants of the *medina*. "It is great to watch her stomp through the market," a friend writes, "looking neither to the left nor the right, ignoring the urgent pleas of mint merchants and lemon vendors as she makes her way to the very best *bakoola* and *smen* to be found. Not to mention listening to her prattle away in Arabic to her two astounded maids named Fatima while she literally throws meals together, waiting for the bread boy to come back from the village oven with the morning bread on a board held over his head."

This book vibrates with that same delicious loving madness. I doubt that anyone who adores good food will be able to resist the book's siren call to Morocco. So one day you will be wandering through the food stalls of Tangier's *medina* maze. You may see a tall intense brunette pinching the quinces and poking the shad, sniffing *smen*, sneering at a battered peach or beaming over a plump squawking chicken. That's Paula. Get her to take you home for lunch.

GAEL GREENE

*Concerning the spices of Arabia let
no more be said. The whole country
is scented with them, and exhales an
odor marvellously sweet.*

—*Herodotus*

Preface

The moment the Yugoslav freighter touched at Casablanca in 1959 I boarded a bus and rushed to Marrakesh, in search of the adventurous and exotic life. I felt immediately that I belonged in this country, and have never gotten over that feeling—I am still enchanted by all things Moroccan.

I lived in Morocco two years, then went on to Paris, where I spent eight years plotting ways to return.

Morocco is the only place I know where there is nothing that I do not love: the music, the great Berber city of Marrakesh, the long sandy coast, Tangier. I love the oases of the pre-Sahara, Fez in the early morning, the *souks* of the *bled* (countryside), the landscape that changes every hundred kilometers, and the Moroccans themselves, whose simplicity and hospitality always touch me and fill me, whenever I am away from them, with nostalgia and a deep longing to return.

And then, too, I love the food. For me it is one of the world's great cuisines, but one that is, unfortunately, hardly known outside North Africa. Even in Paris, what passes for Moroccan food is very disappointing. For these reasons I finally decided, after years of cooking Moroccan dishes, to write a cookbook and reveal all I knew.

But as I began to work, I realized how little that was—there were so many mysteries, so many variations, so many good cooks I could never meet. Soon I changed my mind about writing a definitive work—that seemed an absurd and pretentious task for a foreigner—and, besides, I knew it would take a lifetime to complete.

So this book is not a comprehensive study of Moroccan cookery: rather it is about the "good food" of Morocco, the Moroccan food I like the best. My criteria for including recipes changed, too: it was no longer a question of finding a recipe for every Moroccan dish, but of finding or developing a good recipe for every dish that I felt tasted good.

Many people have helped on this adventure. I owe my greatest thanks to Consul General Abdeslam Jaidi and his American wife, Janet, and to his mother, Khadija Jaidi, in whose Moroccan kitchen I learned so much.

I also want to thank many others who have contributed to this book:

Khadija and Mehdi Bennouna of Tetuán and Rabat; Taleb Jouarhri of Fez; Touria Serraj of the Moroccan Ministry of Tourism; Majoubi and Miriam Ahardan of Oulmes and Rabat; Jaffa El Glaoui of Marrakesh; Abdelaziz Lairini of Tangier; Hadj Mohammed Liludi of Rabat; Fama El Khatib of Tetuán; Alqoh M'hamed, caid of Itzer; Paul Bowles, the writer and the American best versed in Moroccan things; Abouchita Hajouji of Fez; Zohra Lahlimi Alami of Safi; Lydia Weiller of Tangier and New York; James Skelton of Marrakesh; the Minister of Tourism, His Excellency Abderrahmen El Kouhen; Taïeb Amara, Pasha of Safi; Gloria Adelson, designer of this book; M. Ben Gabrit, Pasha of Chaouen; Aziza Benchekroun of Tetuán; Abdelhakim El Bahid, caid of Tineghir; Alan Lapídus of New York; John Hopkins of Marrakesh; Frances McCullough, my editor at Harper & Row; H. Lemdeghri Alaoui, Pasha of Essaouira; Omar Kadir, Mina Kallamni, Rakia Nadi, Corinna Scariot, Fatima ben Lahsen Riffi, Fatima Drissiya—all equally fine cooks; my mother, Frieda Harris, who helped test many recipes; and Bill Bayer, who tasted everything, traveled with me in Morocco, took the color pictures for this book, and shared my excitement in its making.

Important Notes to the Cook

A Moroccan cookbook written for Americans by definition alone must be a form of adaptation. Though I have painstakingly tried to reproduce the authentic flavors of Morocco in these recipes, it has been difficult in some instances to give more than a glimmer of their original tastes, due to the special Moroccan methods of cooking. I have altered these methods to fit into the American kitchen and its capabilities, using high oven temperatures to replace glazing under hot coals, cooking times allowing just enough time for *American* meat and poultry to cook to perfection (i.e., "falling off the bones" or meat that separates easily from the bone), and equipment lists with suggestions for sizes of pots and pans intended to fix the cooking times—these are easily adjustable, of course. I did not include in these lists the obvious kitchen knives, forks, wooden spoons, and so on, which I assume will be at hand when you start to cook.

A note about pronunciation: I have not included a guide because words differ, sometimes dramatically, from region to region. I have chosen the most widely used pronunciation and given a *phonetic* transcription. I beg those who may ever be embarrassed by mispronouncing a Moroccan dish my apologies.

ONE

Moroccan Food

There are people, alas, who do not like Moroccan food. More than a century ago a certain Edmondo de Amicis had a "dreadful experience" in Tangier. He wrote: "The Arab dishes, objects of our intense curiosity, began to circulate. I tasted the first with simple faith. Great Heaven! My first impulse was to attack the cook."

I have met people who have tasted *couscous* at some "*couscous* joint" in Paris and were unimpressed, or who ordered a "Moroccan specialty" at a Moroccan hotel and were served a *tagine* (a stew) consisting mainly of grease. At the Parisian "*couscous* joint" they were undoubtedly served the Algerian version of that great dish, undeniably robust but about as delicate as a fiery curry. And the friends who suffered at the Moroccan hotel endured an infuriating and disgraceful situation: with less than half a dozen exceptions there is no fine Moroccan restaurant in Morocco; in fact, in the gastronomic capital of Fez it is nearly impossible to find a restaurant that serves even halfway decent Moroccan food.

But those fortunate ones who have dined at a Moroccan home, or attended a Moroccan *diffa* (banquet), know what the others have missed. Moroccan food is great, by any definition of that word. It may be the last of the great "undiscovered" cuisines—a situation I hope this book will remedy.

There are at least four Moroccan dishes (and probably many more) that can be compared, without exaggeration, to such great and unique specialties

1

as the sukiyaki of Japan, Peking duck, bouillabaisse, and paella Valenciana.

First there is *couscous*, the Moroccan national dish, which Craig Claiborne has called one of the dozen greatest dishes in the world. I have included here recipes for seventeen versions of Moroccan *couscous* and descriptions of many more. Imagine a platter piled high with fine, light, tender, delicate grains of wheat flour that have been steamed over the broth of a delicately and exotically spiced chicken or lamb and vegetable stew. The grains are served along with the vegetables and meat, and doused with its delicious gravy.

Imagine, too, *bisteeya*,* the most sophisticated and elaborate Moroccan dish, a combination of incredibly tasty flavors representing the culmination of all the foreign influences that have found their synthesis in Moroccan culture. *Bisteeya* is a huge pie of the finest, thinnest, flakiest pastry in the world, filled with three layers—spicy pieces of pigeon or chicken, lemony eggs cooked in a savory onion sauce, and toasted and sweetened almonds—and then dusted on top with cinnamon and sugar.

And then there is *mechoui*, the Berber version of roasted lamb. The entire animal is roasted on a spit after the meat has been rubbed with garlic and ground cumin. When cooked the lamb is fully crisped on the outside, and so tender inside that you can eat it easily with your fingers—which, in fact, is the way Moroccans eat.

Or take *djej emshmel*,† one of the four versions of the famous Moroccan chicken, lemon, and olive *tagine*. The chickens are slowly simmered with soft, luscious olives and tart, preserved lemons in a silken sauce seasoned with saffron, cumin, ginger, and paprika. Like *mechoui,* the final result is meat that can easily be eaten with the fingers.

I could go on, could describe the exalted heights of shad stuffed with dates; spiced balls of ground lamb simmered in a seasoned tomato sauce in which, at the last minute, eggs have been poached; *djej mefenned*, braised chicken covered, at the very end, with a delicate coating of eggs; a rich stew of lamb, prunes, and sesame seeds that looks, when served, like a starry night; chickens and squabs stuffed with *couscous* grains and honey and nuts; Moroccan brochettes; the infinite graces and refreshing tastes of Moroccan salads;

*Sometimes called *bistayla* or *pastilla*.
†Also called *meshmel* and *emsharmel*, depending on the region.

"gazelles' horns," crescent-shaped pastries filled with cinnamon-flavored almond paste; and *m'hanncha* (also known as "the snake"), a sublime coil of stuffed and browned pastry. The list is endless; I have described only the beginning. What about fresh green barley sprouts grilled with wild herbs and served with cold buttermilk? What about fish simmered with tomatoes and green peppers on a bed of celery or fennel stalks? What about the rich *harira* soup of chick-peas, vegetables, lemon, eggs and myriad spices? What about zucchini and tomatoes stuffed with delicately spiced ground meats? All these are part of the extraordinary Moroccan cuisine, and there are many more.

The Prerequisites for a Great Cuisine

To my mind four things are necessary before a nation can develop a great cuisine. The first is an abundance of fine ingredients—a rich land. The second is a variety of cultural influences: the history of the nation, including its domination by foreign powers, and the culinary secrets it has brought back from its own imperialist adventures. Third, a great civilization—if a country has not had its day in the sun, its cuisine will probably not be great; great food and a great civilization go together. Last, the existence of a refined palace life—without royal kitchens, without a Versailles or a Forbidden City in Peking, without, in short, the demands of a cultivated court—the imaginations of a nation's cooks will not be challenged.

Morocco, fortunately, is blessed with all four. In its ever-changing landscape and geographical situation are riches that rival those of France. Situated in the northwest corner of Africa, only a few miles across the straits from Europe, with a Mediterranean coast and an Atlantic coast, with green fertile agricultural belts, five mountain ranges, and encompassing areas of desert, Morocco has every type of environment except tropical jungle. In this small but highly variegated space some of the finest raw ingredients may be found. There are the mint, olives, and quinces of Meknes; the oranges and lemons of Fez and Agadir; the pomegranates of Marrakesh; the almonds, lamb, and *za'atar* of the Souss; the dates of Erfoud; the shad of the Sebou River; rosebuds from the Valley of Dades; walnuts, chestnuts, from the Rif; Barbary figs, also known as prickly pears, from the region of Casablanca; the honey of Tagoundaft; the barley of the Dra; the cherries of Sefrou; the melons of the Doukkala; the fish caught by the men of Essaouira; the seafood collected by the men of Safi; and the spices that for thousands of years have been brought to this country, first by Phoenicians, then by Senegalese traders and caravans that crossed North Africa from Arabia, the Sudan, and the Middle East. It is all there—Morocco is, literally, a land of milk and honey.

As for cultural influences, there have been an enormous number. The indigenous culture is Berber, and Berbers still constitute a good 80 percent of the people. (Berbers are not Arabs; ethnically they are Hamites with a suspected Nordic strain* but they embrace Islam, and it is in fact this common religion that holds the country together.)

In 683 Morocco was invaded by Arabs in what the painter-writer Brion Gysin has so aptly called the "Damascus Thrust." An Arabian conqueror named Ogba ben Nafi reached Morocco in that year, and his invasion was followed by other waves of Arabs bringing the religion of Islam and the cultural influence of Arabia and the Middle East.

The Arabs, as everyone knows, went on to conquer Spain. Their Spanish empire, known as the Andaluz, founded in 711, produced a great and delicate culture, less strong in terms of military might than the kingdom of Morocco, but perhaps more graceful, excelling in such refinements as the art of courtly love and magnificent architectural feats. (Some of the greatest buildings in Morocco, the Koutoubia Mosque in Marrakesh, for example, were designed by Andalusian architects.) For centuries there was cultural exchange between Morocco and Muslim Spain; their reciprocal influences were perhaps as great as the original influence of their Arabian invaders.

Each of the great dynasties of Morocco—the Almoravides, the Almohades, the Merinides, the Saadians, and the Alaouites—included, at one time or another, kings whose power went far beyond the borders of present-day Morocco. Idriss II, the son of an Arabian shrif, founded Fez in the ninth century, and for hundreds of years that city was known as a center of Arab culture. The Almoravides, whose king Yusuf ibn-Tashfin (1061–1106) founded the city of Marrakesh, possessed an empire that encompassed half of Spain, more than half of Algeria, and extended as far south as Senegal. The Saadians were

* C. G. Seligman, *Races of Africa*, London: Oxford University Press, p. 119.

powerful as far south as Timbuktu, and Moulay Ismail (1672–1727), the man who built Meknes, was highly regarded by Louis XIV, with whom he exchanged many letters, including pleas that *le Roi Soleil* convert to Islam.

Morocco, on account of the invasions of Arabs and the exterior adventures of Moorish kings, was strongly influenced by Middle Eastern culture and the culture of the Andaluz. The Arabs learned culinary secrets from the Persians and brought them to Morocco; from Senegal and other lands south of the Sahara came caravans of spices. Even the Turks made a contribution; though their sixteenth-century North African conquest did not penetrate Moroccan territory, their cultural influence was felt within its borders.

From a culinary point of view these cultural influences can be seen quite well in the three gastronomic centers of the land. In the Berber city of Marrakesh the food is basically Berber, with a Senegalese and African influence. In the Arab city of Fez the cuisine shows the influence of the Andaluz. And in the Andalusian city of Tetuán the Spanish influence is strongest, with some Ottoman traces. Portuguese influence may be found in the cuisine of the Portuguese settlement cities on the Atlantic coast, and here Essaouira, a city of white buildings and blue shutters, became the home of a large Jewish population who worked out their own variations on the national cuisine. The Moroccans picked up tea-drinking from the British traders; and the French, from the forty-four years (1912–1956) of their protectorate, left behind some Gallic touches. There are indeed an enormous number of outside influences—the African spice meets the Andalusian chick-pea, the Saharan date confronts Middle Eastern pastry, Berber butter competes with Spanish oil—and then all merge to become Moroccan food.

The greatness of Moroccan culture? This nation had its days when its influence radiated thousands of miles from Fez, a city that was preeminent in theology, astronomy, medicine, mathematics, and metallurgy when Europe was deep in the Middle Ages. Fez was an Athens, a city of enormous vitality and refinement, and Moroccan knowledge of agriculture and irrigation (Marrakesh is basically a huge grove of palms, an enormous man-made oasis) made Spain flourish. In fact, after the fall of Granada and the final expulsion of the Moslems from Spain in 1492, Spanish agriculture began to suffer a reversal.

The high culture of Fez was developed in parallel with the rich folk culture that had strong Berber origins: that mad charge of horsemen known as the *fantasia*; Berber trance-dancing; the great Berber pilgrimages (*moussems*), which are today important tourist attractions; folk music and poetry; and the basic cuisine of the mountains and plains.

This cuisine would certainly be worthy of attention even on its peasant level, but, as developed in the kitchens of the royal palaces of Fez, Meknes, Marrakesh, and Rabat (the four royal cities), it reached summits of perfection. The Moroccan dynasties always originated in powerful warlike tribes, whose leaders, as soon as they obtained power, were quickly refined. Thus the Saadians, who came from the pre-Saharan Valley of the Dra, were transformed from primitive tribesmen into regal monarchs, their tombs in Marrakesh being among the most lavishly decorated in all Morocco. (The garden of these tombs, by the way, is filled with a glorious ambrosia, the result of high, thick hedges of rosemary.) In the same way, in our own time Thami el Glaoui, whose power rivaled and sometimes exceeded the power of the sultan, was transformed from a feudal warlord of the High Atlas stronghold of Telouet, into the pasha of Marrakesh; friend of Winston Churchill, he dealt with premiers and presidents of France, and moved, in the latter half of his long, ruthless, and now generally discredited life, in the most civilized and refined international circles.

These monarchs and lords, as soon as they learned to entertain in regal style, began to make great demands upon their chefs to produce some of the great cosmopolitan specialties of Morocco. A case in point is *bisteeya*, which had humble origins in a simple Berber dish of chicken cooked with saffron and butter. It was combined with the primitive Arab pastry called *trid*, enhanced when later Arabs brought the fine art of Persian pastry making to Morocco, and was further embellished with Andalusian ideas until it became the *bisteeya* we know today.

People still speak with awe of the food served in the king's house. One hears rumors of "mounds of pigeons" each differently stuffed, flowing to diners on golden platters and then being whisked away, only to be replaced by equally luxurious foods. Meknes, a royal city conceived like Versailles as a place devoted to court life, was where much of modern Moroccan cooking reached its final form.

Moroccan Cooking—A Shared Heritage

Unlike her American or French counterpart, a young Moroccan girl, recently married, cannot go to a bookstore and find a text that will teach her how to cook. This cuisine has not been codified; there is no Moroccan culinary establishment, no Moroccan equivalent of the Cordon Bleu. The cuisine developed in the kitchens of the palaces is found throughout the land in less luxurious forms.

It is not surprising that nearly all Moroccan cooks are women, for cooking is considered woman's work, and a Moroccan wife spends much of her time preparing food. The cooking knowledge that is passed from mother to daughter, mother-in-law to daughter-in-law, is also shared in another way. When a family feasts, the female relatives and neighbors will come and help with the work. This constant cross-fertilization, this sharing of culinary knowledge, has kept the culinary art alive in a country where the number of literate people is extremely low. A person who cannot read or write, who cannot note things down or find knowledge in books, must develop his memory to an extraordinary degree.

The Philosophy of Abundance

There is a fine Moroccan restaurant in Marrakesh, called La Maison Arabe, which has sometimes been called one of the greatest restaurants in the world. I think this is an exaggeration, but I cannot deny that La Maison Arabe, run by Madame Larochette, whose dishes are prepared in accordance with the methods of the legendary Rhadija of the household of the Glaoui, is probably the best *Moroccan* restaurant in the world. The food is always fabulous at La Maison Arabe—I have never failed to eat extremely well there— but there is something about this famous restaurant that I do not like. Though the food and decor are Moroccan the spirit is not. One is served, for quite an extravagant price, only as much as one can eat. If you are four people you will get sufficient food for four. The philosophy is French middle class—parsimonious, rigid, and austere. (Once when I asked for a second glass of mint tea I was told that the kitchen was closed, and, besides, the house was out of mint.) This is not the way a dinner in a Moroccan home is served. The thing that is missing at La Maison Arabe is the philosophy of abundance.

Arab hospitality is legendary—an embarrassment of riches, total satisfaction, abundance as an end in itself and as a point of pride for the host. At a Moroccan *diffa* (banquet) so much food is served that you can't imagine who is expected to eat it. Dish after dish is offered, each piled high. After a few bites, if there are many courses—and at a grand *diffa* there can easily be as many as a dozen—these platters will be whisked away. To puritans like us this may all seem vulgar, ostentatious, showy, and chauvinistic. To Moroccans it is the essential requisite of a feast.

At my first few *diffas* I worried about these barely touched, high-piled platters going to waste. Later I learned the truth, that not a speck of them would be wasted, for the kitchen was filled with people—women, children, relatives, servants—all of whom would finish off every crumb.

Moroccans have large, healthy appetites; perhaps it takes them longer to achieve that state of total satisfaction which they call *shaban*. The fact that after an entrée of *bisteeya* or an array of salads, or both, a *mechoui*, a succession of *tagines* (chicken, lamb, and fish), and an enormous platter of *couscous*, there still remain a dessert of fruits and nuts to be devoured and then some glasses of mint tea to be drunk strikes many foreigners as decadently lavish. But even in a poor house such an abundance of culinary riches can be presented when the occasion warrants, because the vegetables vastly outweigh the meat in *tagines*; the sauce is always what counts, and the lack of expensive ingredients goes unnoticed.

Nineteenth-century foreign travelers to Morocco have described some incredible dinners. Walter Harris, a correspondent for the London *Times* around the turn of the century, wrote of a dinner in Marrakesh at which he was served with seventy-seven different dishes (he selected only fifteen to try). A certain Dr. Leared, who wrote a book entitled V*isit to the Court of Marocco* [sic], told of a dinner given by the prime minister at which he was served thirty dishes of meat and poultry, twelve salads, and thirty-two sweetmeats.

Here is an extremely verbose description from a nineteenth-century book about Moroccan cuisine that may give some notion of the Moroccan sense of culinary abundance:

Now the Moorish paradise is a glutton's dream. Its soil, of whitest wheaten flour, is irrigated by rivulets of milk and wine and honey. The musical branches of the immeasureable tuba tree, which adorns the celestial palace-garden of the Prophet of Islam, are laden with exquisite fruits, and ready-dressed banquets of thrice a hundred courses in golden dishes, such as the Slave of the Lamp served up to Aladdin. In short the haven of the Moor is an elysium wrought out of a pastry-cook's shop and a harem where the existence of the blessed will be one eternal "guzzling-bee," somewhat similar to Sydney Smith's description of the future state of beatified epicures—"the eating of *pâtés de foie gras* to the sound of trumpets." No wonder therefore that the Moor's *summum bonum* here and hereafter is repose and abundance.*

Moroccan hospitality is notorious for its flourishes and sweet suffusion, well conveyed in this nineteenth-century dinner invitation:†

To my gracious master, my respected lord. . . . This evening, please God, when the King of the army of stars, the sun of the worlds, will turn toward the realm of shades and place his foot in the stirrup of speed, thou art besought to lighten us with the dazzling rays of thy face, rivalled only by the sun. Thy arrival, like a spring breeze, will dissapate the dark night of solitude and isolation.

After sending out an invitation like that the host was virtually obligated to serve a great succession of exquisite courses.

I have noted that the Moroccan banquet bears a curious and striking resemblance to the Chinese. First, the dining process is communal—many people crowd around a circular table and serve themselves from central dishes. In China the last dish before dessert is always rice; in Morocco it is *couscous*, another and perhaps more fanciful grain. In both countries the number of courses can go very high, and it is a point of pride for the host to offer his guests as many different things as he can. Each cuisine plays games

---

* George D. Cowan, and L. N. Johnston, *Moorish Lotus Leaves* (London, 1883). These same writers, whose love of the literary flourish often exceeds my desire to read their prose, describe *couscous* thus: "The mere sound of the syllables is musical, with a sweet sibilance, suggestive of twin kisses united to the coo of the turtle-dove and the note of the cuckoo."
† Budgett Meakin, *The Moors* (London, 1902).

with its diners' palates, playing off salty against sweet against spicy, and varying the textures of successively offered dishes so that the diner will experience a full range of culinary pleasures. Each also ends its meals with what is basically a ceremony of tea.

There is another resemblance in the actual cooking process, discussed more fully in Chapter 6; the pastry for *bisteeya*, called *warka*, is made precisely the same as the dough for Chinese spring rolls—a method of pastry making unique to these two regions of the world. But the two cuisines differ in their basic ways of preparing food. The key to the preparation of a Moroccan *tagine* (stew) with its spices and accompanying vegetables and fruits is long, slow simmering in a shallow, glazed earthenware pot. In the city of Tetuán there is a saying that food should be cooked until it is "standing in the sauce." The great amount of spices naturally gives Moroccan food a piquant flavor, but not, usually, a spicy-hot one. Your tongue and lips will not be burned, as they would be by the hotter types of Chinese food, such as Szechuan, or those from India or Korea.

An old book on Andalusian cooking describes this process so well that it might well be describing the Moroccan *tagine*-simmering method itself:

> The philosophy of the Spanish [i.e., Moroccan] cuisine is strictly oriental—it is the stew or pilaf. The *prima materia* on which the artist is to operate is quite secondary; scarcity of wood and ignorance of coal prevent roasting; accordingly *sauce* is everything; this may be defined to be unctuous, rich, savory, and highly spiced. . . .*

How to Eat Moroccan Food

With the exception of *couscous* (which is *sometimes* eaten with a spoon) Moroccans eat with the first three fingers of their right hands. This is in the tradition of the Arabs, who always, before they dine, go through an elaborate hand-washing process. At a Moroccan dinner a servant or a young member of the family assists each diner by holding a basin beneath his hands, pouring water over them, and then offering him a towel from an extended arm.

* Richard Ford, *Handbook for Travellers in Spain* (London, 1845).

Bread is very important in Moroccan dining, both as food and as an implement for grasping hold of meat or vegetables, swirling them in the gravy of a *tagine*, and then transporting them to the mouth. Moroccan bread, being highly absorbent, is also ideal for sopping up the savory juices.

Bryan Clarke, in his book *Berber Village*, describes the folklore of eating with the fingers: "To eat with one finger is a sign of hatred; to eat with two shows pride; to eat with three accords with the Prophet; to eat with four or five is a sign of gluttony."

Though *couscous is* sometimes eaten with a spoon, any self-respecting Moroccan will eat his national dish with his fingers—a difficult process for an unschooled foreign visitor. A nineteenth-century travel writer described this process miraculously well:

> With the points of the fingers of the right hand a portion of grains is drawn towards the side of the dish. It is fingered as the keys of a pianoforte till it gathers together; it is then taken up into the hand, shaken, pressed till it adheres, moulded till it becomes a ball; tossed up and worked till it is perfect, and then shot by the thumb, like a marble, into the open mouth.*

However, such delicacy has not always been observed. A very old book entitled *Account of Barbary*, published in 1713, contains the following passage:

> When he (the Sultan) is intent upon a piece of work, or eager to have it finished, he won't allow himself to go to his meals, but orders some of his eunuchs or negroes to bring him a dish of kuscoussoo [*couscous*], which he sits down and eats after a brutish manner; for as soon as he has rolled up the sleeves of his shirt, he thrusts his arms into the dish up to his elbows, and bringing a handful from the bottom he fills his mouth, and then throws the rest into the dish again, and so on till he is satisfied.

A Moroccan meal is best eaten in a traditional dining room, which also doubles for receptions. The walls are lined with luxuriously cushioned divans and a circular table is set up in a corner. After the meal, for the serving and drinking of mint tea, the diners will spread out and lounge on the divans so they can stretch their legs.

Some Moroccan families cover their table with a piece of opaque plastic and simply throw bones and other inedible bits right onto the table. After-

* David Urquhart, *Pillars of Hercules* (London, 1848).

wards the servants simply roll up this plastic sheet—bones, garbage, and all—and carry it away.

All of this may sound barbaric—no pun intended on the word Berber, from which the word "barbarian" originally comes—but it is actually an extremely sensible way to eat, ranking with Chinese chopsticks and Indian hands and fingers, and opposed to the decadence of using all sorts of silver utensils. I find that Moroccan food always tastes better when eaten Moroccan style—the contact between fingers and a hot *tagine*, fingers and a crisp *bisteeya*, fingers and a tender *mechoui*, always adds to the pleasure—and I urge everyone to eat a Moroccan dinner this way. It is sensible, too, in that there will be far fewer dishes to wash, since the cooking vessels (earthenware *tagine slaouis*) double as serving platters and communal plates.

I also urge everyone to make Moroccan bread. It is not at all difficult (see page 51), enhances Moroccan food enormously, and makes eating with the fingers pleasureful and tasty.

Moroccan Regional Specialties

Moroccan food is more or less homogenous; the country is unified, and its cuisine is distinct, even from the other two countries of the Maghreb, Algeria and Tunisia. But, like all countries with great cuisines, Morocco has its regional specialties.

The three great gastronomic capitals, Fez, Tetuán and Marrakesh, have developed their own variations of particular dishes, as well as some dishes that are special and unique. And considering its modest size, Essaouira must also be thought of as a great city of food, as, to a lesser degree, should Tangier, Safi, and Rabat. But it is in the regions of Morocco—the Rif Mountains of the north; the Middle Atlas area, which is totally Berber; the Souss in the southwest; and the pre-Sahara—that one finds the most spectacular differences and inventions in food.

I have not included recipes for all the regional specialties indicated on the map on pages 14–15, but have listed them anyway for the culinary adventurer or adventuress who may travel to some of these places and find an opportunity to eat them. One opportunity, accessible to all, may occur on a Berber *moussem*; foreign visitors are welcome at many of these pilgrimages (including the famous *moussem* of Imilchil), and if you should get to one you will be able to eat some marvelous food in the tents.

The pre-Sahara and the outlying oases are a little harder to get to than Fez or Marrakesh, but they are among the most fascinating places in Morocco, and anyone who has the chance should visit them. In the farthest reaches, wandering Arab tribesmen not only eat camel, but also gazelle and hedgehogs, jackals and desert foxes, which they serve with simple, flat loaves of bread made from Indian millet, wheat, or barley. In some parts of Morocco there is even a bread made with locusts!

The people of the Souss are hard working, and they have huge appetites. There is a tree that grows only in their area, the argan, that produces a nut from which a delicious oil is extracted and then used in various foods. The "hamburger" of the Souss is *asidah*, a pyramid of cornmeal mush served in a wide, shallow wooden dish with a knob of fresh butter on top. Here, too, you may have a chance to eat the famous bluefish, or the tiny, delicious bird called the *ehyell*.

Kimia

Finally, a word about one of the most mysterious things in Morocco—a land, by the way, that according to many of its inhabitants is inhabited by numerous spirits and supernatural powers—a kind of magic called *kimia*. *Kimia*, according to those who know, is the power to multiply food. Thus a person with *kimia* can live on very little; if a man has some *couscous* and *kimia* he can presumably multiply his *couscous* into as much of that grain as he will need in his lifetime, and even into everything else he needs to eat. If you have *kimia*, you must not call attention to your poverty or else your power of multiplication may be lost. *Kimia* is something very personal, something that lies between the person who has it and the universe.

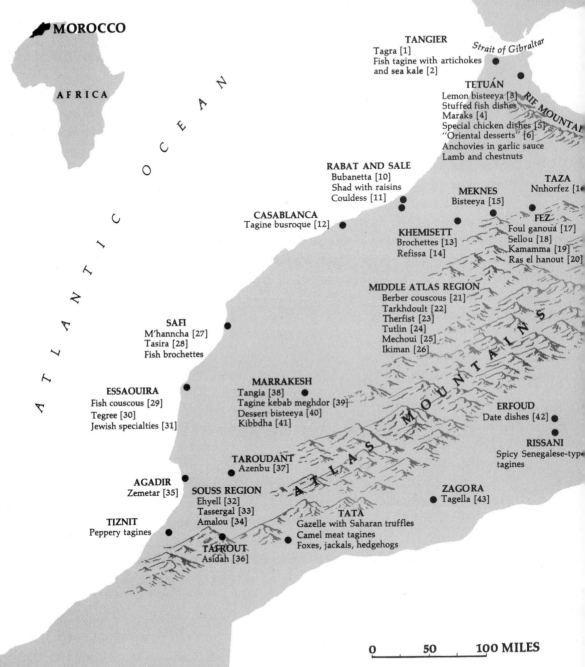

MOROCCO

AFRICA

ATLANTIC OCEAN

S

TANGIER
Tagra [1]
Fish tagine with artichokes
and sea kale [2]

Strait of Gibraltar

TETUÁN
Lemon bisteeya [3]
Stuffed fish dishes
Maraks [4]
Special chicken dishes [5]
"Oriental desserts" [6]
Anchovies in garlic sauce
Lamb and chestnuts

RIF MOUNTAINS

RABAT AND SALE
Bubanetta [10]
Shad with raisins
Couldess [11]

MEKNES
Bisteeya [15]

TAZA
Nnhorfez [1

CASABLANCA
Tagine busroque [12]

KHEMISETT
Brochettes [13]
Refissa [14]

FEZ
Foul ganoua [17]
Sellou [18]
Kamamma [19]
Ras el hanout [20]

MIDDLE ATLAS REGION
Berber couscous [21]
Tarkhdoult [22]
Therfist [23]
Tutlin [24]
Mechoui [25]
Ikiman [26]

SAFI
M'hanncha [27]
Tasira [28]
Fish brochettes

ATLAS MOUNTAINS

ESSAOUIRA
Fish couscous [29]
Tegree [30]
Jewish specialties [31]

MARRAKESH
Tangia [38]
Tagine kebab meghdor [39]
Dessert bisteeya [40]
Kibbdha [41]

ERFOUD
Date dishes [42]

RISSANI
Spicy Senegalese-typ
tagines

TAROUDANT
Azenbu [37]

AGADIR
Zemetar [35]

SOUSS REGION
Ehyell [32]
Tassergal [33]
Amalou [34]

ZAGORA
Tagella [43]

TIZNIT
Peppery tagines

TATA
Gazelle with Saharan truffles
Camel meat tagines
Foxes, jackals, hedgehogs

TAFROUT
Asidah [36]

0   50   100 MILES

JEAN PAUL TREMBLAY

I   N

DITERRANEAN SEA

MOUNTAINS
Brek [7]
Aferfur [8]
Byesar [9]

1. Tagra, a dish of fish, tomatoes, and paprika oil.
2. Fish tagine with artichokes and sea kale, a wild herb found near Tangier.
3. Lemon bisteeya (see recipe page 108.)
4. Maraks, vegetable tagines (see recipes pages 89-95.)
5. Special chicken dishes—that is, chicken stuffed with celery and onions; chicken stuffed with bakoola (a wild herb); chicken with quinces, honey, ambergris, aga wood, and so on. (See page 186 for a list of fifty Tetuanese chicken dishes.)
6. "Oriental desserts," which show a Turkish influence: Ktaif, mulhalabya, taba, and so on (see recipes pages 292-323.)
7. Brek, the Riffian word for the North African brik. (See recipe page 124.)
8. Aferfur, a couscous made with sorgo.
9. Byesar, a soupy puree of favas eaten with green onions.
10. Bubanetta, a sausage made of innards.
11. Couldess, a form of dried salted lamb.
12. Tagine busroque, a tagine of mussels.
13. Brochettes of Khemisett. The economy of this town seems to depend upon the sale of brochettes to travelers on the Rabat-Meknes-Fez road. The main street is nothing but one brochette stand after another.
14. Refissa, a Berber tagine of biscuits soaked in bouillon with onions, salt, and pepper.
15. Bisteeya is served everywhere in Morocco, but the bisteeya of Meknes is as highly regarded as that of its rival, Fez.
16. Nnhorfez, a tagine of turnips.
17. Foul ganoua, a dish of Guinean lentils.
18. Sellou, a special dessert served at weddings, made of flour, grilled sesame seeds, fried almonds, and smen.
19. Kamamma, a tagine of lamb or chicken with layers of onions and tomatoes.
20. The ras el hanout of Fez is quite famous, and may be purchased there in brut form. (See page 25 for an analysis of the twenty-six ingredients.)
21. Berber couscous made with barley grits. (See recipe page 158.)
22. Tarkhdoult, a bisteeya of meat made by Berbers.
23. Therfist, Berber unleavened bread.
24. Tutlin, a Berber version of liver brochettes covered with sheep's caul and served with salt.
25. Mechoui, Berber-style roasted lamb. (Served throughout Morocco, but best at a Berber moussem, or pilgrimage.)
26. Ikiman, a form of cooked wheat.
27. M'hanncha, a coiled pastry stuffed with almond paste and prepared with a glazed honey coating.
28. Tasira, a dish of conger eel, raisins, onions, and cinnamon.
29. Fish couscous, also called baddaz bil hut.
30. Tegree, a dish of dried and spiced mussels.
31. Jewish specialties, among the many of which are sweet meatballs served with couscous, and braewats stuffed with fish.
32. Ehyell, a tiny bird unique to the Souss, served with raisins and onions and said to be delicious.
33. Tassergal, an especially delicious bluefish caught off this coast, which in season people come from far away to eat.
34. Amalou, a great specialty of the Souss, made with honey, almonds, and the oil extracted from the nuts of the argan tree after they have been expectorated by goats.
35. Zemetar, made of wheat germ, honey, and argan oil, and served as a cereal.
36. Asidah, a kind of corn porridge.
37. Azenbu, a special Berber couscous of barley shoots grilled with wild herbs then steamed and buttered. Traditionally accompanied by a glass of cold buttermilk.
38. Tangia, a lamb stew, made with garlic and cumin and lots of oil. (There is a story in Marrakesh about a man who made tangia by mixing pieces of lamb with the meat of hedgehog. He sent it to a community oven to bake, and when he came to fetch it it wasn't there. The baker claimed innocence but the man was angry and took him before the caid. The baker could not explain why there was no tagine in his oven until it came out during the hearing that the man had mixed his lamb with hedgehog. "Ah ha," said the baker to the caid, "that explains everything. The lamb and the hedgehog obviously started a fight, broke the pot and escaped." The caid forgave the baker, and the man who had dared to mix these irreconcilable meats went home hungry.)
39. Tagine kebab meghdor, a delicious Marrakesh specialty in which previously grilled lamb is stewed in a spiced butter sauce. (See recipe page 238.)
40. Dessert bisteeya. (See recipe page 322.)
41. Kibbdha, a liver salad. (See recipe page 88.)
42. There are more than thirty varieties of dates grown in the oasis of Erfoud. Needless to say, the people of Erfoud have many ways of serving them.
43. Tagella, the bread eaten by the Tuaregs, cooked on hot stones.

———◆———

TWO

The Souks

I find American supermarkets seductive—everything is in its place, well-lighted and under one roof, the prices are clearly marked, and I can do my shopping in a few minutes. But I am not seduced, for I miss the chaos of Moroccan *souks*, the endless haggling, the crush of people, the freshly harvested goods so lovingly displayed, the squawks of live poultry, the spice stalls choked with fabulous seasonings and all sorts of dried insects and rare barks alleged to have magical properties.

The Moroccan word *souk* literally means "market," a place where anything is bought and sold. In cities where there is an old, walled *medina*, the section devoted to market stalls is called the *souiqua*. Here, if you have lived in the city for a while, you will know exactly where to make the best deal on a belt, a barrel of olives, a chair, a screwdriver, or even an "underground" item like hashish.

In Fez, for instance, where the *medina* is perhaps the world's most complicated maze, each street seems to have its own trade, and only a born-and-bred Fassi can find his way about. Every time I've gone into the *medina* of Fez in search of some cooking utensil or some special spice, I've gotten lost, had an adventure, and somehow emerged more or less intact, usually with the item I originally wanted to buy, plus, always, many things more.

In Marrakesh, too—where, on the other hand, the maze is less complicated—I've never failed to see something, some inexplicable bit of street action or some inscrutable sight, that has kept me puzzled for days. In these great cities the Moroccans have a life style that is endlessly fascinating, and often very difficult to penetrate and understand.

The country *souks* are marvelous, too, and on a recent trip I was struck again by the honesty of the Berber people. I drove with Madame Jaidi, who had kindly consented to let me work in the kitchen of her traditional Moroccan home, to the little *souk* of Tiflet in the Middle Atlas in search of some thick country honey. It was a hot day, we were both tired, and since the *souk* was built on a hillside we asked a young Berber man if he would help us out. We explained what we wanted, he said he knew a good place to buy, we gave him money, and he disappeared into the crowd. I wandered around, and then, after an hour, when he failed to reappear and we were all set to drive away, he came running down the hill carrying a can of honey and our precise change. Why had it taken him an hour? Because, he explained, that was how long it took him to negotiate a good price. The honey, of course, was delicious, as country food usually is.

In the oasis of Goulimine there is a *souk* devoted entirely to camels. I once spent a morning there watching the furious trading on a flat piece of beige, stony earth, where the camels looked more sure of themselves than the young men who waited in line to consult a medicine man. The haggling over the camels was ferocious, but the medical interviews were grave, with much sympathetic nodding of the head and the inevitable finale, when the medicine man dispensed, no matter what the ailment, a pink packet of French aspirins. I didn't buy a camel, of course, but that may have been the one time I visited a *souk* and returned empty-handed.

Everything Moroccan that I own is combined in my mind with the story of how I bought it, including my favorite rug, which I bought for ten dollars in the town of Chichaoua, where it looked like a flame against the countryside, the people's clothing, the tents, and everything else. In Morocco shopping is an intricate process in which the pleasure and the adventure are forever part of your memory.

Shopping is a crucial matter when it comes to preparing good food, too. Though an absolutely delicious chicken with lemons and olives should, ideally, be made with Moroccan olives, preserved Moroccan *doqq* (a fragrant lemon especially amenable to salt preservation) and Moroccan chickens raised in the Moroccan style and butchered the Moroccan way, it is still possible to make a sublime version of this dish with materials that are available in the United States. The trick, of course, is to shop carefully, to buy always for quality, to use organically grown vegetables if possible, and to settle for nothing less than the finest spices.

That is what this chapter is about: turning the markets of your town into *souks*, searching out the best purveyors of meat, vegetables, spices and fish, buying carefully and selectively so that you can make delicious Moroccan food. Any of the special ingredients you need for my recipes can be bought from the firms listed separately in the back of this book. Do take the trouble —a Moroccan dish may have a totally different flavor if a crucial aromatic is left out. But in the end most of my recipes do not involve the purchase of exotic materials. Moroccan food is basically made of humble things: lamb shanks and chickens, tomatoes and parsley, butter and olives. But they must be well bought, and thus these notes on spices, herbs and aromatics, fragrant waters, olives, oil, butter, eggs, honey, *couscous*, chick-peas, and utensils, with some recipes thrown in on the preparation of some of the basic components—such things as preserved lemons, *smen, ras el hanout,* hot *harissa* sauce, and "coriander water."

SPICES, HERBS, AND AROMATICS

————◆————

Wandering among the spice stalls in a great city like Fez, seeing myriad spices displayed in huge bags, small boxes, and glass jars with cork stoppers, the visitor is struck by the idea that the Moroccans have fallen in love with every spice in the world. In fact, this love of spices is in the tradition of their ancestors, who brought with them, on their great sweep across North Africa from Arabia, a sophisticated knowledge of their use in perfumes and medicines, for the enhancement of food, and as currency for trade. Since biblical times spices have been a symbol of luxurious living in the Middle East, and the earliest practitioners of the spice trade—the ancient Phoenicians, who were among the first foreigners to visit Morocco—began something that the Arabs have embellished and made into a way of life. The caravans that crossed the desert, and brought aromatics to people who treasured them like gold, became one of the economic pillars of the Arabian empire. The Moors taught the Spaniards the value of spices, and thus disposed them to stake the spice-seeking voyages of Christopher Columbus.

There is a misapprehension about spices in our country—the idea that they are used by people in poor nations to cover up the bad taste of corrupted food. The corollary of this belief is that "pure" foods like broiled steak represent some sort of cultural and culinary advance. In fact this is not true at all: spices are used in countries like Morocco and India not to cover up but to *enhance* the taste of food. Cooks in these countries have a deep understanding of how spices should be used. Displaying none of our fearful calculation with measuring spoons and scales, they toss them into food with an apparent abandon that reflects a precise awareness of how far they can go without overwhelming a dish. While we are in awe of spices and use them conservatively, they are lavish with them and yet never push them too far.

Spices cannot help a tomato that has the texture of cardboard, or resuscitate rotten meat, or do much to improve the taste of a chicken so fattened by hormones that it has lost all traces of flavor. Spices can be used to *stretch* the taste of foods, to push them to a certain point without destroying or breaking up their inherent flavors.

THE TEN IMPORTANT SPICES

◆

In Moroccan cooking there are ten important spices that are used over and over again; they appear frequently in recipes, and the prospective cook should always have them on hand: cinnamon, cumin, saffron, turmeric, ginger, black pepper, cayenne, paprika, aniseed, and sesame seeds.

CINNAMON: There are two kinds, Ceylon cinnamon (*Cinnamomum zeylanicum*), called *dar el cini* in Morocco, which is light tan and delicate; and cassia cinnamon (*Cinnamomum lauri*), called *karfa* in Morocco, which usually comes from Saigon, and has a stronger taste than the Ceylonese variety and a little less delicacy of flavor. Cinnamon is used frequently in Moroccan food, as a final dusting in a Berber *harira* soup, in salads, *bisteeya*, *kdras*, *couscous* dishes, and desserts.

CUMIN (*Cuminum cyminum*), called *kamoon* in Morocco. This is one of the indispensable spices. Used frequently in fish and chicken dishes, brochettes, and *mechoui*, it is a most important component for ground-meat dishes (*kefta*). Cumin seeds smell like old hay, but when they are ground in a mortar the released aroma is sensational. They are grown all along the North African coast and also in Mexico, where the taste is the same but the aroma is different.

SAFFRON (*Crocus sativus*), called *zafrane* in Morocco. A very small amount of saffron can totally change the aroma and color of a dish, and, happily, only a small amount is ever needed, since saffron is the most expensive spice. To harvest one ounce you need to raise more than five thousand crocus flowers, each of which supplies only three tiny stigmas. The collection of the crocus stigmas was once a specialty of Moroccan Jews.

Saffron threads should be brittle before being pulverized, or else some of their potency will be lost and too bitter a taste imparted. To make them brittle place them on a plate set over a pan of boiling water or dry in a warm oven. After ten minutes or so, pulverize them in a mortar. A pinch or two is all that will be needed.

Some Moroccan recipes call for "saffron water." To make saffron water soak ¼ teaspoon pulverized saffron threads in ½ cup *hot* water. Saffron water will keep about a week in a refrigerator if covered. If a recipe calls for a pinch of pulverized saffron you can use 2 tablespoons of saffron water instead.

TURMERIC (*Curcuma longa*), called *quekoum* in Morocco. Turmeric comes from the root of a tropical plant of the ginger family, and has a clean, bitter taste. In Moroccan cooking it is sometimes mixed with saffron for reasons of taste and economy. The soup called Harira (page 58) always contains a spoonful.

GINGER (*Zingiber officinale*), called *skinjbir* in Morocco. Ginger has a sweet, peppery flavor and is used often in Moroccan cooking, especially (along with black pepper) in *tagines* and all dishes with a *makalli* sauce. Though there are many qualities of ginger used in Morocco, including the white variety from Japan, which is extremely delicate, all the recipes in this book assume the use of Jamaican ginger, the best quality available in the United States.

BLACK PEPPER (*Piper nigrum*), known in Morocco as *elbezar*. This spice, so familiar and so good, is always added early in the cooking of Moroccan food so its coarse taste has time to mellow.

CAYENNE (*Capsicum frutescens*), known as *felfla soudaniya* in Morocco. This yellow-orange colored spice is used mostly in southern Morocco, where many dishes reflect the influence of Senegalese cuisine.

PAPRIKA (*Capsicum annum*), known in Morocco as *felfla hlouwa*. Though Hungarian paprikas are the best in the world, Spanish paprika is quite good, readily available in America, and the most commonly used variety in Morocco. It appears in Moroccan salads, vegetable *tagines*, *kefta*, virtually all the tomato dishes (except the ones that use cinnamon and honey), and in the indispensable fish marinade known as Charmoula (page 175). Brown paprika is the poorest quality, but one cannot trust bright red purely on sight, since it has often been colored with *cochenille*. The only way to check the quality of paprika is to open up a jar and smell and taste it.

A paprika mixture called *felfla harra* (sharp and aromatic peppers), made up of equal parts of sharp paprika, cayenne, and ground long peppers, is used in some fish dishes, dishes that feature lentils, and in *khboz bishemar*, which I call "Marrakesh Pizza" (page 54).

Paprika doesn't keep well, so I suggest you buy it in small amounts, and store it in a screw-top jar in a dark, cool place.

ANISEED (*Pimpinella anisum*), known in Morocco as *nafaa* or *habbt hlawa*. There are many types, but the best is the green aniseed from Spain, which has a strong, warm flavor. Aniseed is fragrant and tastes like licorice; it is used in Moroccan bread, cookies, and some preparations of fish.

SESAME SEEDS (*Sesamum indicum*), known in Morocco as *jinjelan*. Sesame seeds are cultivated in Morocco and also in the Far East as the source of an important oil. They are used in Moroccan bread and desserts, and when toasted they are a popular garnish for chicken and lamb *tagines*.

NINE SECONDARY AROMATICS

◆

These flavorings—allspice, caraway, cloves, coriander seeds, gum arabic, fenugreek, licorice, honey dates, and orrisroot—are used much less frequently than the ten important spices, and need not be kept on hand unless you choose to execute the one or two recipes in which some of them appear. Others are described here simply as curiosities.

ALLSPICE (*Pimenta officinalis*), called *noioura* in Morocco. This reddish-brown berry, with its special taste that combines the flavors of cloves, nutmeg, and cinnamon, is sometimes used in chicken dishes, in old recipes for *couscous*, in some varieties of *kefta*, and in a *bisteeya* made in Fez.

CARAWAY (*Carum carvi*), called *karwiya* in Morocco. Caraway grows in great abundance in the Rehamma Plain between Casablanca and Marrakesh. It is not used very often, but appears with garlic in Harissa Sauce (page 30), and in the famous snail dish called *boubbouche*, where it joins twelve or fifteen other aromatics in good quantity.

CLOVES (*Eugenia caryophyllata*), called *oud el nouar* in Morocco. Rarely used in Morocco, though it appears in some *couscous* recipes more than a century old.

CORIANDER SEEDS (*Coriandrum sativum*), called *kosbour* in Morocco and *not to be confused* with the herb, green coriander, which grows from these seeds, has a different taste, and is used frequently in Morocco. Coriander seeds are used very infrequently, but when they are it is with great vigor—for example in *mechoui* (Roasted Lamb, page 234), when they are rubbed with garlic and cumin into the lamb flesh, and in the preserved meat called Khelea (page 42).

GUM ARABIC (*Acacia arabica*), known as *mska* in Morocco. This has a strong scent and I love it, especially in almond paste, where I think it can make a decisive difference. It is most popular in Marrakesh pastries and as a flavoring for water; it also turns up in an unusual recipe for scrambled eggs (page 58).

FENUGREEK (*Trigonella foenumgraecum*), known as *helbah* in Morocco. It grows in Morocco and is used by the Berbers in the flat bread called *therfist*. Fenugreek has no taste unless heated, and then it tastes a little like burnt sugar and smells a little like celery. It is very difficult to pound into powder, but is favored anyway by Berbers, who believe this spice makes women pleasingly plump—which is the way they like them.

LICORICE (*Glycyrrhiza glabra*), called *arksous* in Morocco. Used in the famous snail dish, *boubbouche*, and also in a recipe for squid.

HONEY DATES (*Rhamnus zizyphus*), called *nabka* in Morocco. This reddish, shiny, sweet-tasting fruit-seasoning is found in central Morocco, and occasionally turns up in a lamb *tagine*.

ORRISROOT (*Iris germanica*), called *amber el door* in Morocco. When these off-white rhizomes are roasted they taste a little like coffee, and when they are sucked they sweeten the breath.

Ras el Hanout

Ras el hanout, which means, literally, "top of the shop," seems to fascinate everyone, foreigners and Moroccans alike. It is a very old mixture of many spices, sometimes ten, sometimes nineteen, sometimes twenty-six; Moroccans have told me of a *ras el hanout* that contained more than a hundred ingredients.

It is incorrect to think of *ras el hanout* as curry powder by another name. It lacks the abundance of fenugreek, coriander seeds, mustard seeds, poppy seeds, and cumin of commercial curry. Though theoretically almost anything is permissible in *ras el hanout*—even dried garlic and saffron—obviously some mixtures are better than others. The aphrodisiacs (Spanish fly, ash berries, and monk's pepper) that appear in most formulae seem to be the reason why the mere mention of this mixture will put a gleam into a Moroccan cook's eye.

Ras el hanout is used in Moroccan game dishes; in *mrouzia* (Lamb Tagine with Raisins, Almonds, and Honey, page 286), a sweet lamb dish; in the hashish candy called Majoun (page 314); in various rice and *couscous* stuffings; and even in some recipes for *bisteeya*. I bought a packet in the Attarine quarter of Fez, where it is sold in *brut* form, and, after a long analysis, a friend in New York who is a spice importer and I came up with the following list of ingredients:

Allspice	Cubebe pepper[7]
Ash berries[1]	Earth almonds[8]
Belladonna leaves[2]	Galingale[9]
Black cummin seeds[3]	Ginger
Black peppercorns	*Gouza el asnab*[10]
Cantharides[4]	Grains of paradise[11]
Cardamom pods[5]	Long pepper[12]
Wild cardamom pods[6]	Lavender[13]
Cayenne	Mace[14]
Cassia cinnamon	Monk's pepper[15]
Ceylon cinnamon	Nutmeg[16]
Cloves	Orrisroot
Coriander seed	Turmeric

1. *Holarrhen*, called *lissan ettir* in Morocco. A tan, elongated spice that looks like a bird's tongue and is alleged to have strong medicinal and aphrodisiacal properties.

2. *Atropa belladonna*, called *zbibet el laidour* in Morocco, sometimes known as "deadly nightshade." Collected in the Rif Mountain area and often used as an antispasmodic.

3. *Nigella arvensis sativa*, called *habet el soudane* in Morocco. These seeds, which have nothing to do with cumin, have a very sharp, acid taste.

4. *Lytta vesicatoria*, called *debbal el hand* in Morocco. The very sight of these green, metallic beetles, called "Spanish fly," terrifies me.

5. *Elettaria cardamomum*, called *qaqula* in Morocco. This green pod is one of the most expensive spices in Morocco. Inside are roughly a dozen seeds, which are aromatic, clean tasting, sweet, peppery, and bitter. Sometimes used to flavor coffee.

6. *Elettaria cardamomum, var. major*, called *abachi* in Morocco, and popularly known as "bitter black cardamom." Similar to the green cardamom pods but with a completely different appearance, sort of a brown root with a beard at one end that smells to me like old shoes.

7. *Piper Cubeba*, called *kabbaba* in Morocco. Bitter, sharp-tasting berries with a slightly elongated shape. Sometimes called "tailed pepper," this comes from Java.

8. *Cyperus esculentus*, called *tara soudania* in Morocco. They look like small elongated nutmegs, and have a perfumed chestnut taste. In Tangier there is a small Spanish ice-cream parlor that sells *horchata*—a very good iced drink made from earth almonds.

9. *Alpinia galanga*, called *kedilsham* in Morocco. A highly aromatic spice that tastes like a cross between ginger and cardamom. In Indonesia it is frequently used, and is called *laos*.

With a Moroccan girl who lives in New York, I worked out an American formula for *ras el hanout* that obviously lacks some of the rare Moroccan items like cubebe peppers and the aphrodisiacs. Nevertheless, it's a pretty good approximation.

Try to make it yourself if you want; your blender will undoubtedly survive all these nuts, sticks, barks, and seeds, but the aroma will linger on—*ras el hanout* is *strong*. (Follow with a separate grinding of cane sugar and your blender will be clear and clean). Grind the following ingredients in a blender until you obtain a fine mix, then sieve:

4 whole nutmegs	½ teaspoon lavender
10 rosebuds*	1 tablespoon white peppercorns
12 cinnamon sticks	2 pieces galingale
12 blades mace	2 tablespoons whole gingerroot
1 teaspoon aniseed	6 cloves
8 pieces turmeric	24 allspice berries
2 small pieces orrisroot	20 white or green cardamom pods
2 dried cayenne peppers	4 wild (black) cardamom pods

---

10. This is a kind of nut, about an inch in diameter, that is really a spherical cluster of pin-sized white balls. I have not been able to identify its botanical name and am indebted to the Fez cookbook of Mme. Z. Guinaudeau for being able to identify it at all.

11. *Aframomum melegueta*, called *gooza sahraweea* in Morocco. These grains, also called "malagueta pepper," are about half the size of black peppercorns, reddish-brown, and are used as a stimulant and an aphrodisiac. They were called "grains of paradise" in old books which described how they were found along the pepper coast of Africa in Guinea and Sierra Leone. They came to Morocco in caravans from Senegal and Mauretania, and were first used by southern Berbers to spice meat and flavor breads.

12. *Piper longum*, called *dar felfel* in Morocco. They look like elongated and pock-marked black peppercorns.

13. *Lavandula vera*, called *khzama* in Morocco. These small purple flowers have a sweet, lemony aroma, and must be used with care because they are very strong. Sometimes added to tea.

14. *Myristica fragrans*, called *bsibsa* in Morocco. Made from the outer covering of the nutmeg shell, it is an indispensable ingredient in *ras el hanout*.

15. *Agnus castus*, called *kheroua* in Morocco. Another potent aphrodisiac.

16. *Myristica fragrans*, called *gouza* in Morocco. This, of course, is the inner kernel of the nut of which mace is the outer covering; thus the two spices have the same botanical name. Also indispensable in *ras el hanout*.

* *Rosa damascena*, called *rous el word* in Morocco. These come from dried roses grown in the Valley of Dades. They were not in the Fez *ras el hanout*, but they do appear in most formulae.

A rather simple recipe for *ras el hanout*—although far less thrilling to make or use—can be made with the following formula (buying in ounces from a spice merchant and grinding at home):

½ ounce allspice berries
1 ounce black peppercorns
½ ounce galingale or *laos* roots
½ ounce mace blades
1½ whole nutmegs
10 cardamom pods

1½ ounces dried gingerroot
½ ounce stick cinnamon
¼ ounce turmeric
3 rosebuds
1 clove

HERBS

◆

There are nine important herbs in Moroccan cooking: onions, garlic, parsley, green coriander, basil, marjoram, grey verbena, mint, and *za'atar*.

ONIONS (*Allium cepa*), called *sla* in Morocco. Most commonly used in Moroccan cookery, and the one I recommend, is the Spanish onion. Onions are used in great quantity in these recipes, so I recommend that you buy the biggest ones you can find and save yourself a lot of unnecessary peeling.

Sweet red onions are used with tomatoes in Moroccan salads, and fat spring onions, three times larger than our scallions, are delicious in chicken *tagines*.

GARLIC (*Allium sativum*), called *tourma* in Morocco. Moroccan garlic cloves are smaller than ours and pink, but they should not be confused with red garlic, which is milky and chewable. Quite surprisingly, garlic is often used in honeyed dishes, where it helps to balance out the flavors.

PARSLEY (*Petroselinum sativum*), called *madnouss* in Morocco. Moroccans use the flat-leaved Italian variety, which is a little milder than ours, but all my recipes have been adjusted to the curly parsley readily available in the United States. You may be surprised at the large amounts—sometimes several cupfuls—that go into *tagines*, but in the end the flavors balance out and the dishes become vitamin rich.

GREEN CORIANDER (*Coriandrum sativum*), called *kosbour* in Morocco.

For years I have been baffled by food writers who indicate coriander seeds when a recipe obviously calls for green coriander leaves. The taste is completely different, and the one cannot be exchanged for the other. It's sometimes difficult to find green coriander. If you do not live near a Portuguese, Mexican, Spanish, or Latin American market, and if there are no Chinese grocery stores in your vicinity, you can plant coriander seeds and grow your own green coriander. You'll need plenty of it, as it is one of the most important Moroccan herbs and is what gives many *tagines* their special flavor.

Because green coriander is sometimes difficult to find, many people want to know how to preserve it so that they can avoid frequent and difficult trips to obscure stores. I suggest three different ways:

1. Keep it in the refrigerator in an air-tight plastic container (1 week to 10 days).

2. Clean it, chop it, salt it and freeze it. Many people do this and then scoop out a piece whenever they need some for a recipe. My own experience is that, despite freezing, coriander stored this way has sometimes rotted.

3. Make "coriander water"—and I think this method is the best. "Coriander water" will work in all the recipes in this book that call for green coriander except the salads, where the coriander leaves *must* be fresh. To make "coriander water" cut off and discard half the stalks. Wash the leaves well and chop them coarsely. In a blender puree 3 cups of tightly packed leaves with 1½ to 2 cups cold water. Place in an ice tray and freeze into cubes. When frozen, separate the cubes and pack in a plastic bag. Each cube of "coriander water" or "coriander ice" is equivalent to 2 tablespoons of chopped green coriander.

BASIL (*Ocimum basilicum*), called *hboq* in Morocco. Not used in cooking, but I've been told it is used in Moroccan tea. In his book about spices John Parry tells of the superstition that a person will be bitten by scorpions on the same day that he has eaten basil. I find this fascinating, since Moroccan families keep a few pots of basil in their houses to ward off insects.

MARJORAM (*Origanum majorana*), called *mrdeddouch* in Morocco. This is a very common herb in Middle Eastern cooking, but the Moroccans use it less frequently than the Greeks or Syrians. It is found in some recipes for *kefta*, in the snail dish called *boubbouche*, and most often in tea. It is also used as a cure for bronchitis, in a drink of hot milk and sugar.

GREY VERBENA (*Lippia citriodore*), called *louisa* in Morocco. It is used by Moroccans in tea, which it gives a slightly bittersweet taste. Also said to have medicinal qualities.

MINT (*Mentha viridis*), called *nana* in Morocco. This, of course, is the foundation for Moroccan mint tea. Spearmint is best, but any good, fresh bunch of mint will do. The purple-tinged stalks are considered best.

ZA'ATAR (*Origanum cyriacum*). Za'atar, is a sort of hybrid of thyme-marjoram-orégano. Use any of these three commonly available herbs or mix them and substitute for *za'atar* when called for in a recipe. Do not confuse it with the mixture of thyme and sumac that is sold as *za'atar* in some Middle Eastern markets.

FRAGRANT WATERS

◆

The Moroccans use both orange flower water and rosewater in cakes, confections, certain *tagines*, and salads, and also for perfuming themselves after dining. You can buy both in Middle Eastern food shops, imported from either Lebanon or France. (I prefer the French water—it is cheaper and more aromatic.)

In Morocco, of course, the fragrant waters are often homemade. Arabs invented the process of distilling, and their *alambic* or *quettara* stills are basically the same as the distilling apparatus found in a modern chemical laboratory.

Orange flower water, called *zhaar* in Morocco, is usually made from the flowers of the Bergamot orange tree, and rosewater, called *ma ward*, is made from rosebuds collected in the Valley of Dades and sold in the *souks* by the kilo from enormous baskets. It takes seven pounds of rosebuds or orange blossoms to make a gallon of fragrant water.

Both fragrant waters are used throughout Morocco, but there seems to be a preference for rosewater in Marrakesh and for orange flower water in Fez.

Harissa Sauce

This popular relish is served along with many salads, mixed with olives, and, when thinned with a little oil and lemon juice, is sometimes used to flavor brochettes and *couscous*.

You can buy tinned *harissa* paste imported from Tunisia, or substitute the Indonesian spice paste called *sambal oelek*. Or, if you want, you can make your own. When refrigerated, *harissa* keeps 2 to 3 months.

INGREDIENTS	EQUIPMENT
1 ounce dried red chili peppers	Mortar and pestle or electric
1 clove garlic	spice mill
Salt to taste	Clean jar with tight-fitting
Olive oil	lid

Working time: 10 minutes

Cover the peppers with hot water and soak 1 hour, then drain and cut into small pieces. Place in the mortar or spice mill and pound or grind to a puree with the garlic. Sprinkle with a little salt, then spoon into the jar and cover with a layer of olive oil. Cover tightly and refrigerate.

Preserved Lemons

Preserved lemons, sold loose in the *souks*, are one of the indispensable ingredients of Moroccan cooking, used in fragrant lamb and vegetable *tagines*, recipes for chicken with lemons and olives, and salads. Their unique pickled taste and special silken texture cannot be duplicated with fresh lemon or lime juice, despite what some food writers have said. In Morocco they are made with a mixture of fragrant-skinned *doqq* and tart *boussera* lemons, but I have had excellent luck with American lemons from Florida and California.

Moroccan Jews have a slightly different procedure for pickling, which involves the use of olive oil, but this recipe, which includes optional herbs (in the manner of Safi), will produce a true Moroccan preserved-lemon taste.

The important thing in preserving lemons is to be certain they are completely covered with salted lemon juice. With my recipe you can use the lemon juice over and over again. (As a matter of fact, I keep a jar of used pickling juice in the kitchen, and when I make Bloody Marys or salad dressings and have a half lemon left over, I toss it into the jar and let it marinate with the rest.) Use wooden utensils to remove lemons as needed.

Sometimes you will see a sort of lacy, white substance clinging to preserved lemons in their jar; it is perfectly harmless, but should be rinsed off for aesthetic reasons just before the lemons are used. Preserved lemons are rinsed, in any case, to rid them of their salty taste. Cook with both pulps and rinds, if desired.

To make preserved lemons:

INGREDIENTS	EQUIPMENT
5 lemons	Shallow bowl
¼ cup salt, more if desired	Sterile 1-pint mason jar
	Sharp knife
Optional Safi mixture:	
1 cinnamon stick	*Working time:* 10 minutes
3 cloves	*Ripening time:* 30 days
5 to 6 coriander seeds	
3 to 4 black peppercorns	
1 bay leaf	
Freshly squeezed lemon juice, if necessary	

1. If you wish to soften the peel, soak the lemons in lukewarm water for 3 days, changing the water daily.

2. Quarter the lemons from the top to within ½ inch of the bottom, sprinkle salt on the exposed flesh, then reshape the fruit.

3. Place 1 tablespoon salt on the bottom of the mason jar. Pack in the lemons and push them down, adding more salt, and the optional spices, between layers. Press the lemons down to release their juices and to make room for the remaining lemons. (If the juice released from the squashed fruit does not cover them, add freshly squeezed lemon juice—*not* chemically produced lemon juice and *not* water.*) Leave some air space before sealing the jar.

4. Let the lemons ripen in a warm place, shaking the jar each day to distribute the salt and juice. Let ripen for 30 days.

To use, rinse the lemons, as needed, under running water, removing and discarding the pulp, if desired—and there is no need to refrigerate after opening. Preserved lemons will keep up to a year, and the pickling juice can be used two or three times over the course of a year.

VARIATION:

Aziza Benchekroun's Five-Day Preserved Lemon Special

If you run out of preserved lemons, or decide on just a few days' notice to cook a chicken, lamb, or fish dish with lemons and olives and need preserved lemons in a hurry, you can use this quick five-day method taught to me by a Moroccan diplomat's wife. Lemons preserved this way will not keep, but are perfectly acceptable in an emergency.

With a razor blade, make 8 fine 2-inch vertical incisions around the peel of each lemon to be used. (Do not cut deeper than the membrane that protects the pulp.) Place the incised lemons in a stainless-steel saucepan with plenty of salt and water to cover and boil until the peels become very soft. Place in a clean jar, cover with cooled cooking liquor, and leave to pickle for approximately 5 days.

* According to the late Michael Field, the way to extract the maximum amount of juice from a lemon is to boil it in water for 2 or 3 minutes and allow it to cool before squeezing.

OLIVES

———◆———

There are stalls that sell nothing but olives—olives of every flavor, size, quality, and color. An olive's color depends upon the moment in the ripening cycle that it is picked. As it ripens on the tree it turns from pale green to green-tan to tan-violet to violet-red to deep winy red to reddish black and finally to coal black. After that it loses its glistening appearance and begins to shrivel in the sun.

A freshly picked olive is inedible; it must be pickled or cured, and the way this is done will determine whether it is tangy, bitter, salty, lemony or sweet. There are other variables that affect its final flavor—the size of its pit, its shape, its meatiness, and the conditions of the soil and the climate.

Basically, three types of olives are used in Moroccan cooking: unripened green, cracked or whole olives for salads and such dishes as *meslalla*, where they literally "smother" the chicken (or lamb or fish); ripe "midway" olives ranging in hue from green-tan through violet and winy red, used in chicken or lamb *tagines* with lemon and olives and similar fish *tagines*; and salt-cured, shriveled black olives used in Moroccan salads. Note that the very good-tasting, glistening black olives so prevalent in America are not used in this cuisine.

GREEN, CRACKED OLIVES: One type of green olive used in the "smothering" dishes is so unripe when the olives are picked that they must be soaked in a strong brine to draw out their bitterness. In Morocco these olives are then cracked with a stone, hard enough to open the flesh but not hard enough to break the pit. After seven changes of salted brine the bitterness seeps out and a sharp, tangy taste develops inside. Then lemon juice is added to improve the flavor.

Green, cracked olives bottled in brine are readily available in the United States. To use them in Moroccan cooking you must wash, drain, and boil them at least three times to get rid of excessive bitterness. To use them in salads you must also pit them and then marinate them for a few hours in a sauce that contains lemon juice, a clove or two of slightly crushed garlic, some chopped fresh herbs (parsley and green coriander), paprika and cumin in a ratio of 2 to 1, cayenne, and salt to taste. I can't give a precise recipe because the amounts depend on the type of olive—a very bitter Nafpiou, a less bitter Agrinon (both of which are sold cracked), or the Spanish or California unripened green olives, which you can crack yourself. Use a good-sized olive, but stay away from American jumbos and colossals—they are too big.

RIPE OR "MIDWAY" OLIVES: These can be green, but the best ones are tan, russet, violet, or deep purple. I particularly recommend Italian Gaetas and Greek Kalamatas, and I have had excellent luck with Greek Royal-Victorias, which are a little more pungent. You can even use the enormous brown Alfonsos from Spain, but I suggest you stay clear of Italian colossals and Spanish and American ripe green olives—though excellent for eating, they just don't seem to work in Moroccan *tagines*.

You don't have to do anything to these ripe olives except rinse them before adding them to the pot. If you buy them by the quart from barrels, drain them and then store in a solution of the juice of 3 lemons, 1 cup olive oil, a little salt, and sufficient water to cover for 1 quart olives. I am advised by fastidious Moroccans that under no circumstances should you reach into this brine; they claim that fingers will spoil the brine and that the olives must be removed with a spoon.

CURED BLACK OLIVES: These are readily available, and as a matter of fact the salt-cured, shriveled olives sold under the house name of a famous Italian food packager are actually from Morocco. In the olive stalls you often find these olives either partially coated or totally covered with the hot relish called *harissa*.

OIL

————◆————

Many Moroccans cook their *tagines* with amounts of oil that are unacceptable to American tastes. I have reduced the quantities of oil to acceptable limits, but leaving enough so that the *tagines* will properly bind. For those who cannot take oil at all it can be reduced further or the *tagine* can be skimmed before serving.

There are some dishes (with tomatoes and other vegetables) in which all liquid is cooked away until only oil is left in the pan. This procedure follows a principle of Moroccan cooking: the vegetables, having been thoroughly stewed, are allowed, in the final minutes, to fry, producing a firmer texture and a crisper taste.

Salad, vegetable, or peanut oil is used mainly for cooking, and olive oil for cold dishes such as salads. One of the best oils is homemade by Berbers, who extract it from unripened green olives. When scented with wild thyme this green olive oil is exquisite.

A hundred years ago a particular method of cooking with oil was widely prevalent, but it is now confined to a few squab and game bird dishes. The bird, often fully stuffed, is plunged into a pot of terrifically hot oil, searing it instantly and sealing the juices inside. The pot is removed from the fire and allowed to cool, and cooking then continues at a simmer. The oil itself—with a few spoonfuls of water and more butter and some spices—becomes the sauce!

In the Souss region (the southwest), the people often cook with an oil extracted from the nuts of the argan tree,* a plant unique to that region and famous for its attractiveness to goats, who literally climb up into its branches. Argan oil can be mixed with almond paste and honey (fresh walnut oil may be the closest available substitute) to make a delicious almond butter called *amalou* (see next page), or kneaded with grilled wheat germ and honey to make a breakfast gruel called *zematar*.

* *Argania sideroxylon.*

Amalou

INGREDIENTS

EQUIPMENT

½ pound blanched almonds
Salad oil
½ cup French walnut oil
½ teaspoon salt
¼ cup thick honey

Skillet
Electric blender
Stoneware crock

Working time: 10 minutes
Makes: About 1½ cups

An adaptation for the Moroccan *amalou* can be made with fine French walnut oil.

Brown the almonds in a little hot salad oil. Drain and pulverize them in the blender with the walnut oil and the salt. When the mixture is smooth and creamy, spoon the honey into the blender jar and continue blending 20 seconds. Pour the *amalou* into a stoneware crock and store in a cool place. *Amalou* is spread on Moroccan bread or fried breads.

MILK PRODUCTS

———◆———

Zebda, Leben, Smen
(Country-Fresh Butter, Buttermilk, and Preserved Butter)

Moroccan *zebda* (a kind of fresh country butter) is extremely pungent, but should not be confused with the even more potent *smen* (a form of preserved butter that is prepared like the Indian butter-oil called *ghee*), or the rancid butter called *boudra*.

Zebda is made by leaving fresh milk in an earthen jug for two or three days and allowing it to "turn" naturally. It is then poured into an earthen churn called a *khabia,* which though never washed is kept very clean and only used for this purpose. The naturally curdled milk is churned until the butter particles separate out and the liquid turns to buttermilk (*leben*). In southern Morocco the churning is done inside a goatskin bag slung between trees. A woman swings it until she hears splashing sounds inside that tell her that the butter has separated from the milk. *Zebda* is used for cooking, and also to make the infamous *smen.*

Leben, or buttermilk, is much appreciated by Moroccan Berbers, who use it as a thirst-quencher, and often down it with a plate of cold barley *couscous* or fava beans buttered with *zebda.* Since American buttermilk (which *is* different) isn't at all bad, I recommend that you serve it with these Berber dishes.

As for *smen,* it was the *bête noire* of the early travel writers, particularly the British, who time and again referred to it as "rancid," "foul smelling," and so on, and told harrowing tales of how they were forced, at the risk of appearing rude, to eat it for breakfast with their Moroccan hosts. Unfortunately its terrible reputation has continued to this day, and at its very mention some people (again, usually Britishers) will gag and indicate their repulsion with all sorts of sour exclamations and expressions.

My first experience with *smen* came on one of my earliest trips to the pre-Saharan area. Taking the road south from Tiznit we turned off onto a trail in search of Targhist, one of the most beautiful and least known of the Moroccan oases. We finally stumbled into town with two flat tires, and though there was no gas station some people found a boy who knew how to fix bicycle tires and he patched us up. We met a man who worked in Ifni and who spoke Spanish, and he and his wife invited us to join them and their ten children for lunch. On the table was a giant slab of *smen* that had been made with strange wild herbs gathered from the surrounding desert. I thought it was one of the most delicious things I had ever tasted.

I have since learned to make *smen* with sweet fresh butter and easily obtainable herbs; it can be used for cooking, and gives a marvelous flavor to *couscous:*

Herbed Smen

INGREDIENTS

Salt
½ cup orégano or a combination of orégano, marjoram, and thyme
1 pound very fresh sweet butter

EQUIPMENT

Saucepan
Sieve
Shallow bowl
Sterile, airtight glass container

Working time: 5 minutes
Cooking time: 10 minutes
Ripening time: 30 days

1. Boil a small handful of salt and the orégano leaves in 1 quart water. Strain into the shallow bowl and allow to cool.

2. When the blackened "orégano water" has cooled to the point where it will no longer melt butter, add the butter, cut up into pieces, and knead until it has the consistency of mashed potatoes, pressing the mixture again and again against the bottom of the bowl so that every bit has been thoroughly washed. Drain the butter and then squeeze to extract excess water. Knead into a ball, place in the sterile glass container, and cover tightly.

3. Keep the container in a cool place (not the refrigerator) for at least 30 days before using. Once it has been opened, store in the refrigerator, where it will keep 1 to 2 months longer.

In Safi I have tasted *smen* made by washing the butter with water containing cinnamon, ground coriander seeds, and other pickling spices. Of course in the *bled*, or countryside, one finds some extremely potent *smens*. Some Berbers cook it, salt it, and bury it in the ground in earthen jugs for a year, after which it comes up tasting something like Gorgonzola cheese. The rich people of Fez (the Fassis) are the keepers of legendary quantities of *smen*, stored away for years in secret caches in the cellars of their magnificent homes, and brought out on rare occasions in all its pungent, dark-brown glory to be sniffed by honored guests.

Here is another recipe for *smen*, no doubt not to be compared to what may be found in the basements of the Fassis, but nevertheless Moroccan in flavor, nutty on account of the cooking of the butter, and more practical than the herbal *smen* because it will keep much longer:

Cooked and Salted Butter *(Smen)*

It is traditional to add a small spoonful of this to soups, and to mix a few tablespoons with *couscous* grains before serving. It is also excellent in *kdras*.

INGREDIENTS

1 pound sweet butter, cut up
1 tablespoon kosher or pickling salt

EQUIPMENT

2-quart saucepan
Strainer, lined with 4 layers of cheesecloth, over bowl
Sterile, airtight 1-pint glass container

Cooking time: 45 minutes
Makes: About 1 cup

1. Melt the butter over moderate heat, stirring frequently to avoid coloring it. Bring to a boil, lower the heat and simmer, undisturbed, for 45 minutes, or until the butter is clear and the solids on the bottom are light brown.

2. Spoon the clear liquid into the cheesecloth-lined strainer, and to keep the *smen* from turning rancid repeat the straining; the *smen* must be absolutely clear. Discard the milk solids in the saucepan.

3. Stir in the salt, then pour the liquid butter into a jar, cover, and store in a cool place or in the refrigerator.

Note: This will keep a long time, six months or longer.

Moroccan "Yogurt" (*Raipe*)

Raipe is a type of sweetened junket or "yogurt" in which the milk thickens and "firms up" on account of a most unusual ingredient: the hairy centers, or "chokes," of wild Moroccan artichokes. Unfortunately these wild artichokes, called *coques** by the Moroccans, are not available here, but if you get to Morocco and find ten or so of them you should not hesitate to let the chokes dry in the sun, bring them home, and make *raipe*—it's simple to prepare and absolutely delicious.

INGREDIENTS

10 *coques* or wild artichokes
 2 quarts fresh milk
⅓ cup granulated sugar, more or less, to taste
¼ to ½ cup orange flower water to taste

EQUIPMENT

Paring knife
Mortar and pestle
Cheesecloth
Enamel or stainless steel
   saucepan

Working time: 30 minutes
Setting time: 1½ hours
Serves: 8

1. Break off the outer leaves of the *coques* and trim carefully—they are very spiky. Remove the base and set the chokes aside. (If desired, let the chokes dry in the sun for a few days, then crumble them and pack them in a cheesecloth bag.)

2. Heat the milk, with the sugar, to lukewarm.

3. Pound the hairy chokes to a pulp in the mortar. Wrap the pulp in cheesecloth and swirl around in the lukewarm milk, then gently squeeze the bag to extract all the brown juice. Remove and discard the bag, and stir the orange flower water into the milk. Cover and set in a warm place for 1 to 1½ hours, until set. Serve cool or chilled in cups.

* Cynara humilis.

EGGS

———◆———

In country *souks* one finds fresh eggs packed in reed baskets, each one nestled in a bit of straw. When a Moroccan buys an egg he holds it up to the light: if it is translucent he knows that it is absolutely fresh.

Eggs are sold hard-boiled on the streets. The hungry stroller shells them, then dips them in a mixture of salt and ground cumin.

Often a Moroccan will dip a hard-boiled egg into saffron-tinted water, slice it, and then fry the slices as for one Fez version of *tafaya* (lamb cooked with spices, almonds, and decorated with saffron-colored eggs). Sometimes he will hard-boil eggs all night in a meat and bean casserole, as in the Jewish specialty called Sefirna (page 268); this long simmering turns the whites to a soft tan, and gives the yolks a creamy texture.

In Morocco eggs are often treated differently than they are here. For example, we try very hard to keep our eggs from curdling, but curdled eggs are ideal for the most famous Moroccan dish, *bisteeya*. They are deliberately beaten with lemon juice to encourage curds when boiled; otherwise they become stringy and leathery inside the pastry. Other dishes that require curdled eggs are Braewats (page 122) (eggs, onions, and lemon wrapped in pastry leaves and then fried) and *masquid bil beid* (pieces of chicken set within layers of curdled eggs and a spicy sauce).

One of the best family dishes in Moroccan cuisine is a preparation of eggs poached in a spicy tomato sauce with *kefta* (meatballs), or in a buttery onion sauce with bite-sized pieces of lamb.

Every country has its own versions of the omelet, and all the Mediterranean countries have a method of cooking eggs in a skillet with potatoes and onions or other vegetables. Among such dishes the Moroccan *khboz bil beid* is a *ne plus ultra*: it is made with potatoes, parsley, cumin, paprika, and cubes of bread and is garnished with olives and preserved lemon. At the other end of the scale I hear there is an omelet filled with bits of locust!

Eggs are often used to glaze stuffed vegetables, and one of the great tours de force of the Moroccan kitchen is *djej mefenned* (Chicken Braised and Browned and Coated with Eggs, page 215).

MOROCCAN PRESERVED MEAT (KHELEA)

———◆———

Khelea, a preserved beef that bears a close resemblance to Greek or Turkish *bastourma,* is usually prepared in Moroccan homes during the summer months, when the sun shines brilliantly all day. The meat is salted, spiced with ground cumin and coriander seeds, rubbed with garlic, and then dried in the sun—sometimes by hanging it from the clothesline!

Meat being turned into *khelea* is left to dry in the sun for six days, and is brought inside each night so that nocturnal dampness will not cause mold. Once it has dried and the spices have penetrated fully, it is cooked in boiling olive oil mixed with lamb or beef fat and plenty of water. It is then removed to an earthen container, while the oil continues to boil until all the water has evaporated. The remaining grease is used to cover the meat and seal it off from the air.

A well-to-do family might purchase up to 100 pounds of meat at a time to make a year's supply of *khelea.* Moroccans unable to afford such a huge outlay can buy it tinned in the *souks*—or, for that matter, in Arab stores in this country.

Khelea can be used in *couscous* in place of meat or poultry, in Rghaif (page 126), in certain *tagines,* and in a highly spiced dish that also contains dried beans and pumpkin. Because *khelea* is preserved it is often taken on forays into the Sahara, where its spicy flavor warms up the diner on chilly desert nights—though it leaves *me* cold.

If you wish, you can prepare *khelea* in an "instant" version:

"Instant" Khelea

INGREDIENTS
- 1 pound beef round
- ¼ cup ground cumin
- ¼ cup ground coriander seed
- 3 tablespoons chopped garlic
- 3 tablespoons salt
- ¼ pound beef fat
- Salad oil to cover

EQUIPMENT
Large saucepan
Large glass or enameled
  mixing bowl

Working time: 10 minutes
Cooking time: 1 to 2 hours

Rub the beef with the ground cumin, ground coriander seed, chopped garlic, and salt. Melt the beef fat in 1 cup water over high heat. When the water has evaporated, put in the spiced beef and enough oil to completely cover the meat. Cook it slowly, covered, for 1 to 2 hours. Drain the meat and cool the fat. Place the meat in a clean bowl and strain the fat over it.

Note: This "instant" form of *khelea* should keep for 2 to 3 days in a cool place.

HONEY

———◆———

The best Moroccan honey comes from Melilla (in the north) and Tagoundaft (in the Souss). Both honeys are thick and aromatic, sometimes crystallized, and are marvelous in the desserts, glazed dishes, poultry stuffings, and *tagines* where honey is an important ingredient. As substitutes, Spanish rosemary honey is very good, and Mount Hymettus honey from Greece, with its strong thyme flavor, is particularly recommended. If you cannot get any of these I suggest, as a last resort, the clover honeys available everywhere; these impart the correct amount of sweetening, although they lack a good, strong, herbal flavor.

COUSCOUS GRAIN

———◆———

You can buy packaged *couscous* grains in some supermarkets and at nearly all organic food stores and gourmet shops. The best-tasting *couscous*, however, is sold loose, and can be obtained in health food stores and by mail order (see Appendix A). In an airtight container *couscous* grains can be kept for years.

Unfortunately neither the *rough*-grained semolina flour (*smeeda*) used to make the *couscous seffa* nor the very large hand-rolled grains called *mhammsa* are available here, but hopefully that situation will soon change. You really shouldn't follow the directions or recipes on a *couscous* package—the directions are poorly expressed, the recipes are second-rate, and if you follow them you will not have the lightest, tenderest *couscous*.

Beware of packages of "precooked" or "instant" *couscous*. Some are very poor. If the wording on the package indicates that it is imported and can be cooked "the traditional way" as well as "instantly," then it will probably be all right.

CHICK-PEAS

———◆———

There is an interesting theory, developed by Richard Ford, nineteenth-century travel writer and historian, and seconded by Arnold Toynbee, that both the Spaniards and the Berbers are Punic peoples. Ford finds partial proof in their mutual fondness for the chick-pea, and he points out that the Punic love of chick-peas so pleased the Roman playwright Plautus (ca. 200 B.C.) that he introduced a chick-pea-eating character speaking Punic, which is comparable to Shakespeare's use of a toasted-cheese-eating Welshman speaking Welsh.

Be that as it may, the chick-pea is popular throughout the Middle East, especially in the form of *hummous*, and in Morocco it appears over and over again in *couscous* dishes and *tagines*. As for peeling chick-peas, it is not necessary, but I recommend you do it for aesthetic reasons, especially if you use chick-peas that are canned. (In Morocco dried chick-peas are soaked in water, in sunlight, then drained and rubbed against the sides of a reed basket to facilitate the removal of their skins. You can peel them easily by cooking the dried chick-peas separately for an hour and then plunging them into cold water; rub them lightly between your fingers—the skins will come off and rise to the surface.) In all these recipes I have left open the option of using dried or canned chick-peas. The choice is yours, but my own preference is for the dried ones (available at organic food stores), even though they must be soaked the night before preparing the dish.

KITCHEN EQUIPMENT

———◆———

There are rows and rows of market stalls devoted to pots and pans, earthenware *tagine slaouis* (shallow dishes with conical tops), knives, *couscousieres*, brass mortars and pestles, and all the other pieces of equipment used to make Moroccan food. A friend who is a great authority on food tells me that he always visits a hardware store and a cooking equipment store as soon as he arrives in a country; between the two, he says, one can understand a nation's culture.

Despite the great array of equipment for sale in the *souks*, I am constantly amazed by the small number of utensils found in a Moroccan restaurant kitchen or even in a well-to-do home. There will always be a *couscousiere*, a few copper *taouas* (casseroles), a skillet for frying almonds or fish, knives and earthenware, bottles for keeping spices, a simple brazier for charcoal, and a two-burner stove. One rarely sees an oven; in one restaurant I visited, if a *tagine* was to be baked or "gratinéed," an earthenware platter heaped with burning charcoal was placed on top. For extensive baking, a servant or a child is dispatched to a neighborhood oven.

Naturally, this kind of simplicity is more practical in a country where labor is cheap and there are many hands to do the things that we do with the help of gadgets. Nevertheless, it suggests to me the elegant simplicity of Moroccan cooking; with the exception of a few dishes (*bisteeya, trid,* and so on), it is accessible to nearly anyone who wishes to try it, and that cannot be said of French haute cuisine or Viennese pastry.

Another thing that I noticed about Moroccan cooks is their total lack of reliance on any sort of measuring equipment except their noses and eyes. I watched one Moroccan cook time and time again hack off lamb into perfect five-ounce portions (confirmed on my scale) and add amounts of ginger with a wave of her hand that were always accurate to the quarter teaspoon. (I discovered this when we repeated *bisteeya*—the amounts were the same to a fraction.) This kind of consistency comes from years of cooking experience, plus years of observation when she was a little girl. But every good Moroccan cook has this kind of measuring instinct—as do most good cooks almost everywhere in the world.

You will need very little new equipment to cook Moroccan food: a *couscousiere,* of course (a wise investment, since it can be used for steaming all sorts of things—though, if you like, you can substitute a pot and a snug-fitting colander, or use a steamer); perhaps a heavy brass mortar and pestle for pounding (not wood, since garlic and saffron will soon leave their traces); and a few shallow serving casseroles for *tagines* (earthenware, if possible, especially for fish). Enameled cast-iron or tin-lined copper pots will do nicely—though you may have to transfer the food to serving platters, since these pots are rarely shallow enough for dining with the hands *à la Marocaine.*

If you go to Morocco you can buy the real thing, earthenware or copper *couscousieres,* beautiful four-handled brass mortars (*mehraz*), and glazed earthenware *tagine slaouis,* with their marvelous-looking conical hats.

If you become a real Moroccan enthusiast like me you can then buy all sorts of esoteric cookware: a *gsaa,* the wooden or earthen basin used for kneading dough for bread, *rghaifs,* and pastry; a *gdra dil trid,* a domelike utensil of earthenware used for stretching dough to make the pastry leaves for *trid;* a *tobsil*, a large, round, tin-covered copper pan to be placed over charcoal or boiling water when you make the *warka* for *bisteeya* (page 103); a *tbicka*, a large basket with a conical hat used for storing bread and serving *tagines*; the *m'ghazel* skewers, made of silver in Fez, for *kefta* and brochettes; a Moroccan teapot, tea glasses, and tea trays; copper, silver, and brass serving trays; and implements for pouring perfumed water over the hands after eating. And then, if you are really dedicated, you can go to the Valley of Ammeln in the Anti-Atlas and find a special kind of unglazed earthenware pot that I first heard about from Paul Bowles. It looks like a pumpkin with a handle at the top; if you tap it lightly near a small air hole it cracks around the circumference, making a perforated line. Tapping along this line you end up with a perfectly matched top and bottom that fit together and will seal in the juices when you cook *tagines*.

THREE

Bread

*Manage with bread and butter until
God sends the honey.*

—Moroccan Proverb

In North Africa bread is sacred, and is treated with respect. If you see a piece lying on the ground, you pick it up and kiss it and put it some place where it will not be dirtied. A woman who wishes her bread to impart that special kind of God-given luck called *baraka* will send the first three leaves of the unleavened *therfist* to a Koranic scholar. And there is a tale in Morocco of a Negro woman imprisoned in the moon because she defiled a loaf.

The round, heavy-textured, spicy bread of Morocco is quite different from the flat, hollow discs that pass for "Arab bread" in the United States. Chewy, soft-crusted Moroccan bread is highly absorbent, ideal for dipping into the savory sauces of *tagines* and as a kind of "fork" for conveying food when eating with one's hands. Because it is left to rise only once it is extremely easy to make, and is well worth the trouble if you are planning to serve Moroccan food.

The custom at a Moroccan dinner is that only one person distributes the wedges cut from the round loaves; otherwise, there will be a quarrel at the table.

In most Moroccan homes bread is still prepared every morning, kneaded in a large, unglazed red clay pan called a *gsaa* and then sent to the community oven on the heads of children wearing padded caps. The loaves of each family are identified with a wooden stamp, and the bread is returned as soon as it is baked.

To my mind the best bread in Morocco is made with such coarse grains as whole wheat or barley mixed with unbleached flour. But whenever a visitor (and especially an American) is coming to the house, many Moroccans unfortunately feel that it is "finer" to prepare their bread with refined white flour, and the result is, predictably, bland.

Moroccan women knead bending over the *gsaa* while pushing and folding a long roll of dough back and forth until it gains maximum elasticity. The best-tasting breads are the ones most thoroughly kneaded—the yeast is evenly distributed and the bread is protein-rich: my image of bread making in Morocco is concentrated around the memory of myself on my knees kneading in tune to the recorded songs of the great Egyptian singer Oum Kaltsoum.

Besides the classic Moroccan breads called *kisra* or *khboz* (pages 51–55) there is a Marrakesh specialty called *khboz bishemar* (very similar to the pastry called *rghaif* and which I call Marrakesh "Pizza" [page 54]); *therfist*, an unleavened bread that is prepared in sheets, which are often spread with a foamy mixture of fenugreek and water reputed to make Berber women plump; and a kind of bread made by the "blue people" (Tuaregs) of the Sahara, baked on hot sand and called *tagella*.

When Tuaregs share bread with a stranger they sanctify the occasion by saying: "By bread and salt we are united."

Moroccan Bread (*Kisra or Khboz*)

INGREDIENTS

1 package active dry yeast
1 teaspoon granulated sugar
3½ cups unbleached flour
1 cup whole-wheat flour
2 teaspoons salt
½ cup lukewarm milk
1 teaspoon sesame seeds
1 tablespoon aniseed
Cornmeal

EQUIPMENT

Small and large mixing bowls
Electric mixer with dough
　hook (optional)
2 baking sheets
Towels

Working time: 35 minutes
Rising time: 1½ to 2 hours
Baking time: 40 to 50 min-
　utes
Makes: 2 six-inch round
　loaves

1. Soften the yeast in ¼ cup sugared lukewarm water. Let stand 2 minutes, then stir and set in a warm place until the yeast is bubbly and doubles in volume. Meanwhile, mix the flours with the salt in a large mixing bowl.

2. Stir the bubbling yeast into the flour, then add the milk and enough lukewarm water to form a stiff dough. (Since flours differ in their ability to absorb moisture, no precise amount can be given.) Turn the dough out onto a lightly floured board and knead hard with closed fists, adding water if necessary. To knead, push the dough outward. (It will take anywhere from 10 to 15 minutes to knead this dough thoroughly and achieve a smooth, elastic consistency. If using an electric beater with a dough hook, knead 7 to 8 minutes at slow speed.) During the final part of the kneading, add the spices. After the dough has been thoroughly kneaded, form into two balls and let stand 5 minutes on the board.

3. Lightly grease a mixing bowl. Transfer the first ball of dough to the greased bowl and form into a cone shape by grasping the dough with one hand and rotating it against the sides of the bowl, held by the other hand. Turn out

onto a baking sheet that has been sprinkled with cornmeal. Flatten the cone with the palm of the hand to form a flattened disc about 5 inches in diameter with a slightly raised center. Repeat with the second ball of dough. Cover loosely with a damp towel and let rise about 2 hours in a warm place. (To see if the bread has fully risen, poke your finger gently into the dough—the bread is ready for baking if the dough does not spring back.)

4. Preheat the oven to 400°.

5. Using a fork, prick the bread around the sides three or four times and place on the center shelf of the oven. Bake 12 minutes, then lower the heat to 300° and bake 30 to 40 minutes more. When done, the bread will sound hollow when tapped on the bottom. Remove and let cool. Cut in wedges just before serving.

VARIATION:

Khboz Mikla

A flattened circle of the dough is cooked, over an open fire, on a dry earthen griddle called a *mikla* until browned on both sides. To my mind this is absolutely delicious with fresh butter and crystallized honey.

VARIATION:

Holiday Bread

This is a family recipe from Essaouria.

INGREDIENTS

1 package active dry yeast
¼ cup sweet butter, melted and cooled
½ cup granulated sugar
1 cup lukewarm milk or ¾ cup lukewarm milk
    plus ¼ cup lukewarm buttermilk
4¼ cups unbleached flour
2 teaspoons salt
1 tablespoon orange flower water
1½ teaspoons aniseed
1½ teaspoons sesame seeds
    Cornmeal

EQUIPMENT

Small and large mixing bowls
Electric mixer with dough
    hook (optional)
2 baking sheets
Towels

Working time: 35 minutes
Rising time: 1½ to 2 hours
Baking time: 40 to 50 minutes
Makes: 1 twelve-inch round
    loaf or 2 six-inch loaves

1. Prepare the yeast as directed in step 1 on page 51, then add the cooled melted butter, sugar, milk, and enough lukewarm water to the flour and salt to make a stiff dough. Knead well. During the final kneading add the orange flower water and spices.

2. Form and bake as directed in steps 3 through 5 on pages 51–52.

Marrakesh "Pizza" (*Khboz Bishemar*)

It may seem odd to stuff bread with fat and spices, but the idea is extremely ingenious: the fat runs out through holes pricked in the dough, becomes the medium in which the bread is fried, and leaves behind its flavor and an array of spices and herbs that make it taste strikingly like pizza crust.

INGREDIENTS

1 package active dry yeast
¼ pound mutton or beef suet (about 1 cup, tightly packed)
3 tablespoons chopped parsley
½ cup finely chopped onion
¼ heaping teaspoon ground cumin
1 dried red chili pepper
1 heaping teaspoon paprika
2 cups unbleached flour
1 teaspoon salt
4 teaspoons sweet butter, melted

EQUIPMENT

Small and large mixing bowls
Heavy chopping knife or meat grinder
Mortar and pestle
Iron griddle or skillet

Working time: 40 minutes
Rising time: 45 minutes
Cooking time: 20 minutes
Serves: 4

1. Sprinkle the yeast over ¼ cup lukewarm water. Stir to dissolve and let stand in a warm place for 10 minutes, or until the yeast has become bubbly and doubled in volume.

2. Meanwhile, make the filling. Chop or grind suet; pound the parsley, onion, and spices in a mortar or chop finely to a paste. Mix with the suet and set aside.

3. Mix the flour with the salt and make a well in the center. Pour in the bubbling yeast and enough lukewarm water to form a ball of dough. (Add more water if the dough seems hard to handle.) Knead well until smooth and elastic, about 20 minutes. Separate the ball of dough into 4 equal parts.

4. Lightly flour a board. Begin patting the first ball of dough down to a disc shape, stretching and flattening it to make a rectangle approximately

8 x 14 inches. Spread one-quarter of the filling in the center. Fold the right and then the left side of the dough over the filling. Press down on this "package" and begin flattening and stretching it (with the filling inside) until it is the same size (8 x 14 inches) as before. Repeat the folding, this time right side over center and left side under. Repeat with the remaining 3 balls of dough. Set aside, covered, in a warm place for 45 minutes.

5. Heat the griddle. Prick the "packages" with a fork six or seven times on both sides. Place on the griddle—they will begin to fry in the fat released from their fillings. Fry the "packages" 10 minutes on each side, until crisp. Dot each package with a teaspoonful of melted butter before serving.

FOUR

————◆————

Soups

In Morocco soup is usually a supper dish, heavy and well spiced, nourishing and rich. I have known people who lived on nothing but *harira* soup while visiting Morocco.

Harira, of course, is famous as the food eaten at sundown each day during the fasting month of Ramadan. But Moroccans eat it throughout the year, and also a lighter version called *chorba*, which is not thickened with yeast or flour or eggs and which is particularly good in summer.

Harira karouiya (Caraway-Flavored Soup, page 62) is a fortifying curiosity usually served with lamb's head. Then there are the various "medicinal" soups—a peppery concoction of garlic, saffron, thyme, and peppermint recommended for women who are about to give birth, and a soup of lightly toasted aniseed, ground in a mortar and cooked in boiling water with whole-wheat flour, pepper, salt, and butter, which is said to relieve a sore back or a cold. Thyme is added if the cold is complicated by a sore throat, and the anise has an additional effect—it will prevent nightmares and ensure a comfortable sleep.

HARIRA AND RAMADAN

The holy month of Ramadan is one of the most striking features of the Arab world. This ninth month of the Muslim year is called "the month of fasting," and not a bite of food or a drop of water is consumed between sunrise and sunset, which is announced, when it comes, by the report of a cannon.

At the moment of sunset, Moroccans sit down to the traditional Ramadan "breakfast": *harira* soup, dates, *mahalkra* or *shebbakia* (Honey Cake, page 303), and coffee or milk. *Harira* is peppery and lemony, rich with vegetables and meat, and thickened with *tedouira*—a mixture of yeast or flour and water. It is always reddened with tomatoes, and sometimes enriched with beaten eggs.

I have heard that the beaten eggs are often omitted at the royal palace in favor of a more luxurious triumph of the Moroccan kitchen: in silver egg cups sit eggshells, their tops removed, filled with eggs that have been softly scrambled with gum arabic, saffron, cumin, and salt. The diners imbibe this mixture like shots of whiskey directly from the shells, for instant nourishment and while waiting for their *harira* to cool down.

Harira I

This is a city version.

INGREDIENTS

1 cup chopped onion
1 cup chopped parsley
1 tablespoon finely chopped celery leaves
1 teaspoon freshly ground black pepper

EQUIPMENT

Large soup pot
Mortar and pestle or electric
  blender

1 teaspoon turmeric
1 tablespoon *smen* (Cooked and Salted Butter, page 39) or 2 tablespoons fresh butter
½ teaspoon ground cinnamon
½ pound shoulder of lamb, in ½-inch cubes
  Wings, backs and giblets of 1 chicken
½ cup dried lentils
2 tablespoons green coriander leaves
  Salt to taste
2 pounds red, ripe tomatoes, peeled and seeded (see page 71), then pureed (1 tablespoon tomato paste or more is optional for less than perfect tomatoes)
½ cup fine soup noodles
3 tablespoons semolina or all-purpose flour mixed with ½ cup water
  Lemon wedges

Working time: 20 minutes
Cooking time: 2 hours
Serves: 6 to 8

1. In a large soup pot, cook the onion, parsley, celery leaves, pepper, and turmeric in the *smen* for about 3 to 4 minutes, stirring, then add the cinnamon, lamb and chicken. Cook slowly, turning the mixture over and over until golden but not browned (about 15 to 20 minutes).

2. Meanwhile, pick over and wash the lentils. In a mortar pound the green coriander leaves with a little salt into a paste or puree the leaves in an electric blender with a spoonful of water. Add the lentils, coriander paste, and pureed tomatoes to the pot. Cook 15 minutes over low heat, then pour in 1½ quarts water and cook until the lentils are soft and the soup is well blended.

3. Five minutes before serving, salt the soup and add the noodles. Bring to a boil and cook for 2 minutes, then stir in the flour-water mixture. Cook 3 minutes longer, stirring continuously to avoid any flour nuggets forming. Serve at once with lemon wedges.

Note: In Marrakesh the *tedouira,* or flour-water mixture, used to thicken *harira* is prepared a day in advance so that the flour will ferment slightly and impart a musky flavor to the soup.

Harira II

A marvelous version from the *bled* (countryside), thickened with lemony eggs.

INGREDIENTS

½ cup dried chick-peas
1 pound lamb, trimmed and cut into ½-inch cubes
1 teaspoon turmeric
Pinch of pulverized saffron
1 teaspoon freshly ground black pepper
1 teaspoon ground cinnamon
¼ teaspoon ground ginger (optional)
1 tablespoon *smen* (Cooked and Salted Butter, page 39) or 2 tablespoons sweet butter
¾ cup chopped celery leaves and ribs
2 medium yellow onions
½ cup chopped parsley
2 pounds tomatoes, peeled, seeded and chopped (see page 71)
Salt
¾ cup dried lentils
8 small white onions
¼ cup fine soup noodles (optional)
2 eggs beaten with the juice of ½ lemon
Lemon slices and cinnamon for garnish

EQUIPMENT

Sieve
Large soup pot with cover

Working time: 30 minutes
Cooking time: 2 hours or longer
Serves: 8

1. Soak the chick-peas in water to cover overnight. Drain and husk if desired.

2. Put the lamb, spices, *smen*, celery, chopped onions, and parsley in the soup pot and cook, stirring, over moderately low heat for 5 minutes. Then add the tomatoes and continue cooking 10 to 15 minutes longer. Salt lightly.

3. Meanwhile, wash the lentils in a sieve under running water until the

water runs clear. Add the lentils to the pot with 2 quarts water. Bring to a boil, then lower the heat and simmer, partially covered, 1½ hours.

4. Add the small white onions and continue cooking the soup 30 minutes.

5. Five minutes before serving add the soup noodles. When they are tender, pour the egg and lemon juice mixture into the simmering soup and turn off the heat immediately. Stir rapidly to form long egg strands. Taste for seasoning and serve with lemon slices and a light dusting of ground cinnamon.

———————— • ————————

Soup of Chick-peas (*Chorba Bil Hamus*)

This is an excellent soup to serve before *djej mahammer* (Chicken Braised and Browned, page 213) or *djej mefenned* (Chicken Braised and Browned and Coated with Eggs, page 215).

Though chick-peas must be husked (see page 45) if they are going into a chicken *tagine*, the process is optional for soup.

INGREDIENTS	EQUIPMENT
1 cup dried chick-peas or 1 twenty-ounce can cooked chick-peas	5½-quart enameled cast-iron casserole with cover
1 lamb shank	
Wings, backs, and giblets of 2 chickens	*Working time:* 20 minutes
½ cup chopped parsley	*Cooking time:* 2½ hours
Salt	*Serves:* 10
¼ teaspoon freshly ground black pepper	
2 pinches pulverized saffron	
¼ teaspoon turmeric	
¼ teaspoon ground ginger	
⅓ cup grated onion	
3 tablespoons salad oil	
1 tablespoon tomato paste	
1 cup peeled, cubed potatoes	
¼ cup lemon juice	

1. The night before, soak the chick-peas in plenty of water.

2. The next day, drain the chick-peas and place in the casserole with the lamb, chicken, parsley, salt to taste, spices, onion, and oil. Cover with 2 quarts water and bring to a boil. Reduce the heat, cover, and simmer 2 hours, after 1 hour adding the tomato paste.

3. After 2 hours remove the lamb and cut into dice. Return to the soup, along with the diced potatoes, and simmer another 30 minutes. Add the lemon juice, taste for salt, and serve.

Caraway-Flavored Soup (*Harira Karouiya*)

This fortifying soup, traditionally served with lamb's head, is recommended by my Moroccan friends as fare suitable for a "tired voyager." Though I personally find it something less than sublime, I offer it here as a curiosity. When flavored with sugar and a little orange flower water, though, its curds make an excellent stuffing for Braewats (page 122).

INGREDIENTS

3½ quarts fresh milk
½ cup lemon juice
1 heaping tablespoon caraway seeds
1 teaspoon thyme
7 to 8 sprigs fresh mint
1 cup all-purpose flour
Salt
¼ cup granulated sugar

EQUIPMENT

5½-quart enameled cast-iron casserole
Colander
Cheesecloth
Large and small mixing bowls
Mortar and pestle

Working time: 20 minutes
Cooking time: 10 minutes
Serves: 6 to 8

1. Heat the milk in the casserole. Add the lemon juice and bring to a boil. Stir quickly until curds have formed, then remove from the heat. Line the colander with one piece of the cheesecloth. Set the colander over a large bowl and pour in the curds and milk. Holding the ends of the cloth together, let the curds drain well. Pour the milk back into the casserole.

2. Pound the caraway seeds, with the thyme, in the mortar. Sprinkle with water and wrap in another piece of cheesecloth. Add the mint sprigs and cheesecloth bag of caraway and thyme to the milk. Bring to a boil.

3. Mix the flour with 2 cups water and slowly add to the boiling milk, stirring constantly to avoid lumping. When smooth add a *handful* of curds broken into small pieces. Cook 5 minutes then let cool. Remove and discard the mint and the cheesecloth filled with aromatics.

4. Cut the remaining curds into dice and place in a soup tureen. Reheat the soup, add salt to taste and sugar, and pour over the curds. Serve hot.

FIVE

Salads and Vegetables

There are people who come to the *souks* of Morocco to buy silver and gold, caftans and rugs, or who like to wander through the streets of the carpenters, the tailors, the coppersmiths, or the cloth merchants. My favorite *souks* are the markets of fruits and vegetables—the ones in the countryside, where everything is young and tender and fresh, and the endless produce stalls of the great cities.

I love to roam the market of Tangier, where I can feast my eyes on tapering turnips, sweet green peppers, young carrots with their leafy tops, baby eggplants, knobby tan Jerusalem artichokes, and long red radishes. Here I can caress luscious, vine-ripened tomatoes, young and fat spring onions, fine-stalked celery, huge cauliflowers, pale pink heads of garlic, and all manner of greens and gourds. I can run my fingers through shell beans and favas, and then press them lightly against oranges, *clementines*, fresh apricots, red and greengage plums, pink grapefruits, and many kinds of Moroccan grapes. These fruits and vegetables are always lovingly displayed; in the great urban markets one finds row after row of fresh produce, whole rows of stalls that sell nothing but greens. To move among these things, amid a swirl of people buying and selling, bargaining and bustling, is for me one of the great pleasures of life.

Vegetables were not a traditional part of the cuisine of the southern Berber peoples; for them there was little more than pumpkin and gourds, turnips, onions, nuts, and fruit. It is still customary in the south to start a guest off with a plate of dates and a bowl of milk, just as in the *bled* the first offering is usually some kind of biscuit served with honey and *smen*. But around Fez and along the coastal areas vegetables have always been popular. Here one finds the great agricultural districts of the country, the Sais Plain and the Sebou Valley, the Chaouia area stretching from Rabat to Casablanca, and the great gardens of the southern Atlantic coast that culminate in the famous orange groves of Agadir.

In the heartland, around Fez and Meknes, and down this fruit- and vegetable-laden coast, one eats the salads of Morocco. These are not salads in the sense that we think of that word here—not mixtures of greens doused with dressings. Moroccan salads are more like Italian antipasti—dishes of spiced or sweetened, cooked or raw vegetables served at the beginning of a meal to inspire the appetite and refresh the palate.

The glories of these dishes are their unexpected contrasts and combinations of tastes—such things as zucchini flavored with *za'atar*; orange sections, black olives, and garlic; carrots with orange blossom water; and, by extension, meat dishes such as brains with herbs and spices; and salads of cubed liver. They are all delightful and delicious, gems that sparkle in the crown of a great national cuisine. Sometimes they are placed on the table at the beginning of a meal and left there throughout; other times they are whisked off upon the arrival of the first *tagine*. Either way, the memory of their superb flavors stays with the diner, who is rarely served with less than four different types.

EGGPLANT SALADS

Eggplants are used to make a Moroccan version of *ratatouille*, and, when cooked with small chili peppers, a dish closely related to the Tunisian *chatchouka*. One eggplant salad (Zeilook, opposite) is made of fried slices of the vegetable, seasoned with cumin and paprika, mashed to a puree, then fried again until rich and firm. In another (Eggplant Salad, Rabat Style, page 68), the vegetable is first grilled over charcoal and then the pulp is fried until it condenses into a thick black jam. Both salads are delicious, and both keep well for many days.

Eggplants need to be salted before frying to rid them of their bitter juices; then they should be rinsed, squeezed, and dried on paper towels. Try to fry them in olive oil; vegetable dishes served cold taste better that way.

Eggplant Salad (*Zeilook*)

You can play around with this recipe, using whatever you happen to have on hand. For example, you can add two or three zucchinis, sliced, and fry them with the eggplant, or three or four sweet green peppers, which have been grilled, peeled, and diced with the tomatoes. Or you can simply execute the recipe as written below.

INGREDIENTS

2 pounds eggplant
Salt
Olive oil for frying
3 red, ripe tomatoes, peeled, seeded, and chopped (see page 71)
2 to 3 cloves garlic, peeled and chopped
½ scant teaspoon ground cumin
1 teaspoon sweet paprika
1 tablespoon freshly chopped green coriander (optional)
3 tablespoons lemon juice, or to taste

EQUIPMENT

Vegetable peeler or paring knife
Colander
Paper towels
Large skillet
Perforated spatula
Potato masher

Working time: 25 minutes
Cooking time: 40 minutes
Makes: 2 cups

1. Remove 3 vertical strips of skin from each vegetable, leaving the egg-plants striped, then cut eggplant into ½-inch-thick slices. Salt them and leave to drain in the colander for 30 minutes. Rinse well, squeeze gently, and pat the slices dry with paper towels.

2. Heat a good quantity of oil in the skillet and fry the eggplant slices until brown on both sides, removing them when done with the perforated spatula. Reserve the oil in the pan. Mash the eggplant with the tomatoes, garlic, spices, and coriander.

3. Fry the puree in the oil in the pan until all the liquid evaporates and there is only oil and vegetable left. Stirring the puree often to avoid scorching, continue frying 15 minutes. Pour off the oil and season with lemon juice to taste. Taste for salt. Serve warm or cool.

Note: This salad can be kept 3 to 4 days covered in a cool place.

Eggplant Salad, Rabat Style

The eggplant is traditionally grilled over a charcoal brazier; for convenience in this recipe, it is baked in the oven.

INGREDIENTS

- 1 eggplant (1 pound)
- 1 clove garlic, peeled and slivered
- 2 tablespoons chopped parsley
- 2 sprigs green coriander, chopped (optional)
- ½ teaspoon paprika
- ½ teaspoon ground cumin
- 2 tablespoons olive oil
- 1 to 2 tablespoons lemon juice
- Salt

EQUIPMENT

Paring knife
Baking sheet or foil
Potato ricer or food mill
Large skillet
Perforated spatula

Working time: 20 minutes
Baking time: 45 minutes
Frying time: 15 to 20 minutes
Makes: 1 cup (serves 4)

1. Stud the whole eggplant with garlic slivers, using the paring knife to "drill" holes. Bake the eggplant in a 400° oven until very soft (it will seem as if it has collapsed; the skin will be black and blistery). Remove from the oven to cool.

2. When cool enough to handle, rub the skin off the eggplant and squeeze the pulp to release the bitter juices or scoop out the pulp with a wooden spoon and let drain in a sieve. Discard the bitter liquid.

3. Mash or push the eggplant pulp and garlic slivers through a food mill. (Avoid the temptation to use a blender—it destroys the character of the dish.)

4. Add the chopped herbs and spices and mix well. Fry in the oil over moderate heat, turning the eggplant often with the perforated spatula until all the liquid has evaporated and the eggplant has been reduced to a thick black jam. (This turning and frying will take about 15 to 20 minutes.) Sprinkle with lemon juice, taste for salt, and readjust the seasoning to taste. Serve warm or slightly cooled. (You may want to decorate this salad with baby tomatoes.)

GREEN PEPPER AND TOMATO SALADS

———◆———

There is no question that the green pepper and tomato salads of Morocco encompass the same spectrum of seasonings as the *gazpacho* of Spain. In fact, there is a fascinating historical connection between the two series of dishes. *Gazpacho* in Arabic means "soaked bread." The Spaniards first learned of *gazpacho* from the Moors, who made it of garlic, bread, olive oil, lemon juice, salt, and water. Just after the Moors left Spain, Columbus returned from America with tomatoes and peppers, and these two vegetables became the mainstays of the new *gazpachos* that the Spaniards developed. From Spain these two new vegetables came to Morocco to be used in, among other things, Moroccan salads. Thus, a culinary idea exported from Morocco to Spain was changed there by the addition of newly discovered ingredients, which were then in turn reimported into Morocco, where they found their way into a series of unique variations.

When making these dishes try to buy the plumpest, reddest, ripest tomatoes you can find, and be sure your green peppers are sweet. (Nibble on the tip of each one before using it.) The peppers are prepared by grilling them over charcoal or over a gas flame, but you can bake them in the oven if you prefer. Then they must be peeled, and cored.

Tomato and Green Pepper Salad, Fez Style

Exquisite!

INGREDIENTS

3 sweet green peppers
4 large red, ripe tomatoes
1 clove garlic, peeled and crushed
  Pinch of sweet paprika
¼ teaspoon ground cumin
2 tablespoons olive or salad oil
1 tablespoon lemon juice
½ teaspoon salt
¼ teaspoon freshly ground black pepper
¼ preserved lemon (see page 30)

EQUIPMENT

Towel or plastic bag
Sharp paring knife
2-quart saucepan
Glass serving dish

Working time: 15 minutes
Baking time (optional): 20
  minutes
Serves: 4 to 6

1. To prepare the peppers, grill them over a gas flame, turning them until the skins are completely blackened, or bake them as follows: Preheat the oven to 450°; wash the peppers, drain dry, and arrange on an ungreased baking sheet; bake for 10 minutes, then turn over carefully and continue to bake 10 minutes more, or until the skins are black and blistered.

2. Place the blackened peppers in a plastic bag or under a towel and set aside to cool. (This enables the skin to separate from the flesh.) Remove the peppers when cool, core, seed, and slip off their skins. Scrape off any extra

seeds. Cut the pepper flesh into small pieces and set aside.

3. To prepare the tomatoes, bring 2 cups water to a boil; drop in the tomatoes and boil for 15 seconds. Remove the tomatoes and cut out the stem with the sharp paring knife. Peel off their skins, then slice each tomato in half crosswise and squeeze gently to remove the seeds. Cut the tomato flesh into small pieces.

4. Mix the tomatoes and peppers in the glass serving dish, then add all the remaining ingredients except the preserved lemon. Mix well to blend the spices with the vegetables. Rinse the preserved lemon under running water and cut away the pulp. Cut the peel into cubes and sprinkle over the salad. Serve cool.

Tomato and Hot Green Pepper Salad, Essaouira Style

This is hotter than the Fez recipe.

INGREDIENTS

4 large, ripe tomatoes, peeled, seeded, and cubed (see step 3, above)

4 sweet green peppers, grilled or baked, cored, seeded and diced (see page 70)

1 cucumber, peeled, center core removed, and diced, or 3 celery ribs, stringed and diced

1 tablespoon or more chopped chili peppers, cored and seeded

Salt and freshly ground black pepper

1 tablespoon lemon juice

2 to 3 tablespoons olive or salad oil

2 tablespoons chopped parsley

¼ teaspoon ground cumin (optional)

2 cloves garlic, peeled and chopped (optional)

EQUIPMENT

Medium-sized mixing bowl

Working time: 15 minutes
Serves: 4 to 6

Combine all the ingredients in the mixing bowl and blend gently. Refrigerate at least 1 hour before serving.

Hot Chili Relish, Rabat Style

Fry 6 hot green chili peppers in salad oil, then cool them under a towel; when they are cool, skin them and mix with a little lemon juice and salt. Serve whole.

Sweet Green Pepper Relish, Fez Style

Mix 6 grilled, peeled, cored, and chopped sweet green peppers (see page 70) with 2 tablespoons lemon juice, a few tablespoons olive oil, and granulated sugar to taste.

Pickled Sweet Green Peppers (*Filfil Mrakad*), Tetuán Style

Split and clean 2 pounds sweet green peppers. Trim off the stems, then fill the pepper cavities with salt. Pile the peppers into a large sterile jar, add 1 head peeled garlic cloves, and pour in 2½ cups mild vinegar, 2 cups olive oil, and enough water to cover the peppers. Close tightly and store in a warm place 10 days.

Note: After opening store in a cool place. Use a fork to remove peppers.

Sliced Tomato and Onion Salad

INGREDIENTS

6 to 8 red, ripe tomatoes, peeled (see page 71) and sliced crosswise

½ Spanish onion or 1 sweet red onion, sliced into thin rings

¼ cup olive oil

1 tablespoon vinegar

1 clove garlic, peeled and crushed

Salt and freshly ground black pepper

Chopped parsley

Pinch of cumin (optional)

Pinch of paprika (optional)

EQUIPMENT

Medium-sized mixing bowl

Working time: 15 minutes
Serves: 4 to 6

Combine the tomato and onion slices. Make a sauce with the remaining ingredients and pour over the tomatoes and onion.

Cooked Tomatoes and Sweet Green Pepper Salad

This is a rich and satisfying salad—sixteen beautiful, red, ripe, plump tomatoes reduced to a cup and a half of delicious puree. (It takes a lot of attention to avoid burning the mixture during the final fifteen minutes.) In Essaouira the cooks add some hot green chili peppers and chopped parsley, but I generally leave them out.

In Tetuán this salad is used as a fish stuffing. The fish is baked under a layer of sliced tomatoes, onions, and lemons, with chopped olives and chopped preserved lemon peel scattered on top. Paprika-flavored oil (see page 176), salt, a little water, and 45 minutes baking in a 400° oven produce a marvelous dish.

INGREDIENTS	EQUIPMENT
16 red, ripe tomatoes (about 4 pounds), peeled, seeded, and chopped (see page 71)	Large enameled cast-iron skillet
Olive oil for frying	Perforated spoon
9 sweet green peppers, grilled, cored, seeded, and chopped (see page 70)	*Working time:* 15 minutes
2 cloves garlic, peeled and chopped	*Cooking time:* 1 hour
1 teaspoon paprika (optional)	*Serves:* 6
Salt and cayenne to taste	

Fry the tomatoes in a small amount of oil, mashing and turning them with the spoon as they cook down. When they are very thick add the chopped green peppers, garlic, optional paprika, and some salt and cayenne to taste. Continue to reduce the mixture until all the liquid has evaporated and it starts to fry in the released oil. (At this moment you must give the dish your full attention, turning the tomatoes and peppers over and over in the skillet to avoid scorching.) When everything is very thick and has reduced to about 1½ cups, remove from the heat and drain. Serve cool.

OTHER VEGETABLE SALADS

—◆—

Carrot Salad

INGREDIENTS

- 1 pound carrots
- 1 clove garlic
- ⅛ teaspoon ground cinnamon
- ½ teaspoon ground cumin
- ½ teaspoon sweet paprika
- Pinch of cayenne (optional)
- Juice of 1 lemon
- ⅛ teaspoon granulated sugar
- Salt to taste
- Olive oil
- Chopped parsley

EQUIPMENT

Vegetable peeler
1½-quart saucepan
Chopping knife

Working time: 5 minutes
Cooking time: 10 minutes
Serves: 4

1. Wash and peel the carrots. Boil whole in water with the garlic until barely tender. Drain. Discard the garlic and dice or slice the carrots.
2. Combine the spices with the lemon juice, sugar, and salt and pour over the carrots. Chill. Sprinkle with oil and chopped parsley just before serving.

VARIATION:
Sweet Carrot Salad

To prepare the same dish in a much sweeter but equally delicious variation, change the proportions as follows:

For 1 pound carrots: ⅓ cup lemon juice, 3 heaping tablespoons granulated sugar, ½ teaspoon ground cinnamon, ¼ cup chopped parsley, ¼ scant teaspoon ground cumin, and ¼ teaspoon paprika. Boil the carrots as in the preceding recipe. Mix all the other ingredients, add a pinch of salt, and pour over the carrots. Serve cool.

Grated Carrot Salad

INGREDIENTS

7 large carrots, scraped and grated
¼ cup granulated sugar
¼ cup lemon juice
Orange flower water
Pinch of salt

EQUIPMENT

Large mixing bowl

Working time: 5 minutes
Serves: 4 to 6

Mix the carrots with the sugar, lemon juice, orange flower water, and salt. Marinate 1 hour before serving.

Beet Salad I

INGREDIENTS

1 pound beets
1 tablespoon granulated sugar
Juice of 1 lemon
1 tablespoon olive oil
Large pinch of cinnamon
1 tablespoon chopped parsley
Salt to taste

EQUIPMENT

3-quart saucepan
Paring knife
Medium-sized mixing bowl

Working time: 10 minutes
Cooking time: 45 minutes to
    1 hour (depending on the
    age and size of the beets)
Makes: 2 cups (approximately)

1. Wash the beets well, being careful not to break their skins. Cut off the tops, leaving a stalk of about 1½ inches. Boil, covered, until tender. Allow the water to cool, then slip off the skins, trim off the tops, and cut into bite-sized pieces.

2. Mix the remaining ingredients and pour over beets. Let marinate 1 hour before serving.

VARIATION:
Beet Salad II

Prepare as described above, but add 1 teaspoon orange flower water, ⅛ teaspoon cumin, a pinch of paprika, and a little water to the sauce.

Cucumber Salad

INGREDIENTS

2 cucumbers, peeled, seeded, and grated
1 tablespoon granulated sugar
1 teaspoon vinegar
1 tablespoon olive, salad, or peanut oil
¼ teaspoon salt
⅛ teaspoon *za'atar;* or marjoram, thyme, or
    orégano; or a mixture of two or three
  Handful of cured black olives

EQUIPMENT

Medium-sized mixing bowl

Working time: 10 minutes
Serves: 4

Drain off excess liquid from the cucumbers, then combine with the sugar, vinegar, oil, and salt. Crush the *za'atar* (or the substitute herbs) between your fingertips and sprinkle over the cucumbers. Mix well with two forks, then chill. Decorate with the olives just before serving.

Mixed Herb Salad I

In Morocco this dish is made with greens called *bakoola,* which are found growing wild in the fields. *Bakoola* tastes something like a cross between rocket leaves (arugula) and watercress, with a hint of sorrel, and there is no real equivalent for it here. I have experimented with sorrel and dandelion leaves and reasonably successfully with watercress. However, I have had the best luck with arugula, and I recommend it for this exquisite salad. In Morocco this same salad is also prepared with purslane.

INGREDIENTS

4 cups rocket leaves and stalks (arugula) or
    purslane, tightly packed
1 cup parsley sprigs, tightly packed
½ cup green coriander, tightly packed
1 or 2 large cloves garlic, peeled
    Salt
3 tablespoons olive oil
¼ teaspoon paprika
    Cayenne to taste
    Lemon juice to taste
¼ preserved lemon (see page 30); optional
    Black olives

EQUIPMENT

Chopping knife
Couscousiere or steamer
Mortar and pestle
Large skillet
Spatula
Paring knife
Serving dish

Working time: 20 minutes
Steaming time: 15 minutes
Makes: 1 cup salad

1. Wash the rocket leaves under running water. Drain and chop roughly. Fill the bottom of the *couscousiere* with water and bring to a boil. Fasten on the perforated top, add the rocket leaves and steam, covered, for 15 minutes. Remove from the heat and allow to cool, uncovered. When cool enough to handle, squeeze out as much moisture as possible.

2. Wash, dry, chop, and pound the parsley, coriander, garlic, and ¼ teaspoon salt to a paste in a mortar.

3. Heat the oil in the skillet and add the herb paste. Cook 2 to 3 minutes

without burning, then add the rocket leaves and sauté slowly until all the liquid has evaporated, turning the mixture often to avoid burning. Chop the mixture fine and blend in salt, paprika, and cayenne to taste. Cool.

4. Just before serving, sprinkle with lemon juice and adjust seasoning. Rinse the preserved lemon peel and remove the pulp, then slice the peel into slivers. Put the salad in a serving dish with slivered peel and/or black olives. Serve cool.

Note: This salad will keep several days if covered and stored in a cool place.

Mixed Herb Salad II

A mixture of many field greens makes an excellent dish to serve either warm or cooled. Use large handfuls of whatever is available: rocket, purslane, sorrel, Swiss chard, sea kale, watercress, rampion, mustard greens, spinach, dandelion greens, or even celery leaves.

INGREDIENTS	EQUIPMENT
2 quarts field greens, including stalks	Chopping knife
1 or 2 small dried red chili peppers	*Couscousiere*
Salt	5½-quart casserole
10 to 12 cloves garlic	Mortar and pestle
1 cup chopped parsley	
1 cup chopped green coriander	*Working time:* 20 minutes
Salad oil	*Cooking time:* 1 hour
¼ pound cured black olives	*Makes:* 6 cups
2 teaspoons paprika	
2 teaspoons ground cumin	
Juice of 2 lemons	
Lemon wedges	

1. Wash the greens under running water. Drain and cut small. Fill the

bottom of the *couscousiere* with water and bring to a boil. Fasten on the per-forated top, add the greens, and steam, covered, for 30 minutes. Remove from the heat and allow to cool, uncovered. When cool enough to handle, squeeze out as much moisture as possible.

2. Pound the chili pepper in a mortar with 1 teaspoon salt and the garlic. Gradually add the chopped parsley and coriander and continue pounding until it becomes a paste.

3. Heat 3 tablespoons oil in the casserole and slowly cook the olives with the paprika and cumin 2 to 3 minutes. Add the herb paste and the lemon juice, cover, and cook 5 minutes. Pour in ½ cup oil, add the greens and cook together, stirring frequently, for 20 minutes, or until all the moisture has evaporated and the mixture is very thick. Salt to taste. Serve with lemon wedges.

Note: This is also very good with an extra dribble of Harissa Sauce (page 30).

ORANGE SALADS

———◆———

Moroccan oranges are so good that even Florida and California people begrudgingly admire them. They make marvelous, clean-tasting salads, and superbly refreshing desserts.

Orange, Lettuce, and Walnut Salad (*Shlada Bellecheen*)

INGREDIENTS

1 head romaine lettuce
3 navel or temple oranges
2 tablespoons lemon juice
2 tablespoons granulated sugar
Pinch of salt
Cinnamon
1 tablespoon orange flower water
¾ cup chopped walnuts

EQUIPMENT

Paper towels
Small serrated knife
Small mixing bowls
Slicing knife
Glass serving dish

Working time: 15 minutes
Serves: 6

1. Wash the romaine lettuce and section into leaves, discarding the tough outer ones. Drain and wrap in paper towels to dry. Store in the refrigerator until needed.

2. Peel the oranges and remove all the outside membranes, using a small serrated knife and employing a seesaw motion. Section the oranges by cutting away all the membranes from the orange flesh. As you work, lift out each section and place in a small mixing bowl. Squeeze the juice from the remainder of the orange over the sections to keep them moist. Cover and keep chilled.

3. Make a dressing by mixing the lemon juice, sugar, salt, ½ teaspoon

cinnamon, orange flower water, and 2 tablespoons of the orange juice. Blend well, then taste—the dressing should be sweet.

4. Just before serving, shred the lettuce and arrange in a glass serving dish. Pour the dressing over and toss. Make a design around the edges with overlapping sections of orange, then sprinkle the salad with the chopped walnuts and dust with cinnamon. Serve immediately.

VARIATION:

Orange and Chopped Dates Salad

Prepare as in the recipe above, using ¾ cup chopped dates and almonds in place of the chopped walnuts.

Orange Salad with Rosewater

Oranges, rosewater, and cinnamon make an outstanding combination. The orange sections are arranged in a pattern of overlapping circles, and the rosewater is spooned on top. This salad also makes an excellent dessert.

INGREDIENTS

  6 navel or temple oranges
1½ teaspoons rosewater
  2 tablespoons confectioners' sugar
    Cinnamon

EQUIPMENT

Small serrated knife
Glass serving dish

Working time: 15 minutes
Serves: 6

Peel and section the oranges as described on page 81. Arrange the sections in a pattern of overlapping circles in the serving dish, then sprinkle with the perfumed water, sugar, and ¼ teaspoon cinnamon. Taste for desired sweetness and adjust as necessary. Chill until ready to serve. Just before serving, dust with more cinnamon.

Note: Orange flower water can be substituted for the rosewater.

Orange and Radish Salad

INGREDIENTS

2 to 3 bunches long or round red radishes
   2 tablespoons granulated sugar
     Juice of 1 lemon
   1 tablespoon orange flower water
     Salt
   2 navel oranges
     Cinnamon

EQUIPMENT

Electric blender
Glass serving dish
Small serrated knife
Mixing bowl

Working time: 20 minutes
Serves: 4 to 6

1. Wash and trim the radishes. Place in the blender jar and "grate" by turning the machine on and off. *Do not puree.* Remove and drain off the excess liquid. Place in the serving dish and sprinkle with the sugar, lemon juice, perfumed water, and salt to taste. Toss lightly and chill.

2. Peel and section the oranges as described on page 81. (Save the juice for some other dish.) Just before serving, mix the orange sections with the grated radishes. Dust lightly with cinnamon and serve at once.

Orange and Black Olive Salad

3 navel or temple oranges
1 cup ripe black olives, pitted
2 tablespoons olive oil
2 cloves garlic, chopped (optional)
½ teaspoon paprika
   Cayenne to taste
½ teaspoon salt
   Pinch or two of granulated sugar
   Pinch of cumin
2 tablespoons chopped parsley

EQUIPMENT

Small serrated knife
Small mixing bowl
Glass serving dish

Working time: 15 minutes
Serves: 4 to 6

1. Peel and section the oranges as described on page 81.
2. Arrange the olives and oranges attractively in the serving dish. Make a dressing of the olive oil and remaining ingredients, pour over the olives and oranges, and serve at once.

Note: In some Moroccan homes 4 large preserved or fresh lemons are used in place of the fresh oranges.

Orange and Grated Carrot Salad

INGREDIENTS

1 pound carrots
1 navel orange
1 teaspoon cinnamon
2 to 3 tablespoons lemon juice
1 tablespoon granulated sugar
1 teaspoon orange flower water
Pinch of salt

EQUIPMENT

Vegetable peeler
Grater
Large mixing bowl
Glass serving bowl

Working time: 10 minutes
Serves: 4 to 6

1. Clean and grate the carrots. Peel and section the oranges as described on page 81, reserving the juice.

2. Mix the leftover orange juice with the remaining ingredients. Stir in the carrots and orange sections, then chill. Before serving, partially drain.

MEAT SALADS

———◆———

Though these dishes are not built around vegetables, they are nevertheless treated as salads and served as part of a Moroccan "antipasto."

Brain Salad I (*Mohk*)

When I first watched Moroccan cooks prepare brains I was shocked that they did not do all the things I'd been taught were de rigueur in my first lessons in classical French cooking. They did not soak the brains, or parboil them before proceeding with other steps; they simply held them under running water, pulled off *some* of the membranes, and went on from there. Now that I've read *Let's Cook It Right* by Adelle Davis, I see that the Moroccan method may be the best after all; prolonged soaking and parboiling, according to Miss Davis, can remove many of the vitamins and minerals that make brains so nutritionally rich.

Mohk, presented here in two slightly different versions, makes an excellent appetizer when teamed with a mixed herb salad, a salad of tomatoes and green peppers, and one of grated carrots or radishes. The contrasting textures and flavors make an interesting start to a Moroccan feast.

INGREDIENTS

   1 pound calves,' lamb, or beef brains
  ¼ cup freshly chopped green coriander
  ¼ cup freshly chopped parsley
  ½ teaspoon cumin

EQUIPMENT

3-quart enameled cast-iron or
   stainless steel casserole
   with cover
Glass serving dish

1 teaspoon paprika
2 to 3 cloves garlic, peeled and cut up
  ¼ cup olive or salad oil
  ⅓ cup lemon juice
  1 preserved lemon (see page 30), rinsed
    and diced
  Salt to taste

Working time: 15 minutes
Optional soaking time: 2
  hours
Cooking time: 1 hour
Serves: 4 to 6

1. Wash the brains under running water, removing the membranes and as much blood as possible. (If you feel squeamish, soak the brains in salted water to cover for 1 to 2 hours, changing the water three times.) Place the rinsed brains in the casserole with the herbs, spices, garlic, and oil. Pour 1½ cups water over and bring to a boil. Reduce the heat, partially cover the pan, and simmer 30 minutes.

2. Add the lemon juice. Then, without removing the brains from the casserole, mash them into small pieces with the back of a wooden spoon. Continue simmering another 30 minutes, stirring often.

3. Ten minutes before the dish is finished add the diced preserved lemon. Taste for salt, and readjust the seasoning. Cool before serving.

VARIATION:

Brain Salad II (*Mohk*)

Follow the instructions for the preceding recipe precisely, substituting 1 small tomato, peeled, seeded and cubed, for the preserved lemon and adding a pinch or two of cayenne pepper along with the spices.

Cubed Liver Salad (*Kibbdha*)

Although this recipe is very popular with Moroccans, it may not survive the American palate.

INGREDIENTS

¾ to 1 pound thick slices of calves', lamb, or beef liver

1 clove garlic, peeled and crushed

1½ heaping teaspoons sweet paprika

1 teaspoon salt

Cumin

¼ cup mixed chopped parsley and green coriander

½ cup lemon juice

Flour, preferably semolina flour

Salad oil for frying

EQUIPMENT

Medium-sized mixing bowl

Large skillet

Spatula

Serving dish

Working time: 15 minutes

Marinating time: 1 hour or longer

Cooking time: 15 minutes

Makes: 2 cups

1. Wash the liver and marinate in a mixture of the garlic, paprika, salt, ¾ teaspoon cumin, half the mixed herbs, and half the lemon juice for 1 hour, or longer.

2. Drain the liver well, reserving the marinade. Dust with semolina flour (preferred by Moroccans because they say it "holds on to the food" best when frying) and fry in ½ inch of hot oil for 5 minutes, turning each piece over with the spatula when browned. Drain the liver and pour off all but 3 or 4 tablespoons of the oil. Cut the liver into ½-inch cubes and return to the skillet to refry for about 1 minute, tossing the cubes in the pan so they brown on all sides.

3. Pour in the marinade and ½ cup water and bring to a boil. Stir and cook down for 1 minute. Pour in the remaining lemon juice and herbs. Stir once or twice and cook 1 minute longer. Remove from the heat and dust with a little cumin. Put in a serving dish and serve at room temperature.

OTHER VEGETABLE DISHES

◆

Besides the salads there are a number of other Moroccan vegetable dishes worthy of note. Among these are the all-vegetable *tagines*, called *maraks*, of Tetuán, where they are usually served after an array of salads.

One of the more interesting of these *maraks* is *marak silk* (Tagine of Swiss Chard, page 90)—not to everybody's taste—simmered down with onions, spices, and herbs, and thickened with rice. *Marak matisha bil melokhias* (Tagine of Okra and Tomatoes, page 91) might normally be considered a "salad," but in Tetuán this savory combination of tomatoes adorned with a "necklace" of young okra is treated as if it were an entrée. There are other *maraks* built around such things as cabbage (known as a "*marak* of rags") and cauliflowerets flavored with cumin and paprika, and there is one *marak* made with pumpkin, raisins, white beans, and bastourma (*khelea*) cooked with a whiff of cinnamon and sugar.

I have included a recipe for the famous Berber vegetable dish known as *byesar* (Puree of Fava Beans, page 92), which in Tangier is made with dried split peas, and, finally, a recipe for a Moroccan Jewish dish, Eggplant Stuffed with Brains (page 94), from the town of Sefrou.

Tagine of Swiss Chard (*Marak Silk*)

In Tetuán this dish is often accompanied by a cup of boiled lentils.

INGREDIENTS

12 cups finely chopped stalks and leaves of Swiss chard (about 4 bunches)
1 cup chopped onion
½ cup chopped green coriander
½ cup salad oil
1 teaspoon sweet paprika
  Salt and freshly ground black pepper
¼ cup raw rice

EQUIPMENT

4-quart enameled cast-iron casserole with tight-fitting lid

Working time: 20 minutes
Cooking time: 50 minutes
Serves: 4

Place the chopped Swiss chard in the casserole with the onion, coriander, oil, paprika, salt, pepper, and ¼ cup water. Cook, covered, 30 minutes. Add the rice and continue cooking until all the liquid has gone and the mixture has become a thick sauce slightly filmed with oil, about 20 minutes. (The lid of your casserole must be tight-fitting so that the rice will cook in the water released by the vegetables.) If you are afraid the rice will burn, stir it from time to time and add water by the spoonful, if necessary, or bake the dish in the oven. Serve warm.

Tagine of Okra and Tomatoes (*Marak Matisha Bil Melokhias*)

In Tetuán the cooks who make this dish want to be able to stir the tomato sauce without breaking the okra that is poaching inside. As always, Moroccan ingenuity has found a way: the okra is strung together with needle and thread into a long "necklace"; when the cook wants to stir the sauce she pulls up the "necklace," stirs, and then drops the okra back in to continue its poaching.

INGREDIENTS

½ pound fresh okra
4½ pounds fresh red, ripe tomatoes, peeled, seeded, and chopped (see page 71)
2 tablespoons chopped parsley
1½ teaspoons sweet paprika
1 teaspoon chopped garlic
Salt
3 tablespoons vegetable oil

EQUIPMENT

Needle and thread
3½-quart stainless steel or enameled cast-iron saucepan
Serving dish

Working time: 15 minutes
Cooking time: 45 minutes
Serves: 5 to 6

1. Wash, top, and tail the okra and string together with thread into a "necklace."

2. Over high heat, cook the tomatoes with the parsley, paprika, garlic, salt, and oil, mashing down the tomatoes as they cook. After 10 minutes lower the heat to moderate, add the okra and begin to poach it in the sauce. From time to time lift up the "necklace" to stir. After the okra is tender, remove and keep warm. Continue to reduce the tomatoes until all the water is evaporated and the oil is released. Fry the tomatoes in this released oil, stirring continuously to avoid scorching. Gently pull out the thread, then place the okra in the serving dish. Pour the sauce over. Serve hot or lukewarm.

Puree of Fava Beans (*Byesar*)

Byesar is the North African cousin of the famous Middle Eastern *hummous* made of chick-peas. It is a dish for the lovers of olive oil, a soupy mixture best eaten with Arab bread. First you sprinkle some mixed spices (see below) on your bread, then dip it into the *byesar* and scoop the puree into your mouth. The dish is so popular among Berbers that Madame Guinaudeau, in her book on Fez cooking, was able to record the following conversation:

> A gentleman from Fez to a Berber mountaineer: "What would you do if you were the sultan?"
> The mountaineer's reply: "I would eat *byesar* every day."

In Tangier *byesar* is made with split green peas and scallions, and in some parts of the country it is cooked with cabbage and flavored with paprika, cumin, garlic, and salt.

The best *byesar* is laced with olive oil made from green, *unripe* olives.

INGREDIENTS	EQUIPMENT
½ pound dried fava beans	2-quart enameled cast-iron or
3 cloves garlic, peeled	stainless steel casserole
1 teaspoon cumin seeds	Food mill or electric blender
Best quality olive oil	
Salt	*Working time:* 10 minutes
¼ teaspoon *za'atar* or thyme, marjoram, or orégano	*Cooking time:* 2 hours (approximately)
	Serves: 4 to 6

1. The night before, soak the fava beans in 3 to 4 times their volume of cold water. Discard any favas that float.

2. The following day, drain, skin, and cover with fresh water. Cook gently, with the garlic and cumin seeds, until the beans are tender (about 2 hours, depending upon the age and quality of the beans). Drain.

3. Puree the beans in a food mill or an electric blender. Stir in enough olive oil, and a little water, to give the puree a soupy consistency. Sprinkle with salt to taste and beat well. Heat just before serving with a little more olive oil and a sprinkling of crushed *za'atar*. Serve with Arab bread and a bowl of "mixed spices" (ground cumin, cayenne, and salt).

Eggplant Stuffed with Brains

This is a Moroccan Jewish specialty.

INGREDIENTS

½ pound lamb, calves', or beef brains
2 or 3 small eggplants (¾ pound)
    Salt
¼ cup salad oil
2 red, ripe tomatoes (½ pound)
2 cloves whole garlic, peeled
    Freshly ground black pepper
1 tablespoon chopped parsley
3 eggs

EQUIPMENT

Large and small mixing
    bowls
Paring knife
Colander
Paper towels
Large skillet
Spatula
Whisk
1-quart saucepan
Small, shallow ovenproof
    serving dish
Serving platter (optional)

Working time: **40 minutes**
Cooking time: **45 minutes**
Serves: **4 to 6**

1. Soak the brains in salted water to cover for 1 to 2 hours, changing the water at least three times. Remove the membranes and any traces of blood.
2. Remove the eggplant stems. With a thin-bladed paring knife, remove ½-inch vertical strips from each eggplant, leaving them striped. Halve lengthwise and scoop out the center pulp, carefully leaving a ¼-inch-thick wall of flesh in each half shell. Cube the pulp.
3. Sprinkle each half shell and the cubed eggplant with salt and let drain at least 30 minutes in the colander. Squeeze gently, then rinse well under running water. Pat dry with paper towels.
4. Heat the oil in the skillet and fry the shells, on both sides, over low heat

until soft. Remove and drain. Set aside all but 1 tablespoon of the oil. (Since eggplant tends to soak up oil, you may need to add the reserved oil later.)

5. Peel and cube the tomatoes (see page 71). Place in the colander and press lightly to drain. Sauté the tomatoes and eggplant cubes in the 1 tablespoon oil with the garlic, salt and pepper to taste, and chopped parsley. Cook a few minutes so that the flavors blend, then place the mixture in a bowl. Discard the garlic cloves.

6. In the saucepan simmer the brains in salted water for about 10 minutes. Drain and cut into small cubes. Add to the tomato-eggplant mixture and mash together.

7. Preheat the oven to 350°.

8. Stuff the eggplant shells with the brain-tomato-eggplant mixture. Place the shells in a lightly oiled ovenproof serving dish, packing tightly so they don't fall over. Beat the eggs to a froth and pour over the stuffed eggplant. Sprinkle with salt and pepper and bake for 30 minutes. Serve directly from the dish or loosen the sides of the firmly set eggs and then invert onto a serving platter. Cut into long slices and serve warm or at room temperature.

———◆———

SIX

Savory Pastries

Bisteeya* is so intricate and so grand, so lavish and so rich, that its extravagance always reminds me of *The Arabian Nights*. The traditional *bisteeya* of Fez is an enormous, flaky pigeon pie never less than twenty inches in diameter. Beneath a perfectly crisped pastry top covered with cinnamon and sugar are layers of shredded squab or chicken, two dozen eggs curdled in a lemony and spiced onion sauce, and sweetened almonds. The whole is enclosed—top, bottom, and sides—in miraculous, tissue-thin pastry leaves called *warka*.

The concept of pastry enveloping meat mixed with spices and nuts was brought to Morocco from the Middle East sometime after the first wave of Arabs swept across North Africa. The paper-thin leaves came from Persia with the third wave of invaders, and, quite possibly, the Persians learned how to make them from the same Chinese who taught them the secrets of ice cream and sherbets. Moroccan *warka* (called *maslouqua* in Tunisia and *dioul* in Algeria) is made precisely the same way as Chinese spring roll skins.† Though many people confuse this type of pastry with Greek phyllo dough and Hungarian strudel leaves (both of which, by the way, will make an adequate *bisteeya*) the *warka*-spring roll skin type is found only in China and North Africa.

* Sometimes called *bistayla*.
† See *The Joy of Chinese Cooking* by Doreen Yen and Hung Feng (London: Faber & Faber). In Canton this type of pastry is called *chun gun*: it should not be confused with the thicker egg roll skin.

The third wave of Arab invaders had been exposed to Persian culture, and the pastry leaves they brought with them were eventually adapted in one form or another by nearly all the countries of the Mediterranean. As Waverly Root wrote in *The Food of Italy*:

> You could draw a map of the limits of Moslem invasion by plotting the places where, during the Middle Ages, their fine flaky pastry became established. It is the *pastilla* [*sic*] of Morocco; the rustic *tourtière* and the aristocratic *millefeuille* of France (where they got as far as Poitiers); the *Strudel* of Central Europe (where they reached the Adriatic and threatened Vienna); and in Italy the *millefoglie* of Sicily and the *sfogliatelle* of Naples.

The process of making *warka* (which I shall explain later in great detail) is in principle quite simple: a soft, elastic, spongy mass of well-beaten flour and water is pressed lightly against a hot, flat pan; it is immediately removed, leaving a thin film of pastry to be lifted off. In the Middle East a similar type of pastry (the Turkish *cadaif*) is made by pushing the dough through a sieve onto the hot metal pan; this, too, is immediately removed and the result, instead of being a thin, flat leaf, is a finely spun type of pastry that resembles shredded wheat.

I wondered for a long time if this process was the original and basic way of pastry making; whether France, Italy, Hungary, and Greece developed their own pastry-making methods later on. When I discovered the striking similarity between *warka* and the ancient Chinese process for making spring roll skins, I became convinced that this, indeed, is the case.

Bisteeya is a totally Moroccan delight; it is not found anywhere else in the world. For me everything great in Moroccan culture (the influence of the Arabs and the Spanish Muslims, and the indigenous culture of the Berbers) is represented in this extravagant dish. Many authorities believe *bisteeya* was totally created in Andalusia, where the music, architecture, and literature of the Moors flourished so brilliantly, and they seem to base this theory on the similarity of the word *bisteeya* to the Spanish word *pasteles*, which means "pastry confections."

I resisted this theory for many reasons, chief among them the fact that there is no trace of *bisteeya* in Spain today, and it seemed inconceivable to me that so great a recipe would totally vanish, not leaving behind even some variant form. I had my own ideas about the origins of *bisteeya,* and became enormously excited one day when I found my first bit of evidence in an old book. I was working in the great private library devoted to Berber culture in the Rabat home of Mr. Majoubi Ahardan, formerly the Moroccan Minister of Defense and now head of the Moroccan Berber Party. Suddenly, as I was glancing through a lexicon,* I came across the Berber word *bestila,* which I learned was the name for chicken cooked in butter and saffron, the base layer of the three-layered *bisteeya* pie.

Clearly the Andalusian theory, which was based on the chance similarity between the words *bisteeya* and *pasteles,* was now in doubt, for the Berber word *bestila* not only had an even more similar sound, but had an actual connection in meaning.

Beginning there, I began to reconstruct the history of this fabulous dish.

First there was the Berber *bestila,* the chicken cooked with butter and saffron. Then the first wave of Arab invaders arrived bringing the Arabian *trid,* which was said to have been the Prophet's favorite food. *Trid* is a primitive form of pastry made by stretching dough over a hot surface. In Morocco it was merged with the Berber *bestila:* the chicken cooked with butter and saffron was placed between layers of *trid,* making a dish similar to the *trid* served in Morocco today, and that is sometimes called "poor man's *bisteeya.*" Finally, the third wave of invaders arrived with the Persian method for making *warka.* This finer pastry was substituted for the *trid,* the chicken cooked with butter and saffron remained inside, and over the years the lemony eggs of Tetuán and sweetened almond layers of the Souss were added until the final glory of the dish was achieved.

I dispute the Andalusian theory on another count. Andalusian cooking is not based on butter at all, but is totally a cuisine of oil. In fact, up to two hundred years ago the only butter to be found in Spain was sold in pharmacies as a kind of ointment. But the Berber cooking of most of Morocco is based on butter, though oil is used for frying. And, too, there is the fact that, despite the existence of a perfectly acceptable Spanish puff pastry called *hojaldres,* made with lard, Spanish pastry is markedly inferior to Moroccan. In Tetuán, the city of refugees from Moorish Spain, where the cuisine of

* E. Laoust, *Mots et Choses Berbères Dialetes de Maroc* (Editions Challamel, 1920).

Moorish Andalusia still survives, one finds that the pastries (aside from the traditional Moroccan ones) are based more on the Middle Eastern models than on anything even vaguely Spanish.

But enough of history—the dish is the thing, and what a thing it is! Besides the great and classic *bisteeya* of Fez there are numerous variations, though I have observed that Moroccans are so chauvinistic about the *bisteeyas* of their mothers and hometowns that they are shocked when I tell them the dish is prepared differently elsewhere. In the Middle Atlas there is a *bisteeya* called *tarkhdoult*, made with minced beef or lamb and cinnamon and eggs—unfortunately overloaded with *smen*. In Tetuán the *bisteeya* is made with lemon-flavored onion sauce and chicken and eggs, but without the sweetened almonds and without sugar. There is an amusing story about a Tetuanese lady who never left her native city until, in her old age, she had occasion to visit Fez. When she returned to Tetuán she told everyone what the Fassis had done. "They are so ashamed of their *bisteeya*," she said, "that they hide their mistakes with a layer of sugar!"

In Rabat there is a *bisteeya* served both as a first course and as a dessert: the *warka* leaves surround rice enriched with almond milk and perfumed with orange flower water. And, finally, there is *keneffa* (Sweet Bisteeya with Milk and Almonds, page 322), of Marrakesh, a dessert version in which a sort of custard of milk and orange flower water is poured between casually arranged layers of fried and crisped *warka* leaves.

There are other regional variations, of course, including special *bisteeyas* served in Meknes and Essaouria. I even read of one, in John Gunther's *Inside Africa*, served at a banquet given by the late Pasha el Glaoui of Marrakesh, that, according to Gunther, contained such things as mussels and brains. I wonder about that, but in Morocco anything is possible, and it occurs to me that the pasha might have ordered the invention of a new *bisteeya* merely for the purpose of flabbergasting an American guest.

The other savory pastries—*briks*, *braewats*, and *trid*—are less dramatic but unusual and delicious.

PASTRY LEAVES

———◆———

Bisteeya can be made perfectly well with commercially bought Hungarian strudel leaves, Greek phyllo dough, and even Chinese spring roll skins, with some reservations, but if you want to make it absolutely authentic you should learn to make *warka*.

The major things to remember when using these substitute ingredients are (1) the leaves tend to dry out quickly and must be doused with butter, and (2) the *bisteeya* is baked in the oven rather than fried, as is the usual case with *warka*.

The relative proportions for a twelve-inch *bisteeya*: approximately 40 eight-inch *warka* leaves (for a full-sized Moroccan *bisteeya* of 25 inches the *warka* would be double this in size) equals ½ to ¾ pound phyllo or strudel leaves.

STRUDEL: Packages of strudel leaves are easily obtainable at gourmet shops and Hungarian bakeries. Their great advantage is that they can be frozen or kept refrigerated for at least 1 week. While *warka* leaves are paper thin and slightly crisp, strudel leaves are soft, so strudel leaves used in the inner part of the *bisteeya* must be crisped in a slow oven before inserting in the pie. (The outside of the pie will become crisp anyway during the final baking.) Strudel leaves are very strong, and as a result are useful when making Braewats (page 122).

PHYLLO: These pastry leaves are sold at nearly every Greek and Middle Eastern food store. They are made almost exactly like strudel, but since they are stretched a little differently they are thinner and more fragile. I have made excellent *bisteeyas* with phyllo, handling the dough the same way I handle strudel, crisping the leaves for inner layers in a slow oven before use.

CHINESE SPRING ROLL SKINS: Obtainable at Chinese grocery stores. Though these skins are created the same way as *warka*, they are made with wheat starch instead of semolina flour or plain flour, and as a result they do not bake or reheat well and tend to become leathery and tough rather quickly. I do not particularly recommend them for *bisteeya*, but they are perhaps the next best thing to *warka* for Braewats and Briks (pages 122–125). As with *warka*, any pastry made with spring roll skins is better fried than baked.

WARKA: Where I live in Tangier, there is a famous cook named Mina who prepares *bisteeya* for a living—she is enormously fat and her bulk, as far as Moroccans are concerned, gives testimony to her culinary skill. Mina is always busy, cooking for every important wedding, birth, and party in town. One time, when she was hired by a friend to make two enormous *bisteeyas*, I asked if I could watch her, but she adamantly refused, doubtless on the grounds that no *nasrani* had a right to know her secrets.

I must confess that, though I did not find it difficult to make good *bisteeya*, I was always in awe of the process of making *warka* leaves, and so I usually bought mine, as do many Moroccan cooks, from women who specialized in making them. Finally I decided that this was ridiculous, that I was a perfectly good cook, and despite the rebuffs of Mina, and a line I had read in a cookbook that said, in effect, that no one could learn to make *warka* who was not brought up in a Moroccan home, I resolved to decipher the mysteries of this pastry.

My first attempts were farcical: among the descriptions I received from those who had witnessed the inscrutable process was that the dough was "thrown" or "flung" at the heated pan, an instruction I dutifully obeyed to the detriment of my clothes, my hair, and my entire kitchen, which was soon covered with dabs of "flung" dough.

The dough, of course, is not "flung" or "thrown" but is gently tapped against the pan. I soon figured this out, but still I continued to fail, until I learned the method properly from Madame Jaidi in Rabat. She explained to me something that no cookbook writer had bothered to mention: that the first five or so *warka* leaves rarely work out, and that to give up after that, just as the pan has become properly "seasoned," is to give up before real *warka* making begins.

To make 40 eight-inch *warka* leaves (enough to make 1 twelve-inch *bisteeya*):

1. It is best to do the kneading on the floor, with a big, shallow wash basin in front of you (henceforth to be referred to as the *gsaa*) and a bowl of warm, lightly salted water at your side. Dump 4 cups hard-wheat flour (or semolina, bread, or strudel flour, or a mixture of semolina and all-purpose flour) into the *gsaa*. Work in the warm water, enough to make a softish bread dough. Knead and fold the dough onto itself, at the same time adding water to the *gsaa*, spreading the dough *over* the water and then punching down with your fists, making squishy noises as the water is worked in. (The dough will begin to look like a sponge.) Pick the dough up, turn it over, and rub it with the heel of the hand, as you do a *fraisage* in French pastry.

2. Keeping your hands wet, beat the dough for 1 or 2 minutes against the *gsaa*, up and down, until it begins to perform like a Yo-yo. Then break off a bit of dough, dip it in the water, fold it back into the remaining mass, and then punch down and knead again. Repeat this step three or four times during the next 5 to 10 minutes, building elasticity by lifting the dough with the sway of the hand until you are lifting it about 12 inches above the *gsaa*. Then let the dough "rest" a few hours in a warm place, under a film of 2 tablespoons warm water and a towel. After a 3-hour "rest" you can start to make *warka*, or you can refrigerate the dough and make *warka* the next day.

3. In Morocco, charcoal is heated in a brazier (*kanoun*) and then covered with a flat pan called a *tobsil del warka*, which has an inner lining of copper and a top surface of tin. To duplicate this in an American kitchen, boil water in a shallow, straight-sided pan covered with a large, upside-down cake pan or large, smooth-bottomed skillet.

4. Wrap a nugget of sweet butter in cheesecloth and set it next to the pan. Rub the *tobsil* with butter and immediately wipe it off with a clean towel.

5. Try out the dough: wet your hands and then, twisting with the wrist as you would twist a baton, twist off a small amount of dough about the size of an apricot. Start flipping this piece in your palm, moving your whole arm back and forth until the dough becomes a sphere that bounces away from your hand and then immediately springs back. (If the dough does not become a ball it is

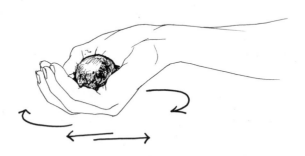

not yet ready; replace the small piece of dough, wait 10 or 15 minutes, and then try again.)

6. Turn your palm upside down, still moving it gently, and begin, *gently*, to tap the dough sphere against the hot *tobsil*, about 1½ inches from the edge. Make several soft, slow taps to form a large circle of pastry. (Each time the dough touches the hot pan it should leave a thin, circular film of pastry.) Tap eight or nine times, so as to make a pastry leaf, and then tap against any places where there are holes and where the separate dabs have not joined well.

7. Allow the pastry leaf to dry slightly around its edges and then carefully lift it up, picking at the edges with your fingernails to loosen it from the pan. You will be able to peel it off after lifting approximately one-third of the leaf. If you are working alone, you may have trouble because your hands will be occupied, one keeping the *tobsil* steady and the other holding onto the sphere of dough, which should be kept in motion. In this case set the sphere down, quickly dip your hand in water, and then peel off the leaf.

Miscellaneous Notes on Making Warka

1. As I've said, your first five or six leaves will probably not succeed. Do not give up.

2. It is important to remember that, when you tap the *tobsil* with the dough, the dough does not really leave your hand; because of the very gentle downward motion of your hand the spherical mass stretches to touch the pan and then snaps back into your inverted palm. If you do this properly, not too fast, you will never lose control of the dough.

3. If you use a spatula to peel off the pastry, the leaf will tear.

4. Because the first five or six leaves will not work out, you need a method for scraping off your mistakes. If the pastry sticks to the pan rub it with a little butter; then rub off the failed leaf with a paper towel.

5. As you accumulate leaves, set them on top of one another and cover them with a clean towel. *Do not let them dry out.* They will keep 1 or 2 days wrapped in foil. If any of your leaves have thick spots, turn these over and let them dry for half a minute or so before piling them on top of the rest.

6. If the *tobsil* is too hot, the *warka* leaves will stick to the pan, and you may not be able to get your nails under their edges to peel them off.

7. If the dough skims the pan, you haven't properly wiped off the butter.

8. Every time you pick up the *warka* dough, wet your hands. But do *not* add any water to the dough itself.

9. A *warka* leaf is cooked on only one side, unless it is excessively thick. A finished leaf should be slightly crisp.

10. Making *warka* is a labor of love. It may take you as long as 3 hours to make 40 leaves. If you are not up to this much effort, make your *bisteeya* with strudel or phyllo dough—you will still obtain a good result.

Bisteeya

Note that *bisteeya* is made either with pigeons (squabs) or chicken; I do not recommend Cornish hens—they are too dry. In Morocco the poultry inside a *bisteeya* is often left unboned, and the bones usually end up strewn all over the table. However, I can think of no earthly reason why the bones should not be removed before the poultry is placed inside the pie.

Bisteeya is customarily served as a first course, and should be hot to the fingertips. To eat it Moroccan style, plunge into the burning pastry with the thumb and first two fingers of your right hand and tear out a piece as large or as delicate as you want. You will burn your fingers, of course, but you will have a lot of fun and the pain will be justified by the taste.

Note that the sugar and cinnamon design on the top is always abstract; it is definitely *not* traditional to stencil on pictures of animals or other recognizable motifs—Muslim practice forbids it. Lattice designs of crisscrossed ground cinnamon always look good.

INGREDIENTS	EQUIPMENT
6 squab pigeons, or 5 pounds chicken legs and thighs	5½-quart cast-iron enameled casserole with cover
5 cloves garlic (approximately), peeled	12-inch skillet
Salt	Paper towels
1 cup chopped parsley, mixed with a little chopped fresh green coriander	Rolling pin or nut grinder
1 Spanish onion, grated	Mixing bowls
Pinch of pulverized saffron	Whisk
¼ teaspoon turmeric	Colander
1 rounded teaspoon freshly ground black pepper	Small saucepan
1 rounded teaspoon ground ginger	13-inch cake pan, or pizza pan, or paella pan
3 cinnamon sticks	Large baking sheet (at least 12 inches wide)
1 cup butter	Spatula
¼ cup salad oil	Serving plate

1 pound whole, blanched almonds
Confectioners' sugar
Ground cinnamon
¼ cup lemon juice
10 eggs
½ to ¾ pound phyllo pastry or strudel leaves, or
40 *warka* leaves (approximately)

Working time: 1½ hours
Cooking time: 1 hour 20 minutes
Baking time: 30 to 40 minutes
Serves: 12 (as part of a Moroccan dinner)

1. Wash the poultry well and pull out as much fat as possible from the cavities. Crush the garlic and make a paste of it with 2 tablespoons salt. Rub the poultry with the paste, then rinse well and drain. Put the squabs or chickens in the casserole with the giblets, herbs, onion, spices, half the butter, a little salt, and 3 cups water. Bring to a boil, then lower the heat, cover, and simmer for 1 hour.

2. Meanwhile, heat the vegetable oil in the skillet and brown the almonds lightly. Drain on paper towels. When cool, crush them with a rolling pin until coarsely ground, or run them through a nut grinder. Combine the almonds with ½ cup confectioners' sugar and 2 teaspoons ground cinnamon. Set aside.

3. Remove the poultry, giblets, cinnamon sticks, and any loose bones from the casserole and set aside. By boiling rapidly, uncovered, reduce the sauce in the casserole to approximately 1¾ cups, then add the lemon juice. Beat the eggs until frothy, then pour into the simmering sauce and stir continuously until the eggs cook and congeal. (They should become curdy, stiff, and dry.) Taste for salt and set aside.

4. Remove all the bones from the squabs or chickens. Shred the poultry into 1½-inch pieces and chop the giblets coarsely.

5. Heat the remaining butter. When the foam subsides, clarify it by pouring off the clear liquid butter into a small bowl and discarding the milky solids. *Up to this point the dish can be prepared in advance, even the day before.*

6. Preheat the oven to 425°.

7. Unroll the pastry leaves, keeping them under a damp towel to prevent them from drying out. Brush some of the clarified butter over the bottom and sides of the cake pan, then cover the bottom of the pan with a pastry leaf. Arrange 6 more leaves so that they half cover the bottom of the pan and half extend over the sides. (The entire bottom of the pan should be covered.) Brush the extended leaves with butter so they do not dry out. (If you are using *warka*, arrange about 15 to 18 leaves around the bottom and sides; there is no need to butter extended leaves.)

8. Fold 4 leaves in half and bake in the oven for 30 seconds, or until crisp but not too browned, or fry the leaves on an oiled skillet. (This is unnecessary if using *warka*.)

9. Place chunks of poultry and giblets around the inner edges of the pan, then work toward the center so that the pastry is covered with a layer of shredded poultry. Cover this layer with the well-drained egg mixture from step 3, and the four baked or fried pastry leaves (or *warka* leaves).

10. Sprinkle the almond-sugar mixture over the pastry. Cover with all but 2 of the remaining pastry leaves, brushing each very lightly with butter.

11. Fold the overlapping leaves in over the top to cover the pie. Brush lightly with butter. Put the remaining 2 leaves over the top, lightly buttering each, and fold these neatly under the pie (like tucking in sheets). Brush the entire pie again with butter and pour any remaining butter around the edge. (Use the same procedure for *warka*.)

12. Bake the pie in 425° oven until the top pastry leaves are golden brown, about 20 minutes. Shake the pan to loosen the pie and run a spatula around the edges. If necessary, tilt the pan to pour off excess butter (which should be reserved). Invert the pie onto a large, buttered baking sheet. Brush the pie with the reserved butter and return to the oven to continue baking another 10 to 15 minutes, or until golden brown. (You can bake the pie made with *warka* leaves, but it is more traditional to gently fry the pie over low heat until golden brown on both sides.)

13. Remove the *bisteeya* from the oven. Tilt to pour off any excess butter. Put a serving plate over the pie and, holding it firmly, invert. (The traditional upper filling is always the almond layer.) Dust the top of the pie with a little confectioners' sugar and run crisscrossing lines of cinnamon over the top. *Serve very hot.*

This makes a superior—but more expensive—*bisteeya*.

Proceed as directed above, but double the quantity of almonds. Partially drain the browned almonds and run through a meat grinder, then knead with sugar and cinnamon (to taste) to form an oily paste. Roll the paste into 1-inch nuggets. Arrange the nuggets over the baked pastry leaves and proceed as directed in step 10.

Bisteeya, Tetuán Style

This is the *bisteeya* known to the old lady from Tetuán who was shocked at the Fez variation. In the north the people prefer the dish more tart than sweet.

Note that you have the option of adding a small amount of preserved lemons—an addition I highly recommend if you have them on hand, but one that is not absolutely necessary.

This dish will work out best if you perform steps 1 through 4 the morning of the day the *bisteeya* is to be served: the better the eggs are drained, the better the *bisteeya* will be—crispy on the outside and moist within.

INGREDIENTS

  4 pounds chicken parts, with giblets
  5 cloves garlic (approximately), peeled
    Salt
  1 cup grated onion
  2 good pinches pulverized saffron
  ¼ teaspoon turmeric
  ½ teaspoon freshly ground black pepper
  ½ teaspoon ground ginger
  2 large cinnamon sticks
 11 tablespoons sweet butter
  2 large Spanish onions, quartered and thinly sliced lengthwise (about 4 cups)
 1½ cups chopped parsley
  ½ cup lemon juice
8 to 10 eggs, well beaten
 1½ preserved lemons (optional; see page 30)
½ to ¾ pound phyllo pastry or strudel leaves or 40 *warka* leaves (page 103)
    Ground cinnamon

EQUIPMENT

5½-quart cast-iron enameled casserole with cover
Colander
Mixing bowls
Paring knife
Small saucepan
Towel
12- or 13-inch cake pan, pizza pan, or paella pan
Pastry brush
Baking sheet (at least 12 inches wide)
Spatula
Serving plate

Working time: 1½ hours
Cooking time: 1 hour 15 minutes
Baking time: 20 minutes
Serves: 12 (as part of a Moroccan dinner)

1. Prepare the poultry with the garlic and salt as described on page 109.

2. Place the rinsed and drained poultry in the casserole with giblets, grated onion, 1 pinch of the saffron, the spices, and 6 tablespoons of the butter. Pour in 1½ cups water. Add salt to taste and bring to a boil. Reduce the heat and simmer 1 hour, covered.

3. Remove the chicken, giblets, cinnamon sticks, and any loose bones from the casserole. By boiling rapidly, uncovered, reduce the sauce to about 1 cup. Add the sliced onions, parsley, more pinches of pepper and saffron, and a few tablespoons water. Cook uncovered, stirring often, until the onions are soft and reduced to a thick mass.

4. Add the lemon juice and eggs and continue cooking until the eggs become curdy and dry. Transfer this mixture to a colander set over a bowl and let drain all day if possible. Reserve the liquid.

5. Shred the chicken into chunks and discard all the bones.

6. Rinse the preserved lemons and discard pulp. Dice the peel and set aside.

7. Heat the remaining butter. When the foam subsides, pour off the clear liquid into a small bowl, leaving the milky solids. *Up to this point the recipe can be prepared in advance.*

8. Preheat the oven to 425°.

9. Unroll the pastry leaves and place them under a damp towel to prevent them from drying out. Cover the bottom of the cake pan with half the pastry leaves, overlapping as directed in step 7 on page 109. Every few layers of pastry should be moistened with 2 tablespoons of the lemon-egg liquid (in place of the melted butter used in the previous recipe).

10. Place chunks of chicken and giblets around the inner edges of pan and then work toward the center so that pastry is covered with a layer of poultry. Cover this layer with one of onions and eggs. Sprinkle with the preserved lemon peel and about ¼ teaspoon ground cinnamon.

11. Cover with the remaining pastry leaves, brushing the remaining lemon-egg liquid on each, but without using more than 3 tablespoons. Fold the leaves as directed in step 11 on page 110. Dribble the clarified butter over the top and sides of the pie.

12. Bake as directed in steps 12 and 13 on page 110 and serve at once, with a mild dusting of ground cinnamon.

Bisteeya Filled with Almond-Flavored Rice (*Bisteeya Bil Roz*)

This is an adaptation of a dish in which rice, simmered in almond milk and perfumed with orange flower water, becomes the filling for a *bisteeya* pie. Unfortunately, strudel leaves and phyllo dough cannot stand a great deal of weight and moisture, so I have had to reduce some of the rich creaminess of the filling. If you want to try the original recipe, follow the instructions for *Roz bil hleeb* (Moroccan Rice Pudding, page 318), partially drain, and make this *bisteeya* with the stronger *warka* leaves. Moroccans serve this dish as a first course, but it can also be used as a dessert. Thanks to the blender, we do not have to pound the almonds by hand in a brass mortar—a long, arduous procedure in a Moroccan kitchen.

INGREDIENTS

¼ cup whole, blanched almonds
3½ quarts milk
   Confectioners' sugar
¼ teaspoon almond extract
1 large cinnamon stick
¾ cup washed raw rice (small grain [imported] or medium grain)
   Salt to taste
   Sweet butter
1 to 2 tablespoons orange flower water
½ to ¾ pound phyllo pastry or strudel leaves, or 35 to 40 *warka* leaves (page 103)
1 egg
   Ground cinnamon

EQUIPMENT

Chopping knife
Electric blender
Sieve
Mixing bowls
3½-quart enameled cast-iron saucepan with cover
Small saucepan
10-inch cake pan
Baking sheet
Pastry brush
Whisk
Spatula
Serving plate

Working time: 1½ hours
Cooking time: 1 hour
Baking time: 25 minutes
Serves: 6

1. Coarsely chop the almonds, then liquefy in the blender with ½ cup very hot water. Strain into a mixing bowl, pushing down with the back of the wooden spoon to extract as much liquid as possible. Return the almond pulp to the blender and add another ½ cup very hot water. Repeat and discard the pulp.

2. Bring 2 cups of the milk to a boil. Add the almond milk, ¼ cup confectioners' sugar, the almond extract, cinnamon stick, rice, salt, and 2 tablespoons of butter. Return to a boil, stir once, partially cover, and let simmer over low heat for 45 minutes, or until all the liquid is absorbed.

3. Slowly, in 4 successive additions, stir in the remaining milk, stirring well and adding more *only* after the rice has completely absorbed the previous amount. Be careful not to scorch the rice; it should be creamy, soft, and very thick. Remove cinnamon stick. Stir in the orange flower water and more confectioners' sugar, to taste. Set aside, with one or two dabs of butter on top to prevent a skin from forming. Let cool. (This makes about 2½ cups filling.)

4. Preheat the oven to 425°.

5. In the small saucepan, melt ¼ cup of sweet butter.

6. If using strudel or phyllo pastry, butter the cake pan and in it arrange half the pastry leaves, one on top of the other so that they overlap the edges, quickly brushing melted butter between every other layer. (If you are using *warka*, see note below.)

7. Spread out the rice in one even layer over the pastry base, then cover with the remaining leaves, brushing melted butter in between. Fold the overlapping leaves up and cover with the last leaf, as directed in step 11 on page 110. Brush the top and sides with butter.

8. Beat the egg with a little water and cinnamon and paint the top of the pastry. Bake 10 minutes, or until golden brown, then invert as directed in step 12 on page 110. Continue baking until golden brown. Invert again, onto the serving plate and decorate the top with confectioners' sugar and crisscrossing lines of ground cinnamon.

Note: If you are using *warka*, scantily brush in between the layers with melted butter and, preferably, fry the pastry over gentle heat until golden on both sides.

One cup whole blanched almonds browned in oil and crushed with a rolling pin, mixed with some cinnamon and confectioners' sugar, can be spread over the rice before covering and baking.

VARIATION:

Packets of Almond-Flavored Rice (*Klandt*)

Klandt is a delightful variation on *bisteeya bil roz*, tiny tea cakes that are also served as a first course in Morocco. In Marrakesh the rice is simply steamed and then mixed with butter, raisins, and grilled chopped almonds before being wrapped in the pastry leaves.

INGREDIENTS

Same as for *Bisteeya bil roz* (Bisteeya Filled with Almond-Flavored Rice, page 116), but substituting 8 phyllo or strudel leaves or 24 Chinese spring roll skins, or *warka* leaves (page 103) and increasing the amount of melted butter to ½ cup (less for spring roll skins or *warka*)

plus

Flour and water paste
Salad oil for frying (for spring roll skins or *warka*)

EQUIPMENT

Same as for *Bisteeya bil roz*
plus
Large skillet

Working time: 50 minutes
Cooking time: 1 hour
Makes: 24 *klandt*

1. Follow steps 1, 2, and 3 on page 117.
2. Roll out the first pastry leaf or spring roll skin. (Brush phyllo or strudel pastry with a little melted butter.) Cut into 3 sections lengthwise. Place about 2 tablespoons rice filling about 1 inch from the bottom of each strip. Fold

the sides lengthwise over the filling. Fold the bottom over, and roll up like a rug. Fasten the last inch of pastry with flour and water paste.

3. Fry in oil until golden brown on both sides. (If using phyllo or strudel dough, bake in a 375° oven for about 35 minutes, turning them over midway. Brush the tops with butter for a golden crust.)

4. Dust with confectioners' sugar and cinnamon before serving. Serve hot or warm.

Trid

Trid, the "poor man's *bisteeya*," is said to have been the Prophet's favorite dish. I have to admit that *trid* is difficult and time consuming to prepare, and though I have found it delicious, I have not found it quite so delicious as *bisteeya*, which is easier to make. I include it here mainly as a curiosity, and because if you read the recipe you will see that *trid* is clearly a primitive form of the great pigeon pie.

Trid is served at Moroccan feasts, sometimes even with the same filling as *bisteeya*, or with a *tagine* of chicken, ginger, pepper, and preserved lemons. In Fez the crêpes are left whole, and in Safi they are torn into small pieces.

INGREDIENTS	EQUIPMENT
2 pounds all-purpose flour	Shallow basin, large mixing bowl, or *gsaa*
Salt	
Salad oil	Electric beater with dough hook (optional)
1 whole chicken (4 pounds), cleaned	
5 cloves garlic (approximately)	5½-quart enameled cast-iron casserole with cover
1 Spanish onion, grated	
½ teaspoon freshly ground black pepper	Large marble or formica workspace

(*continued*)

2 three-inch cinnamon sticks
½ teaspoon ground ginger
1 teaspoon whole black peppercorns
2 to 3 pinches pulverized saffron
½ cup sweet butter
10 sprigs of green coriander, tied together with a thread

Smooth-bottomed skillet or cake pan set over casserole or *gdra del trid* set over a brazier
Large, flat ovenproof serving dish

Working time: 4 hours (for the leaves)
Cooking time: 1 hour (for the sauce)
Serves: 10 to 12 (as part of a Moroccan dinner)

1. Prepare the dough for 60 pastry leaves by combining the flour with enough lightly salted lukewarm water to make a dough. Knead 5 minutes, then add ¼ cup vegetable oil by spoonfuls, kneading well before adding more. Knead the dough 15 to 20 minutes, until it is very elastic and smooth. (You can use an electric beater with a dough hook to do the job in 10 minutes.) Separate the dough into 3 equal parts, coat with more oil and cover with a cloth. Set aside for 1 hour.

2. Make a paste of the garlic and 2 tablespoons salt and prepare the chicken as directed on page 109.

3. Place the rinsed, drained chicken in the casserole with the onion, 1½ teaspoons salt, the spices, butter, coriander, and 6 cups water. Bring to a boil, then reduce the heat, cover, and simmer 1 hour. Remove the chicken and, by boiling rapidly, uncovered, reduce the sauce to a thick gravy of about 1¾ cups. Return the chicken to the sauce and keep warm.

4. After 1 hour place one of the three balls of dough on your marble workspace and flatten by stretching and rubbing outward with the palms of your hands. Knead and roll the dough until smooth. Repeat with the other two balls.

5. Rub the work surface sparingly with oil. Twist the first ball of dough in half and start to work it as follows: press and rub the dough in your hands,

forming a cylinder, make a small circle with your thumb and forefinger, push the cylinder through, and twist off small balls the size of a prune. Repeat until you have popped 10 "prunes" through your thumb and forefinger. Repeat with remaining half and the other two balls. Then flatten each piece into a 3-inch disc by tapping with oily fingertips.

6. Invert a large skillet or cake pan over a casserole of boiling water, or set a *gdra del trid* (a glazed earthen dome) over hot coals. Oil your fingers and start tapping and stretching the first pastry disc until you obtain a paper-thin circle approximately 8 inches in diameter. Lightly oil the bottom of the skillet or *gdra* and place the first leaf on to dry; turn after 30 seconds. Meanwhile, stretch and oil the next leaf. Place the second leaf directly on top of the drying first leaf, wait a second or two and then flip over so that second leaf will start to dry, too. Continue in this manner until 10 flattened discs or leaves are piled together, cooking and drying on the skillet bottom or *gdra*. Fold the pile loosely in half and then loosely in half again so that the ends will have a chance to dry. Remove and keep warm while continuing with the next batch. Continue until 6 sets of dried leaves have been prepared.

7. Preheat the oven to 350°.

8. Reheat the chicken and cut into serving pieces, removing any loose bones. Separate each leaf of pastry, tearing off and discarding any raw ends. Place one-third of the leaves, in two layers, on the serving dish. Dribble ⅓ cup of the sauce over the leaves. Cover with the second third of leaves, cover these with another layer of sauce, and top with the final leaves. Arrange the pieces of chicken in the middle and spoon the remaining sauce over. Bake 10 minutes and serve.

Note: In some parts of Morocco sugar and cinnamon and a bowl of cold milk is served on the side.

BRAEWATS AND BRIKS

———◆———

Braewats are small pastry envelopes stuffed with such things as rice pudding, *kefta* (cinnamon-flavored ground meat), brains, ground fish and spices, spicy sausage, and the fillings normally used in Bisteeya (page 108), without the almonds, or Bisteeya, Tetuán Style (page 114). A platter piled high with *braewats* on the buffet table is a handsome sight.

A variation on *braewats* is the *brik*. Though most people associate *briks* with Tunisia, where they are extremely popular and sold on the street, they are also prepared in Morocco, in the Rif Mountains. A *brik* is basically just another kind of filled pastry, but it must be served like a soufflé—immediately.

Braewats Filled with Eggs, Chicken, and Lemons

INGREDIENTS

Same ingredients as for Bisteeya, Tetuán Style (page 114) but using half the specified amounts with the exception of the pastry leaves (use ½ pound phyllo dough, or strudel leaves, or 40 *warka* leaves) (page 103) or spring roll skins.

EQUIPMENT

Same equipment as Bisteeya, Tetuán Style (page 114)

Working time: 1 hour 15 minutes
Cooking time: 1 hour
Baking or frying time: 20 to 25 minutes
Makes: 40 *braewats*

1. Follow steps 1 through 4 on page 113.

2. Shred the chicken fine and combine with the egg-and-onion mixture. Fold in the diced, preserved lemon peel and ¼ teaspoon ground cinnamon. (This should make approximately 3 cups filling.)

3. To make the *braewats*, spread a pastry leaf in front of you, keeping the other leaves under a clean cloth. Cut phyllo or strudel leaves vertically into three equal parts. Fold in three lengthwise. (Leave 7-inch spring roll skins or *warka* leaves whole.) Brush with oil or melted butter. Place approximately 1 tablespoon filling on each piece, 1 inch from the bottom. Fold the left-hand corner over the filling so as to make a triangle. Fold the triangle straight up, then fold upward to the left and continue folding as you would a flag until you reach the end and have a triangular *braewat*. Tuck in any loose ends and brush the *braewats* with butter or oil. Keep covered in the refrigerator until you are ready to bake.

4. Preheat the oven to 350°.

5. Bake until golden, then turn to bake on other side. The *braewats* will be done in approximately 20 minutes. (If you are using spring roll skins or *warka*, fry in plenty of oil until golden on both sides.) Serve warm, with a sprinkling of ground cinnamon.

Tunisian Briks

In Tunisia almost anything may end up inside a *brik*—tuna fish and anchovies are especially popular. In Morocco *briks* are nearly always filled with an egg, some salt and pepper, a pinch of Harissa Sauce (page 30), and a little sprinkling of ground cumin or chopped green coriander.

If you do not feel like making *warka*, the best pastry for *briks* is Chinese spring roll skins. All you do is spread out the leaf, break a raw egg onto one half, add the flavorings, fold the leaf diagonally and then "glue" the edges with a little frothy egg white. The *brik* is then deep fried in hot oil, turned over when brown and fried some more, and then drained on a paper towel. The *brik* should be devoured immediately. To eat it, grasp it by its corners, being careful not to let any egg run down your face.

This recipe is basically Tunisian, and therefore, strictly speaking, it does not belong in this book. But I included it anyway, because it is North African in spirit, and utterly delicious and unique.

INGREDIENTS

- 1 tablespoon sweet butter
- 1 small onion, finely chopped
- ¼ pound canned tuna, drained and mashed
- 1 to 2 tablespoons chopped parsley
- Salt and freshly ground black pepper
- A few capers, drained, rinsed, and mashed
- 1 to 2 tablespoons grated Parmesan cheese
- 4 Chinese spring roll skins or *warka* leaves (page 103)
- 4 medium or small eggs
- 1 egg white, lightly beaten, or flour and water paste
- Salad oil for frying
- Lemon wedges

EQUIPMENT

Small and large skillets
Perforated spoon
Spatula

Working time: 10 minutes
Frying time: 2 minutes for each *brik*
Serves: 4 (as a snack)

1. Melt the butter in a small skillet and cook the onion over very gentle heat until soft but not browned. Add the tuna, parsley, salt and pepper to taste, capers, and cheese. Mix well and separate into 4 equal parts.

2. Spread out the pastry leaves. Place one-quarter of the filling on one half of each leaf. Break an egg over each portion of filling. Fold each pastry leaf over to form a half circle or triangle, glue the edges with beaten egg white or flour and water paste. Fold each rim over ½ inch for a firmer rim, being careful not to break the egg yolk.

3. Put oil to a depth of 1 inch in a large skillet and heat until hot (but not smoking). Slide the *briks*, one at a time, into the skillet. Spoon hot oil over top while frying. When the underside is nicely browned, turn and continue frying. Remove and drain. Serve at once, with lemon wedges.

Note: An electric frying pan set up wherever you are serving the *briks* works perfectly for cooking and serving.

RGHAIF

———◆———

Rghaif is to Moroccans what *madeleines* were to Marcel Proust—a dish that opens up all sorts of sweet memories of childhood and home. Many Moroccans living in New York have told me that from time to time they feel an inexplicable longing for *rghaif*.

In 1968 my son Bato (he was then six) visited the mountain village of Joujouka to witness the annual celebration of the "rites of Pan." (The music of Joujouka was recorded by the late Brian Jones, of The Rolling Stones, and is now available on a record, with fascinating album notes by Brion Gysin.) When Bato returned he was full of stories of a man dressed in animal skins who danced with a fiery branch. But the thing he remembered best was being awakened in the morning by haunting flute music and being fed what he called "an airy pancake." He begged me to make it for him, but it took me quite a while to figure out that the "airy pancake" he liked so much was actually a type of *rghaif*.

Rghaif is a primitive form of pastry, sometimes served with honey and butter for breakfast, sometimes coated with confectioners' sugar, sometimes stuffed with almonds, or, best of all to a Moroccan, stuffed with spicy preserved meat, *khelea*. It bears a certain resemblance to the much finer French *pâte feuilletée*, in which firm butter is folded into pastry in complicated ways to build up many fine, thin butter layers, or "flakes." Actually *rghaif* is made with either oil or melted butter, which is spread over dough that is only folded in three twice. I should mention that for me *rghaif* can be very good if served hot, but quite ordinary and tough when cold.

Miklee

Miklee is the kind of *rghaif* served most often for breakfast. If the dough is properly worked, these airy pancakes can be quite good.

INGREDIENTS

½ package active dry yeast
1 teaspoon granulated sugar
3½ cups flour (approximately), preferably bread or strudel flour
1½ teaspoons salt
Salad oil
¼ cup sweet butter
½ cup honey

EQUIPMENT

Small and large mixing bowls
Electric beater with dough hook (optional)
Formica or marble workspace, at least 20 x 20 inches, or *gsaa*
Heavy cast-iron skillet
Paper towels

Working time: 45 minutes
Cooking time: A few minutes for each *miklee*
Makes: 18 (approximately)

1. Sprinkle the yeast over ¼ cup sugared lukewarm water. Stir to dissolve and set in a warm place for 10 minutes, until bubbly.

2. Mix the flour with the salt and make a well in the center. Pour in the bubbling yeast and enough lukewarm water to make a soft ball of dough. Knead the dough well, adding more water if kneading becomes difficult. (The dough, at first, should be sticky and soft, but after a good 20 minutes of kneading it should become highly elastic and smooth. If you have an electric beater with a dough hook attachment, set it on slow speed and knead about 10 minutes.)

3. Lightly grease your hands, the working space, and the dough with oil. With thumb and forefinger, squeeze off small balls of dough about the size of

large prunes. Coat each ball with oil. Take the first ball and pat down to a disk shape. Flatten with the oiled palms and fingers of both hands, stretching the disk as you flatten it. If you have kneaded the dough well (until it is very elastic), it will practically slide outwards. Avoid tearing the dough as it becomes paper thin, and try to keep it consistently thin.

4. Stretch out the dough to a paper-thin rectangle 10 x 9 inches, then coat with oil. Fold the ends of rectangles so they meet in the center. Turn halfway and fold again. Pat down slightly with oiled fingers. Set aside and repeat with the other balls of dough.

5. Fill the skillet to a depth of ¾ inches with oil and heat. Press the "package" out a bit and slip it into the pan. Fry the first package in oil until it puffs and its bottom becomes golden brown. Spoon a little hot oil over the top, then turn it over and continue frying for 1 minute. Transfer to paper towels to drain. Serve warm, with butter and honey.

VARIATION:
Almond Miklee

Follow the recipe above and fold an almond paste nugget inside the package.

Mtsimen

In this version of *rghaif*, dough is prepared as for Miklee (page 127), then the paper-thin disk is folded in half and then in half again, so that you end up with a shape like a wedge of pie. It is then fried on a lightly greased griddle (called a *mikla*), and when it browns (like a crêpe) it is served with honey and butter or butter and jam.

Meelowi

For this dish the *rghaif* pastry (prepared as for Miklee, page 127) is folded differently but fried the same as Mtsimen (see above). A piece of dough is squeezed into a long cigar shape. With oiled fingers and palms it is then flattened on a pastry board until it is a long, flat, thin strip. One end, which is flattened very thin, is rolled up the length of the pastry, a procedure like rolling up a rug, except that as you roll you keep stretching the unrolled part. When you are finished you flatten the whole thing into a round pancake and then fry it on the griddle. It is very good hot, with butter and honey.

Azut Cadi

This form of *rghaif* is the most difficult to execute well. The dough (prepared as for Miklee, page 127) is worked into a thin thread. While it is worked and being stretched, the completed portion is kept wrapped around a finger. When the thread is completed it is left for 20 minutes, then is flattened and fried in a small amount of oil. After frying it is pressed down, which loosens the pastry and makes it look like a plate of spaghetti. It is served with butter and dark country honey.

——◆——

SEVEN

Couscous

A thousand tiny pellets of grain, light, separate, and tender, doused with a *tagine*, arranged into a pyramid, and then served upon a platter at the end of a meal—that is *couscous*, the Moroccan national dish.

The *couscous* concept is simple and it is brilliant. Take a container with a perforated bottom, fill it with grain, and place it above a bubbling stew; the steam from the stew will swell the grains and at the same time flavor them with its vapors. When served together—the grain and the stew—the result is extraordinary; with the possible exception of *bisteeya*, *couscous* is the crowning achievement of Moroccan cuisine.

The word *couscous* actually has two meanings: the complete dish and the granules of semolina with which it is usually made. But *couscous* can also be made with other grains—barley, corn, millet, sorgo, green wheat, green barley shoots or sprouts, even crushed acorns and bread crumbs. These things become *couscous* when they are steamed above a boiling *tagine* in the top half of a *couscousiere*.

The derivation of the word *couscous* is obscure. Some believe it is onomatopoeic, a verbal approximation of the hissing sound as steam is forced through the holes into the grain. There are other theories, too, but the one fact that no one denies is that the dish itself is Berber.

Though everyone knows what you mean when you say you want *couscous*, they usually call it by other words. Most Moroccans say *seksu*; some Berbers call it *sikuk*; in the Souss region they say *sksu*; it is *sexsu* in the Rif Mountains, *utsu* in Figuig near the Algerian border, *ta'am* in Algeria, and *kouski* in Tunisia. And then there are variants beyond the Maghreb: in Trapani, in Sicily, where it is served with fish stews, they call it *cuscusu*; in Senegal, where it is substantially the same as in Morocco, it is *keskes*; and, strangest of all, it turns up in Brazil, where there are at least three types made with stone-ground cornmeal, rice, or tapioca, served with such things as shrimps, sardines, and chicken, all called *cuscuz*. (It probably reached Brazil via Portuguese slave ships carrying West Africans, who had learned it from Senegalese traders, who had learned it, in turn, from Berbers.)

Originally the Berbers served *couscous* with preserved butter and downed it with a cup of milk. They called this preparation *sikuk*, and in the Middle Atlas, little by little, they began to elaborate upon it, adding chick-peas, and then, as agriculture and husbandry developed, pumpkins and gourds, other vegetables, then chicken, and finally meat. Today there are nearly as many varieties of *couscous* as there are cooks: the dish can be a simple and pure Berber type, or an elaborate and spectacular extravaganza such as those allegedly served in palaces, great pyramids of semolina concealing mounds of pigeons, each stuffed in turn with *couscous* and other mysterious things.

In Morocco *couscous* is traditionally served for Friday lunch, or when it is warranted by a special occasion—or, of course, whenever anyone feels like eating it. It is so much a part of life that it is always served at feasts honoring weddings, births, and circumcisions, and when someone dies it is prepared by friends and neighbors, then placed in the home of the bereaved to be handed out to the poor during the mourning period. *Couscous* is the central image in a famous Moroccan proverb about the virtues of almsgiving:

A handful of *couscous* [given in charity] is better than Mecca and all its dust.*

As for wedding feasts, the Moroccan author, Ahmed Sefriou, in his charming book on the great Berber pilgrimage of Imilchil, tells how a bride of the Ait Hiddous tribe will use her silver brooch to separate grains, apportioning *couscous* between her husband's family and her own. By sharing the *couscous* in this way she symbolizes the "sharing of happiness."

In Morocco *couscous* is rarely served at the evening meal; also—and many people don't realize this—it is not considered a main course. At a Moroccan

* Edward Westermarch, *Wit and Wisdom of Morocco* (New York, 1931).

diffa it is served at the end of a string of courses to finally and fully satiate the hunger of the guests, and, in this sense, it is similar to the bowl of rice offered at the end of a Chinese banquet. No guest must go home hungry—the basic premise behind Arab hospitality—and, although this idea is often carried to the point of absurdity when, after being offered course after course, the possibility of going home hungry is out of the question, still satiation is symbolized by the appearance of a mound of *couscous*, highly flavored, laden with vegetables and meats, served at the end so that the guest will achieve *shaban* (total satisfaction) and know that his host has held back nothing that would give him pleasure.

Moroccan *couscous* is different from the *couscous* served in Paris. French *couscous* is derived from the Algerian variation: the vegetables, the meat, the broth, and the grain are served to the diner on separate plates. Algerian *couscous* is good, strong in taste, and often flavored with sausage, but it lacks the subtleties of the Moroccan types, whose spices are delicately blended, whose broth is pure ambrosia, and whose variations are infinite and sublime. Tunisian *couscous* is spicy and robust, and the recipes with seafood and fish are excellent and have found some Moroccan admirers. But really no country—Algeria, Tunisia, France, Sicily, Brazil, or Senegal—can begin to approach the exalted heights of Moroccan *seksu*.

In parts of Morocco, for example, you can find *couscous* that is both spicy and sweet at the same time, the two contradictory tastes interacting and tantalizing the tongue. There is spicy *couscous* in which chili peppers and ground pepper is the predominating note, or the great classic sweet *couscous* of Fez, in which onions, raisins, chick-peas, and lamb are served together in perfect harmony. One can prepare Moroccan *couscous* in the Berber style, with chicken, turnips, and creamy milk or as a dessert with dates, cinnamon, and sugar. There is *couscous* with fish, wild turnips, and fennel stalks, as prepared in the coastal town of Essaouira; *couscous* with a lamb's head, fava beans, and carrots, as served on the day after the Festival of the Sacrifice of the Lamb (Aid el Kebir); or *couscous* with lamb, chicken, and seven vegetables in a great and spectacular modern variation. There are *couscous* dishes in the styles of Rabat, Marrakesh, Tangier, Tetuán, and other cities and regions, all of them so delicious that it is impossible to choose a favorite because the last one eaten always seems the best.

HOW TO COOK COUSCOUS

In 1711 a Monsieur Mouette visited Fez and wrote the following description of the making of *couscous*:

They take a great Wooden Bowl, or Earthen Pan, before them, with a Porringer full of Flower [flour]; and another of Fair Water; a Sieve; and a Spoon. Then they put two or three Handfulls of the Flower into the Bowl, and pour three or four Spoonfulls of Water on it, which they work well with their Fingers, every now and then sprinkling it with Water, till it all runs into little Lumps like small Pease, and this they call Couscousou. As it rolls up they take it out of the Bowl and put it into the Sieve to separate the Flower that may remain loose; and there are some Women so expert at making it, that it is no bigger than Hail shot, which is the best. In the meanwhile they boil a great deal of good Meat, as Pullets, Beef, and Mutton, in a Pot that is not above a Span open at the Mouth, and so narrow at the bottom that it may sink two Inches within the Mouth of the other, the bottom whereof is full of holes like a Cullender. Into this last Pot they put the Couscousou over the other Pot the Meat boyls in, when it is almost Ready, leaving it so about three quarters of an Hour, close cover'd with a Napkin, and a wet Cloth with a little Flower, being wrapped about the Mouth of the other Pot, that no Steam may come out that way, but all ascend to pierce the Couscousou. When ready they turn it out into a Dish, and stir it about, that it may not cling together, but lie loose in Grains: Then they Butter it, and lastly pour on the Broth and all the Meat.

One hundred fifty years later, in 1873, Amelia Perrier published her almost identical description of the *couscous*-making process in a book entitled *A Winter in Morocco*. The making of *couscous* is an age-old process that has changed little through the centuries; in fact, a nontechnical description of *couscous*-making would read more or less the same today.

But please don't follow the instructions on *couscous* packages or those that come with *couscousieres:* they're often confusing or short-handed, and they can be extremely frustrating.

Couscous cooking looks difficult, but actually it's easy once you understand the technique of handling *couscous* grains. If you follow these steps, and use them when indicated in the *couscous* recipes that follow, your grains will always be perfect: soft, light, separate, not lumpy, not sticky, not heavy, even though swelled by steam and cold water.

Equipment

The basic piece of equipment you need is a *couscousiere*. The lower part, the pot that holds the bubbling stew, is called the *tanjra* or the *gdra*; the upper part with the perforated bottom that holds the grains is called the *kskas*. Berber *couscousieres* are made of unglazed earthenware, and the bourgeois Fassis use copper *couscousieres* lined with tin. But the aluminum ones sold in America are good, even though they sometimes come with a top, which is unnecessary, since *couscous* is steamed without a cover.

The only other thing you need is a substitution for the Moroccan *gsaa*, a large shallow basin of earthenware or wood in which the *couscous* is worked and where it dries. I have found that a large roasting pan, with sides at least 1½ inches high, is ideal. I've used baking sheets, but sometimes when I've circulated grains too much they've ended up on the floor.

Handling Couscous Grains

These are the master instructions for handling *couscous*, to be followed when indicated in the recipes. Though they look complicated, the principle behind them is very simple: all the wetting, drying, raking, aerating, and steaming of semolina grains is done with the purpose of swelling them with as much water as possible without allowing them to become lumpy or soggy. But you must be careful: the smaller and fresher the *couscous* grain, the less water is needed.

1. *First washing and drying of couscous:* Wash the *couscous* in a large, shallow pan by pouring water over the grain in a ratio of 3 parts water to 1 part grain (that is, if the recipe calls for 2 cups of *couscous*, use 6 cups of water, and so on). Stir quickly with the hand and then drain off excess water through a sieve. Return the *couscous* grains to the pan, smooth them out, and leave them to swell for between 10 and 20 minutes. After roughly 10 minutes, begin, with cupped, wet hands, to work the grains by lifting up handfuls of grain, rubbing them gently and letting them fall back into the pan. This process should break up any lumps that may have formed. Then rake the *couscous* with your fingers to circulate it and help the grains to swell.

Note: Freshly rolled *couscous* is simply dampened and immediately steamed as directed in step 2.

2. *First steaming of the couscous:* Dampen a strip of cheesecloth, dust it with flour, and twist into a strip the length of the circumference of the rim of the bottom part of the *couscousiere*. Use this to seal the perforated top or colander on top of the pot. Check all sides for effective sealing: the top and bottom should fit snugly, so that steam rises only through the holes. *The perforated top should not touch the broth below.* Slowly dribble one-quarter of the swollen *couscous* grains into the steamer, allowing them to form a soft mound. Steam 5 minutes and gently add the remaining *couscous*. When all the grains are in the steamer, lower heat to moderate and steam 20 minutes. *Do not cover the couscous while it steams.*

3. *Second drying of the couscous:* Remove the top part of the *couscousiere* (or the colander). Dump the *couscous* into the large, shallow pan and spread out with a wooden spoon. Sprinkle ½ to 1 cup cold water and 1 teaspoon salt over the grains. Separate and break up lumps by lifting and stirring the grains gently. Oil your hands lightly and rework the grains—this helps to keep each grain separate. (Some people oil the grain *before* steaming, but this results in a tougher texture.) Smooth the *couscous* out and allow it to dry for at least 10 minutes. If the *couscous* feels too dry, then add another cup of water by handful sprinkles, and rake the *couscous* well before each addition. If you are preparing *couscous* in advance, at this point let it dry and cover it with a damp cloth. It can wait many hours. (*Very important note:* If the stew in the bottom of the *couscousiere* is fully cooked and well seasoned and the sauce reduced to the proper amount prior to the final steaming of *couscous* grains, you should transfer the stew and sauce to a separate saucepan, keeping it warm, and perform the final steaming over boiling water.)

4. If you want to serve right away, allow the *couscous* to dry for 10 minutes, then pile it back into the *couscousiere* top, being sure to reseal the two containers with cheesecloth, for its final steaming of 20 minutes. If you have prepared steps 1–3 in advance, 30 minutes before serving break up lumps of *couscous* by working the grains lightly between your wet fingers. Steam the *couscous* in the *couscousiere* top for 20 minutes, as previously directed.

Note: Each time you place the top or colander over the pot, use cheesecloth to reseal the top two containers.

COUSCOUS RECIPES

———◆———

Pumpkin Couscous

This is a superb lamb *couscous* and makes a brilliant follow-up to *djej mechoui* (Roasted Chicken, page 212). I like the fact that it is both ultra-refined and rustic at the same time: ultrarefined because its relatively few ingredients suggest a great purity of gastronomic thinking, and rustic because the inclusion of pumpkin is reminiscent of the earliest vegetable *couscous* preparations of the Berbers.

INGREDIENTS

½ cup dried chick-peas or ½ twenty-ounce can cooked chick-peas
4 cups *couscous* (1½ pounds)
1½ pounds lamb neck, cut into 5 pieces
4 to 5 large Spanish onions
1 tablespoon salt
1½ to 2 teaspoons freshly ground black pepper to taste
1 teaspoon ground ginger
2 pinches pulverized saffron
½ teaspoon ground turmeric
1 cup sweet butter
1 pound carrots
1½ pounds pumpkin
¼ cup granulated sugar
½ pound black raisins

EQUIPMENT

Large saucepan
Mixing bowl
Large, shallow pan
Sieve
Couscousiere
Cheesecloth
Vegetable peeler
Chopping knife
Perforated spoon
Large serving dish

Working time: 30 minutes
Cooking time: 2 hours
Serves: 6 to 8 (as part of a Moroccan dinner)

1. Cover the dried chick-peas with water and soak overnight.

2. The next day, drain the chick-peas and cook in fresh water 1 hour. Drain, cool, and remove the skins by submerging them in a bowl of cold water and gently rubbing them between the fingers. The skins will rise to the top of the water—discard them. (If using canned chick-peas, peel them and set aside.)

3. Prepare the *couscous* by following step 1 (first washing and drying of the *couscous*) in the master instructions (page 136).

4. To prepare the broth, place the lamb in the bottom of *couscousiere*. Quarter and slice the onions lengthwise. Add to the lamb, along with the salt, spices, half the butter, 2 quarts water, and the drained chick-peas. (Canned chick-peas should not be added until 30 minutes before serving.) Bring to a boil, then reduce the heat, cover, and simmer 1 hour.

5. Meanwhile, prepare the vegetables: scrape the carrots, halve lengthwise, and cut into 2½-inch lengths. Peel and core the pumpkin, then cut into 2-inch chunks.

6. Follow steps 2 and 3 (first steaming and second drying of *couscous*) in the master instructions (page 136).

7. Add the carrots, sugar, and raisins to the broth. Continue cooking 30 minutes. *Up to this point the dish can be prepared in advance.*

8. Thirty minutes before serving, add the pumpkin and the drained peeled canned chick-peas (if using them) to the broth. Bring to a boil, reseal the two containers with cheesecloth, and steam the *couscous* another 20 minutes.

9. Dump the *couscous* onto a large serving dish and toss with the remaining butter, using a fork to smooth out any lumps. Spread out and form a well in the center. With a perforated spoon lift out pieces of meat (discarding loose bones). Cut the meat into small pieces and place in the well. Cover with the vegetables. Taste the broth for seasoning and readjust. Strain the broth over the *couscous* and vegetables and serve at once.

Note: Some people sprinkle a little cinnamon over the vegetables just before serving.

Omar's Couscous

This is not a classical Moroccan *couscous*, but a combination of some of the best ideas in many *couscous* recipes, plus a Tunisian touch—a peppery *harissa* sauce. My friend Omar Kadir invented this dish when we were trying to decide whether to serve a *couscous slaoui* or a modern Fez *couscous* at a large dinner party. The result was excellent—a vegetable *couscous* of lamb, raisins, onions, and almonds, sweet and spicy at the same time.

INGREDIENTS

- ½ cup dried chick-peas or ½ twenty-ounce can cooked chick-peas
- 11 medium yellow onions
- 1½ to 2 pounds lamb neck or shoulder, cut into 2-inch chunks
- 2 pinches pulverized saffron
- ¼ teaspoon turmeric
- 1 cup sweet butter
- Salt
- Freshly ground black pepper
- Ground cinnamon
- 5 carrots
- 4 small zucchini
- 4 tomatoes or 1 eight-ounce can peeled tomatoes
- 4 cups *couscous* (1½ pounds)
- ½ cup black raisins
- ½ teaspoon ground ginger
- ¼ cup granulated sugar
- 4 to 5 sprigs parsley and 2 to 3 sprigs of green coriander, tied together
- Salad oil for frying
- 1 cup whole, blanched almonds

EQUIPMENT

3½-quart saucepan
Mixing bowl
Chopping knife
Couscousiere
Vegetable peeler
Large, shallow pan
Sieve
Cheesecloth
Small skillet
Perforated spoon
Large serving dish

Working time: 45 minutes
Cooking time: 2½ hours
Serves: 6–8 (as part of a Moroccan dinner)

1. Soak the dried chick-peas overnight.

2. The next day, drain the chick-peas, cover with fresh cold water, and cook, covered, 1 hour. Drain, cool, and remove the skins by submerging the chick-peas in a bowl of cold water and gently rubbing them between the fingers. The skins will rise to the top of the water. Discard them and set the well-rinsed chick-peas aside. (If you are using canned chick-peas, peel them and set them aside.)

3. To prepare the broth, quarter 3 of the onions and place in the bottom of the *couscousiere* with the lamb, 3 quarts water, half the saffron and turmeric, 5 tablespoons butter, 1 tablespoon salt, 1 teaspoon pepper, and ½ teaspoon ground cinnamon. Bring to a boil, then reduce the heat, cover, and simmer 1 hour over moderately high heat.

4. Meanwhile, prepare the vegetables: scrape the carrots and clean the zucchini; halve both lengthwise and cut into 2-inch lengths. Peel, seed, and chop the tomatoes (see page 71). Cut the remaining onions into ¼-inch-thick "quarter moons." Set the vegetables aside in piles.

5. To prepare the *couscous*, follow step 1 (first washing and drying of *couscous*) in the master instructions (page 136).

6. Begin the preparation of the glazed topping. After the lamb has been cooking 1 hour, transfer 2 cups of the simmering lamb broth to a saucepan. Add the raisins to the broth, along with the onion "quarter moons," remaining saffron and turmeric, ground ginger, sugar, 3 tablespoons of the butter, 1½ teaspoons ground cinnamon, salt, and freshly ground black pepper to taste. Cook, covered, 1 hour, then remove cover and continue cooking until liquid has evaporated and the onions have a glazed appearance (about 30 minutes). Set aside, uncovered.

7. While the glazed topping mixture is cooking, add the tomatoes, the drained chick-peas (do not add canned chick-peas until 30 minutes before serving), herbs, and, if necessary, more water to the bottom of the *couscousiere*. Then follow steps 2 and 3 (first steaming and second drying of *couscous*) in the master instructions (page 136). Add the carrots to the lamb broth. Continue cooking the broth 30 minutes. *Up to this point the dish can be prepared in advance.*

8. *Thirty minutes before serving*, with wet hands break up lumps of *cous-*

cous by working the grains lightly between your fingers. Add the zucchini (and drained and peeled canned chick-peas if using them) to the lamb broth. Bring to a boil, reseal the two containers with cheesecloth, and steam the *couscous* another 20 minutes.

9. Reheat the glazed onions and raisins. Heat the oil in the skillet and fry the almonds until golden brown. Drain and set aside.

10. Dump the *couscous* onto the serving dish and toss with the remaining butter. Use a fork to smooth out any lumps. Spread out and form a well in the center. Place 2 cups drained lamb and vegetables in the well. Cover the lamb and vegetables with the glazed onions and raisins and dust with ground cinnamon. Decorate with the almonds, then moisten the grain with strained broth. Serve with extra lamb and vegetables in an accompanying tureen and Red Pepper Sauce (see below) in a small bowl on the side.

Note: The *couscous* may be tossed with 2 tablespoons *smen* (Cooked and Salted Butter, page 39) instead of the remaining sweet butter.

Red Pepper Sauce (*Harissa*)

INGREDIENTS

1 cup lamb broth from the *couscous* pot
1 teaspoon Harissa Sauce (page 30) or *sambal oelek*
1 tablespoon lemon juice
1 to 2 tablespoons olive oil
Pinches of cumin to taste
Sprinkling of freshly chopped parsley and green coriander

EQUIPMENT

Saucepan
Small serving bowl

Working time: 4 minutes
Makes: 1 cup

Combine all the ingredients in small saucepan over high heat. Beat well and pour into a small serving bowl. Serve at once.

Couscous with Seven Vegetables in the Fez Manner

Fez is one of the great gastronomic centers of Morocco, and there are many people who think the best food is to be found in Fassi homes. The traditional Fez *couscous* is made with chick-peas, raisins, and onions; the modern Fez variation employs seven vegetables (onions, pumpkin, zucchini, turnips, chili peppers, carrots, and tomatoes), two kinds of meat (chicken and lamb), and both sweetness (raisins) and spiciness (*harissa*). This assemblage is rich and glorious, and if you want you can even add other things: cabbage (early in the cooking), peeled baby eggplant and fava beans (30 minutes before serving), or even potatoes (which should be cooked separately with the pumpkin). However, in Fez the number 7 is considered lucky, and it is probably best to keep the vegetables down to that number.

According to Robert Landry, in his *Les soleils de la cuisine*, it is extremely chic to serve a Moroccan *couscous* with seven-year-old *smen*, seven vegetables, and seven spices.*

INGREDIENTS	EQUIPMENT
1 cup dried chick-peas or 1 twenty-ounce can cooked chick-peas	Large saucepan
	Mixing bowl
4 cups *couscous* (1½ pounds)	Large, shallow pan
2 lamb shanks or 2 pounds beef chuck, trimmed	*Couscousiere*
	Sieve
2 sets chicken wings and backs	Cheesecloth
¾ cup sweet butter (or 2 tablespoons salad oil and 10 tablespoons butter)	Vegetable peeler
	Small saucepan
2 tablespoons salt	Perforated spoon
1 tablespoon freshly ground black pepper	Very large serving dish
Pinch of pulverized saffron	Chopping knife

(*continued*)

* I have yet to taste seven-year-old *smen* (though one-year-old *smen* is fairly common). As for seven spices, the only recipe I have found is one noted down by the great English travel writer, Budgett Meakin, in his book *The Moors*, published seventy years ago. He describes a *couscous* flavored with pepper, ginger, nutmeg, coriander seeds, allspice, turmeric, and saffron.

½ teaspoon ground turmeric
2 medium yellow onions, quartered
2 cinnamon sticks (optional)
1 small bundle herbs (green coriander and parsley sprigs tied together with a thread)
4 to 5 red, ripe tomatoes, peeled, seeded and quartered (see page 71)
1 pound carrots
1 pound turnips
1 pound zucchini
½ pound pumpkin
1 fresh chili pepper (optional)
Handful of black raisins

Working time: **45 minutes**
Cooking time: **2½ hours**
Serves: **6 to 8 (as part of a Moroccan dinner)**

1. Soak the dried chick-peas overnight.

2. The next day, drain the chick-peas, cover with fresh, cold water, and cook, covered, 1 hour. Drain, cool, and remove the skins by submerging the chick-peas in a bowl of cold water and gently rubbing them between the fingers. The skins will rise to the top of the water. Discard them and set the peeled chick-peas aside. (If you are using canned chick-peas, peel them and set them aside.)

3. To prepare the *couscous*, follow step 1 (first washing and drying of *couscous*) in the master instructions (page 136).

4. To prepare the broth, place the trimmed meat and chicken in the bottom of the *couscousiere* with half the butter (or the oil and ¼ cup of the butter), the salt, pepper, saffron, turmeric, the quartered onions, the cinnamon sticks, herbs, and quartered tomatoes. Cover and cook gently over low heat for 10 minutes, giving the pan a swirl from time to time. Then add 3 to 4 quarts of water and the drained chick-peas (do not add canned chick-peas until 30 minutes before serving) and bring to a boil. Simmer 1 hour, covered.

5. Meanwhile, prepare the vegetables: scrape the carrots and turnips and cut them into 1½-inch lengths. Cut the zucchini into quarters. Peel and cut up the pumpkin.

6. Follow steps 2 and 3 (first steaming and second drying of the *couscous*) in the master instructions (page 136). Add the carrots and turnips to the lamb broth. Continue cooking the broth 30 minutes more. (The broth has now cooked 2 hours, so add more water if necessary.) Cut the meat into chunks, discarding the bones. *Up to this point the dish can be prepared in advance.*

7. Thirty minutes before serving time, cook the pumpkin, in a separate pan, in lamb broth-flavored water until tender. Add the zucchini, optional chili pepper, raisins, and canned chick-peas (if using them) to the lamb broth. Bring to a boil, reseal the two containers with cheesecloth, and steam the *couscous* another 20 minutes. Dot the *couscous* with the remaining butter during the last 5 minutes of steaming.

8. Dump the *couscous* onto the serving dish and toss with butter or *smen*. Use a fork to smooth out any lumps. Spread out and form a large well in the center. With the perforated spoon, transfer the meat and vegetables into the well. Add the drained pumpkin slices. Taste the broth for seasoning and adjust, then strain. Moisten the grain with the strained broth. Serve with Red Pepper Sauce (page 144) on the side.

Note: I have heard that some Fassis use stewed quinces in place of raisins—an interesting idea.

VARIATION:

Couscous in the Marrakesh Manner

Follow the instructions for Couscous with Seven Vegetables in the Fez Manner (page 145), but leave out the chick-peas and chicken and use any number (up to seven, for good luck) of the following vegetables: onions, fava beans, tomatoes, sweet potatoes, pumpkin, turnips, carrots, zucchini, sweet and hot peppers, cabbage.

Couscous with Dates and Seven Vegetables

Follow the instructions for Couscous with Seven Vegetables in the Fez Manner (page 145), but replace the chicken and lamb with 2 pounds beef chuck, cut into 2-inch chunks, and the butter with 3 to 4 tablespoons beef drippings, and 30 minutes before serving place ½ pound pitted dates in the steamer, pile the *couscous* grain on top and steam them together 30 minutes. To serve, decorate the platter by arranging the dates around the rim of the *couscous*. This is a strong dish that warms the insides—it is usually made in winter.

Couscous with Lamb's Head and Seven Vegetables
(Seksu Raseen Bahar)

In Fez this is a popular *couscous* on Friday, said to make the diner strong and smart. Prepare exactly the same as Couscous with Seven Vegetables in the Fez Manner (page 145) but substitute two lambs' heads—previously soaked in water, halved, well cleaned, and tied together—for the chicken and the lamb. The tongue is meaty and the brains are delicate and sweet. As for the eyes (everything but the pupils), they are considered the best part, and are plucked and handed to the guest of honor! *Chacun à son goût.*

Small Family Couscous

This recipe is not unlike those before and some that follow: what makes it unique is its size. Most *couscous* recipes are scaled to feed a mob and require some intricate preparation. This one is simple and geared to last-minute preparation: it was prepared to celebrate the surprise arrival in Tangier of my editor, who came to help me finish this book.

On the opposite end of the *couscous* scale one hears of the *couscous* prepared in the Doukkala region of Morocco: up to sixteen people (and perhaps more) with arms spread out along the sides of a huge heavy cloth carry a *couscous* prepared for hundreds. This gigantic *couscous* is decorated with not only the ingredients listed below in enormous quantities, but with hard candies of all hues and boiled eggs dyed red, blue, yellow, green, and orange.

INGREDIENTS

- 1 pound *couscous*
- ¼ cup salad or peanut oil
- 2 tablespoons *smen* (Cooked and Salted Butter, page 39)
- 1 small whole chicken, plus the giblets
- Salt
- 1¾ teaspoons freshly ground black pepper
- ½ teaspoon ground ginger
- 3 pinches pulverized saffron
- 1 Spanish onion, sliced
- Small bouquet of parsley, tied together with thread
- ¼ pound large black raisins
- 1 pound sweet red onions
- ¼ cup sweet butter
- 1 teaspoon ground cinnamon
- 2 tablespoons granulated sugar

EQUIPMENT

Large shallow pan
Sieve
Couscousiere
Small mixing bowl
Chopping knife
Heavy-bottomed 2-quart
   saucepan

Working time: 30 to 40 minutes
Cooking time: 2 hours
Serves: 4 to 5

(continued)

2 tablespoons honey
¼ pound blanched almonds
  Salad oil for frying

1. To prepare the *couscous*, follow step 1 (first washing and drying of *couscous*) in the master instructions (page 136).

2. To prepare the broth, place the oil, *smen*, chicken, 2 teaspoons salt, 1½ teaspoons black pepper, ¼ teaspoon ginger, 1 pinch of saffron, and the sliced Spanish onion in the bottom of the *couscousiere*. Cook gently, covered, over low heat, for 15 minutes, swirling the pot from time to time to avoid burning any of the ingredients. Pour in 2 cups water, add the parsley sprigs, cover again, and allow to simmer gently 1 hour.

3. Soak the raisins in water to cover. Slice the red onions and place in the heavy-bottomed saucepan with a little salt and half the butter. Cook, covered, for 10 minutes, then add the remaining ginger and black pepper. Stir in the cinnamon, sugar, and another pinch of saffron. Continue to cook 15 minutes more, covered, then transfer ¾ cup of the chicken broth from the *couscousiere* to the onions. Uncover and cook until thickened.

4. Follow steps 2 and 3 (first steaming and second drying of the *couscous*) in the master instructions (page 136).

5. Drain the raisins and add to the onion sauce. Remove the chicken when tender and allow to drain.

6. Preheat the oven to 450°.

7. Brush the chicken with the honey and set in the oven to glaze. Reduce the onion sauce to a syrupy glaze.

8. Meanwhile, wet your hands and break up lumps in the *couscous* by working the grain lightly between your fingers. Reseal the steamer top and steam the *couscous* again for 15 to 20 minutes.

9. Fry the almonds in oil until golden brown and add to the onion glaze. Blend the remaining butter with another pinch of saffron and dot the steaming *couscous*, then dump the *couscous* out onto a large serving dish and toss well so that it becomes a pale yellow color. Use a fork to smooth out any lumps. Spread out and form a well in the center. Place the glazed chicken in the well and cover with the onion-almond-raisin glaze. Taste the broth for seasoning, then moisten the grain with it. Serve the *couscous* at once.

Couscous from Rabat and Sale (*Seksu Slaoui or Seksu Tafaya*)

This sweet *couscous* is similar to the traditional *couscous* of Fez, and is excellent after a lemony chicken *tagine* or a spicy fish *tagine*. It is a classic dish in which the onions caramelize with sugar or honey, and the *couscous* grains are bright yellow from an additional touch of saffron just before serving.

INGREDIENTS

6 cups *couscous* (2¼ pounds)
2 pounds lamb neck, cut into 5 to 6 pieces
1 tablespoon salt
1½ teaspoons freshly ground black pepper
2 pinches pulverized saffron
¼ teaspoon ground turmeric
6 large Spanish onions, quartered
1 cup sweet butter
3 sprigs green coriander, tied together with a thread (optional)
2 cinnamon sticks
1½ teaspoons ground cinnamon
1 cup honey or granulated sugar
¼ pound black raisins

EQUIPMENT

Large, shallow pan
Sieve
Mixing bowl
Couscousiere
Cheesecloth
Heavy-bottomed 3½-quart casserole with cover
Perforated spoon
Large serving dish

Working time: 45 minutes
Cooking time: 2½ hours
Serves: 10 to 12 (as part of a Moroccan dinner)

1. To prepare the *couscous*, follow step 1 (first washing and drying of *couscous*) in the master instructions (page 136).

2. To prepare the broth, place the lamb, 2 teaspoons of the salt, 1 teaspoon of the pepper, a pinch of pulverized saffron, the turmeric, 1 quartered onion, 3 tablespoons of the sweet butter, the green coriander, and cinnamon sticks in the bottom of the *couscousiere*. Melt the butter over low heat, swirling the pan once or twice to let the spices and meat mix gently. Cover with 2 quarts water and bring to a boil. Cover and simmer 1 hour.

3. Meanwhile, slice the remaining quartered Spanish onions and place in the heavy-bottomed casserole with 2½ cups water, cover tightly, and steam 5 minutes. Remove the cover and drain the onions well.

4. To prepare the glazed topping, when the lamb has cooked for 1 hour, transfer about 1 cup simmering broth to the heavy-bottomed casserole. (Add more water to the bottom of the *couscousiere* if necessary.) Put the drained onions, ground cinnamon, the remaining ½ teaspoon black pepper, the remaining teaspoon salt, 5 tablespoons of the butter, and the honey or sugar in the casserole. Mix well to blend and cook, uncovered, 5 minutes. Add the raisins, cover, and simmer 30 minutes.

5. Follow steps 2 and 3 (first steaming and second drying of *couscous*) in the master instructions (page 136). (The broth has now cooked 1½ hours.) Continue cooking over very gentle heat 30 minutes, adding water if necessary.

6. Meanwhile, remove the cover from the casserole and continue cooking until all the liquid has evaporated and the onions have reduced to a thick syrupy glaze. Set aside uncovered. *Up to this point the dish can be prepared in advance.*

7. Thirty minutes before serving, with wet hands break up lumps of *couscous* by working the grains lightly between your fingers. Bring the broth to a boil, reseal the steamer top, and steam the *couscous* 20 minutes. Reheat the onion glaze. Blend the remaining butter with the remaining pinch of pulverized saffron and dot the *couscous* with the tinted butter during the last 5 minutes of steaming. Dump the *couscous* onto the serving dish and toss well so that the *couscous* becomes a lovely pale yellow. Use a fork to smooth out any lumps. Spread out and form a well in the center of the *couscous*. Place the drained lamb in the well and cover with the glazed onions. Taste the broth for seasoning and readjust, then strain. Moisten the grain with the strained broth and serve at once.

Another Couscous from Rabat and Sale

Follow the instructions for the preceding recipe, but substitute 2 small pigeons (squabs) or 1 trussed chicken for the lamb. Just before serving remove the birds from the broth and glaze in a hot oven with a little honey or grape jelly. Serve under the onion glaze.

Traditional Fez Couscous

Follow the instructions for Couscous from Rabat and Sale (page 151), but add ½ pound chick-peas (prepared as instructions on page 154) to the broth.

Tangier Couscous (*Seksu Tanjaoui*)

INGREDIENTS	EQUIPMENT
1 cup dried chick-peas or 1 twenty-ounce can cooked chick-peas, drained	3½-quart saucepan
4 cups *couscous* (1½ pounds)	Large shallow pan
1½ pounds lamb neck or lamb shank	Sieve
2 teaspoons salt	Mixing bowl
2 rounded teaspoons freshly ground black pepper	*Couscousiere*
1 rounded teaspoon ground ginger	Cheesecloth
¼ teaspoon pulverized saffron mixed with turmeric	Perforated spoon
	Large serving dish

(continued)

Pinch of cayenne
3 quartered medium onions
2 sprigs each parsley and green coriander, tied together with thread
1 cup sweet butter
1 large Spanish onion, quartered and thinly sliced lengthwise
½ cup raisins

Working time: 30 minutes
Cooking time: 2 hours
Serves: 6 to 8 (as part of a Moroccan dinner)

1. Soak the dried chick-peas overnight.

2. The next day, cover the chick-peas with fresh, cold water and cook, covered, 1 hour. Drain, cool, and remove the skins by submerging the chick-peas in a bowl of cold water and gently rubbing them between the fingers. The skins will rise to the top of the water. Discard the skins and set the chick-peas aside. (If you are using canned chick-peas, peel and set aside.)

3. To prepare the *couscous*, follow step 1 in the master instructions (page 136).

4. To prepare the broth, place the lamb, the salt, pepper, ginger, saffron, turmeric, a pinch of cayenne, the quartered onions, herbs, and half the butter (or less, if desired) in the bottom of the *couscousiere.* Melt the butter over low heat, swirling the pan once or twice to let the spices and meat mix gently. Cover with 2½ quarts water and bring to a boil. Add the drained chick-peas, cover, and simmer 1 hour. (Canned chick-peas should not be added until 30 minutes before serving.)

5. Follow steps 2 and 3 in the master instructions (page 136). (The broth has now simmered 1½ hours.) *Up to this point the dish can be prepared in advance.*

6. Thirty minutes before serving, with wet hands break up lumps of *couscous* by working the grains between your fingers. Remove the lamb shank bone and discard, then cut the lamb into bite-sized pieces. Add the thinly sliced onions, chick-peas, raisins, and the lamb cubes to the broth. Bring to a boil, reseal the two containers with cheesecloth, and steam the *couscous* another 20 minutes. During the last 5 minutes of steaming, dot the *couscous* with the remaining butter.

7. Dump the *couscous* onto a very large serving dish, tossing to distribute the butter. Smooth out any lumps with a fork. Spread out and form a well in the center. Place the lamb in the well and cover with the onions, raisins, and chick-peas. Cover slightly with the *couscous* to give a pyramid effect. Taste the broth for seasoning and readjust, then strain. Moisten the grains with the strained broth and serve.

VARIATION:

Tangier Couscous with Vegetables

Follow the directions for Tangier Couscous (above), but add a small bunch of quartered carrots and turnips 30 minutes after the lamb has begun cooking, then add 3 small quartered zucchini just before the last steaming.

VARIATION:

Tangier Couscous with Chicken

To make this dish with chicken, follow the recipe for Tangier Couscous (above), excluding the chick-peas, doubling the amount of ginger and turmeric, tripling the amount of herbs, and substituting a 3- to 3½-pound chicken, quartered and with giblets, for the lamb shank.

Berber Couscous (*Seksu Bidaoui*)

This is the kind of *couscous* you will find in small villages in the foothills of the Middle Atlas Mountains, and it is extraordinary. It is served in the spring, when everything that grows is fresh and young and tender, and it has a miraculous, clean taste. Everything in it should be as fresh as possible, except of course the *smen*, which, ideally, should be about a year old. But I think a month-old *smen* made with orégano water (Herbed Smen, page 38) makes an excellent substitution.

INGREDIENTS

EQUIPMENT

4 cups *couscous* (1½ pounds)	Large, shallow pan
1 small chicken, freshly killed	Sieve
2 teaspoons salt	Mixing bowl
2 teaspoons freshly ground black pepper	*Couscousiere*
½ cup sweet butter	Cheesecloth
1 good pinch pulverized saffron mixed with a little turmeric	Electric blender or food mill
2 large, ripe tomatoes, peeled and chopped (see page 71)	Large serving dish
8 sprigs each parsley and green coriander, tied together with a thread	*Working time:* 40 minutes
1 Spanish onion, quartered	*Cooking time:* 1¾ hours
1 cinnamon stick	*Serves:* 6 to 8 (as part of a Moroccan dinner)
8 white baby onions, peeled	
1 pound small, tender white turnips, cut into large chunks	
1½ pounds small zucchini, quartered	
2 cups baby peas, fava beans, or lima beans	
1 fresh green or red chili pepper (optional)	
2 to 3 tablespoons Herbed Smen (page 38) or 4 to 5 tablespoons fresh butter	
1 pint medium cream or fresh, creamy milk	

1. To prepare the *couscous*, follow step 1 (first washing and drying of *couscous*) in the master instructions (page 136).

2. Wash the pullet or chicken well under running water, then drain. Remove all excess fat.

3. Melt the butter in the bottom of *couscousiere* without browning. Add the salt, spices, half the chopped tomatoes, the herbs, quartered onion, and

cinnamon stick. Take the pot in your hands and give it a good swirl. Add the pullet or chicken, cover the pan, and cook gently 15 minutes. Pour in 1 quart water, cover, and simmer 30 minutes more. Then add the peeled white onions.

4. Follow steps 2 and 3 (first steaming and second drying of *couscous*) in the master instructions (page 136).

5. Add the turnips to the simmering broth and cook 15 minutes. (The broth has now cooked 1 hour 20 minutes—add more water if necessary.) *Up to this point the dish can be prepared in advance.*

6. Thirty minutes before serving, puree the remaining chopped tomato in an electric blender or food mill. Add the puree, zucchini, peas, and optional chili pepper to the broth. Bring to a boil, reseal the two containers with cheesecloth, and steam another 20 minutes.

7. Dump the *couscous* out onto a large serving dish and mix in the *smen* with your fingertips, working it in gently. Smooth out any lumps with a fork. Make a well in the center and place the pullet or chicken in the well. Cover with the vegetables. Meanwhile add the cream or milk to the broth and bring to a boil. Turn off the heat. Strain the broth and use some of it to moisten the *couscous*. (The remaining broth can be served to guests in small cups for additional moistening of individual portions, or as a soup.) Serve at once.

Note: To avoid burning the chicken and the vegetables, give the kettle a swirl from time to time and add more water whenever necessary.

Berber Couscous with Barley Grits (*Cheesha Belboula*)

If you want to make a *couscous* unlike any other, try this. It is precisely the same as the Berber *couscous* in the preceding recipe, except that instead of semolina it is made with barley: the flavor is nutty, rustic, and extraordinarily good. The first time I tasted this *couscous* it was served on a wooden tray—the vegetables looked very bright piled over the pearl-colored grain, and there was one, a long pale green squash called a *slaoui*, that I had never tasted before, which I later found at an Italian market in New York. This is all by way of introduction to special instructions on the steaming and handling of barley grits. The grain is different in texture from semolina, and requires three steamings. If you like this dish you can substitute barley grits (available in all organic and health food stores) for semolina in any of the *couscous* recipes, *using these notes on its handling.* The most important thing is to remember that water must be added to this kind of grain *very slowly,* as described in step 3 below.

INGREDIENTS	EQUIPMENT
Same as preceding recipe, but substitute 4 cups barley grits (1½ pounds) for the *couscous*	Same as preceding recipe

1. Prepare the broth as in steps 2 and 3 on page 156.
2. Wash the barley grits in a large, shallow pan by pouring 6 cups water over them, stirring and then draining off the excess water. Let stand 3 minutes. Meanwhile, butter the inside of the upper container of the *couscousiere.* Squeeze the barley grits to extract excess water and slowly add the grits to the top container by rubbing them between your palms as you drop them in. Before sealing the top container with cheesecloth, make sure there is plenty of liquid in the bottom of the *couscousiere.* Steam the grits 20 minutes.
3. Dump the grits out into a large roasting pan and break up the lumps with a fork. Add 1 tablespoon butter. *Slowly,* add water while raking and working

the grains to help them swell and separate. It should take about 3 minutes to add 2 cups water. Do not let the grits become soggy. Rake and toss them, smooth them out, and let them dry for 10 minutes.

4. Pile the barley grits back into the top container, reseal with cheesecloth, then steam for 20 minutes.

5. Dump the grits back into the roasting pan and break up the lumps. Allow to stand 15 minutes, working the grits from time to time to keep them separate and prevent them from becoming lumpy. *Do not add water.*

6. Add the turnips as in step 5 on page 157. *Up to this point the dish can be prepared in advance.*

7. Thirty minutes before serving, add the vegetables as in step 6 of the preceding recipe, reseal the two containers, and steam the barley grits 20 minutes.

8. To serve, dump the barley grits into the serving dish. Add the *smen* and work in lightly. Form a mound and then a well, pushing the grits away from the center. With a perforated spoon transfer the vegetables and chicken to the well. Taste the sauce and, after adding the milk, readjust for seasoning. Strain the hot, creamy broth over the grits and vegetables to moisten well. Serve at once.

Barley Grit and Fava Bean Couscous (*Cheesha Sikuk*)

This simple recipe was given to me by Mr. Abdeslam Bennis, president of a gastronomic society in Morocco. It is very Moroccan, very elegant, and should be made only in the spring, when the fava beans are tender and fresh. Here is my adaptation.

INGREDIENTS

¼ pound fresh fava beans
1 pound barley grits
2 scallions, sliced
   Salt and freshly ground black pepper
½ cup butter

EQUIPMENT

Large, shallow pan
Couscousiere
Large roasting pan
Saucepan

Working time: 20 minutes
Cooking time: 1 hour
Serves: 4

1. Shuck the fava beans.
2. Steam the barley grits three times, over plain boiling water, as directed in steps 2–5 (pages 158–159).
3. Boil the fava beans with the scallions, a small amount of water, salt, and pepper. Drain and serve with the freshly steamed barley grits, which should then be buttered. Serve with an iced glass of buttermilk.

Note: Some people sprinkle a little sugar over the barley.

Berber Couscous with Barley Shoots (*Azenbu*)

This *couscous*, made with barley shoots or green barley, is considered one of the most delicious in Morocco, though it is available only in the Rif and in the Souss. Admired for its purity and utter simplicity, it is *the* ultimate country dish. Unmatured barley is grilled in a pan with *za'atar*, then cracked and sieved. The smaller grains are used in soup, and the larger grains are steamed over boiling water, placed on a platter, buttered, and served with a bowl of cold milk or buttermilk in the Berber style.

Fish Couscous with Cornmeal (*Baddaz Bil Hut*)

This is a specialty of the southern coastal city of Essaouira—a spicy *couscous* in which a *tagine* of fish, tomatoes, wild turnips with their tops, onions, fennel, and carrots is used to steam hand-rolled pellets of stone-ground cornmeal or hominy.

Rabat Couscous with Acorns

In the winter months in Rabat a *couscous* is made in which crushed and ground acorns are substituted for semolina, and steamed above various *tagines*.

Large-Grain Couscous (*Mhammsa*)

A hand-rolled semolina *couscous* called *mhammsa*, which is twice the size of the regular packaged grain, unfortunately is not available in the United States at this time. It is extremely popular in the southern part of Morocco, particularly the Souss area, where it is prepared with chicken, onions, chickpeas and raisins as a holiday dish. More often it is served with the preserved meat, *khelea*. Since *mhammsa* is so large, it must be steamed 5 times before it becomes light and tender. With each steaming some *smen* is worked in, and during the final steaming it is garnished with chopped or quartered hard-boiled eggs. Even by Moroccan standards *mhammsa* is considered heavy fare, but for people who rise at five A.M. and dine on their first *tagine* by ten o'clock in the morning, it is a good and substantial dish.

Fine-Grain Couscous with Chicken or Lamb (*Seffa* Merdurma*)

Seffa is the opposite of *mhammsa*, an extremely fine *couscous* grain of great delicacy, which is also, unfortunately, not available in America at this time. Until it does become available I suggest you perform this recipe with regular *couscous* and steam it an extra time to obtain extra lightness. If you use real saffron threads and chicken meat or lean pieces of lamb, you will just barely be able to get away with calling this dish *seffa merdurma*, an expression suggesting a particularly fine dish that might be served at the palace. With giblets it runs under the plebeian title of *seffa miftoon*.

INGREDIENTS	EQUIPMENT
2 pounds *couscous* or *seffa*	Large, shallow pan
Sweet butter	Sieve
1½ pounds chicken thighs, lean lamb cut into	Mixing bowl

* Or *sfaa*.

small pieces, or chicken giblets, wings, and
  necks
  Salt
½ teaspoon freshly ground black pepper
½ teaspoon ground ginger
  Pinch of pulverized saffron
¼ teaspoon turmeric
¾ cup grated onion
 3 two-inch cinnamon sticks
¼ pound sweet butter
 3 cups hot chicken stock
  Confectioners' sugar
  Ground cinnamon

Couscousiere
Cheesecloth
4½-quart casserole with
  cover
Large serving dish
Large spoon

Working time: ½ hour
Cooking time: 1 hour
Serves: 10 (as part of a
  Moroccan dinner)
       or
6 (as a supper dish)

1. If using *seffa*, dampen the grain very lightly with salted water, but if substituting *couscous* wash and dry it as directed in step 1 (first washing and drying of *couscous*) of the master instructions (page 136).

2. Fill the bottom of the *couscousiere* with water and bring it to a boil. Rub the steamer heavily with butter, seal to the bottom with cheesecloth, and steam as in step 2 (first steaming of the *couscous*) of the master instructions (page 136). (*Seffa* is covered loosely with a cloth while steaming.)

3. Meanwhile, cut up the poultry or lamb into 1-inch pieces, discarding skin, bones, excess fat, and gristle. Place the poultry or lamb pieces in the casserole (*not* the *couscousiere* bottom) with some salt, spices, grated onion, cinnamon sticks and 3 tablespoons of the butter. Cook gently, covered, for 5 minutes, then add the hot chicken stock. Bring to a boil, cover again, and simmer 45 minutes.

4. Dump the *seffa* or *couscous* into a large, shallow pan. Sprinkle with 1 cup water by quarter cupfuls and "work" the grain for the greatest absorption, before adding more water. Add 2 tablespoons of the butter and toss well. Return to the container top, reseal, and steam again for 20 minutes over boiling water.

5. If using *seffa*, ignore this step. If using *couscous*, dump it out and work it again, adding more water, but avoid making the *couscous* soggy. Dry for

10 minutes, then return the *couscous* to the container top and steam again for 10 minutes.

6. Remove the poultry or lamb and keep warm. By boiling rapidly, uncovered, reduce the broth to ¾ cup. Discard the cinnamon sticks.

7. To serve, dump half of the *seffa* or *couscous* onto a large serving dish. Dot with half the remaining butter and ¼ cup of the sauce, then toss. Spread out to make a flat cake. Arrange the pieces of poultry or lamb on the grain in one layer. Spoon over another ¼ cup sauce. Toss the remaining butter and sauce with the remaining *seffa* or *couscous* in the container and place over the poultry or meat. Making sure no meat is visible, form into a hemisphere, then sprinkle with a little confectioners' sugar and decorate with lines of cinnamon. Serve with a bowl of confectioners' sugar on the side.

Note: Homemade *seffa* can be made by moistening 1 pound *rough-grained* semolina flour and a pinch of salt with 2 tablespoons saffron water. The semolina is rubbed into tiny pellets and then pressed through a fine-wired sieve. It is then steamed 20 minutes, loosely covered with a kitchen cloth. The *seffa* is then returned to the *gsaa* and "worked" with ½ cup saffron water added very slowly by handfuls. A final sieving through a fine colander or coarse-wired sieve prepares the grain for a second steaming just before serving. Homemade *seffa*, as opposed to commercial varieties, must be steamed twice.

SHERIYA

Sheriya is an inch-long noodle very similar to vermicelli, formed between the thumb and forefinger from pellets of dough. Moroccans use them in soups and in various other dishes, where they are treated precisely as if they were *couscous* grains. They are steamed at least three times for 20 minutes, and between each steaming they are "worked" with cold water so that they will remain separate and soft.

Steamed Noodles with Meat (*Sheriya Miftoon*)

You can make *sheriya miftoon* by breaking the thinnest spaghetti you can find (vermicelli, cappellini, or use soup egg noodles) into one-inch pieces and then treating them as if they were *seffa* or *couscous* by steaming them over boiling water three times. (Follow the master instructions on pages 136–137, but boil the egg noodles and drain well.) To serve, use the *sheriya* to cover and conceal various spicy bits of cooked lamb, pigeon, chicken or giblets, and then garnish with a sprinkling of cinnamon.

Steamed Noodles with Sugar and Cinnamon (*Sheriya Bahara*)

Another *sheriya* dish that I first tasted in a home outside Rabat is simple to make. Again, steam inch-long pieces of vermicelli or cappellini over boiling water three times. Then butter them heavily, pile them into a mound, criss-cross them with lines of ground cinnamon, and serve with a bowl of loaf sugar powdered into dust. The dish is eaten with large spoons, washed down with cold milk, and is delicious in the evening.

EIGHT

◆

Fish

One hears curious stories about the coastal region between Agadir and Tiznit. Here, near the estuary of the Massa River, the great seventh-century Arab warrior and proselytizer Ogba ben Nafi is said to have ridden his horse into the sea and proclaimed that there were no more lands to conquer or Berbers to convert. He is said, too, to have saluted "the subjects of Jonah," for it is here, a little north of the place where the Massa River meets the Atlantic, that Jonah is supposed to have been disgorged by the whale. Jonah is remembered in these parts as "the fish man," and if you ask a shepherd he may show you a stone, covered with meager offerings (handfuls of grain, a few tufts of wool), where Jonah took his first step onto dry land.

The coast of the Souss, from Essaouira to a point south of Tiznit, is fishing country, and here, near the end of summer, people come to eat the *tassargal*, a large and tasty bluefish that rivals in popularity the shad caught in the Sebou River near Fez. Fish is popular on the Atlantic Coast of Morocco, in Casablanca, Safi, and Essaouira, and in the Rif Mountains that rise from the Mediterranean the *Riffian* people have a saying: "If a man is with God he can put his arm into the water and by each of its hairs pull up a fish."

When I first heard this proverb I thought, Yes, and if you are talking about the fish market in Tangier each of the fish hanging from your hairs will be different. In that wet, noisy place I used to find skate, whitings, shad, red mullets, porgies, Saint Pierres, sardines, eels, anchovies, sea breams, turbots, sole, *changuetes,* one inch long and a quarter inch wide, crabs, lobsters, angel-fish, shrimps, baby clams, mackerel, squids, swordfish, tuna, *loup,* weevers, gurnards, and God knows what else. Once I decided to cook a different fish in a different way each day, and actually went three weeks before my family balked and put an end to my marathon.

As everyone knows, the success of fish cookery depends in great part upon the freshness of the ingredients. In a land where refrigerators are an enormous luxury, absolutely fresh fish is taken for granted. I wish that were the case in the United States.

There is no doubt in my mind that fish cooked in earthenware tastes better than fish cooked in ovenproof glass or enameled cast-iron. As for tin-lined copperware and aluminum, they definitely alter the flavor.

Of the many Moroccan fish recipes I have collected I offer here the ones I particularly like—such delights as *hut benoua* (Fish Baked with Almond Paste, page 171), a richly textured and delicately perfumed preparation that should be served at the precise moment that the crusty almonds are slipping off the fish into the onion sauce, and *hut tungera* (Fish Tagine with Tomatoes, Potatoes, and Green Peppers, page 173), a spicy robust *tagine* to which the tomatoes, potatoes, and green peppers impart an Andalusian mood.

Fish Baked with Stuffed Fruit

This is my adaptation of a recipe originally published in *Fez vu par sa cuisine* by Z. Guinadeau. Madame Guinadeau calls this dish one of the "great marvels of Moroccan cooking," and she is absolutely right—it is delicious.

It is made with the shad that run the Sebou River near Fez in winter. The shad are stuffed with dates, which in turn have been stuffed with chopped almonds and spices. Lacking the large luscious fleshy dates of the Tafilalet region (and there are over thirty varieties, including the famous delicate and small-pitted *bu-et-tob*), you can substitute California dates or large, fleshy prunes. If you can't get shad, use any freshwater fish; I particularly recommend carp, which can absorb a good deal of seasoning, or sea bass.

INGREDIENTS

1 shad, carp, or sea bass (about 4 pounds),
    cleaned, scaled, center backbone removed,
    and undersection gutted and split, but
    with head and tail intact
Salt and freshly ground black pepper
2½ tablespoons granulated rice ("cream of
    rice")
Scant ½ cup whole, blanched almonds
    (about 5 ounces)
Ground ginger
Granulated sugar
6 tablespoons sweet butter
1 pound pitted dates (2 cups) or 2 cups pitted
    prunes
2 tablespoons chopped onion
Ground cinnamon

EQUIPMENT

Paper towels
Small saucepan
Electric blender or nut
    grinder
Needle and thread
Large, shallow ovenproof
    serving dish (preferably
    earthenware)

Working time: 45 minutes
Baking time: 1 hour
Serves: 6

1. Wash the fish rapidly under running water. (Shad shouldn't be soaked, but carp must be—about 15 minutes.) Pat dry with paper towels, then rub with salt and pepper.

2. Bring ¾ cup water to boil in the small saucepan. Sprinkle with salt and quickly pour in the granulated rice. Boil for 30 seconds, beating well. Turn off the heat and allow to stand, covered, a few minutes, then cool before using.

3. Grind the almonds and mix with the cooled rice mixture, reserving 2 tablespoons ground almonds for later use. Add a scant ½ teaspoon ground ginger, 2 to 3 teaspoons sugar, ¼ teaspoon freshly ground black pepper, and 1 tablespoon of the butter to the almond-rice mixture. Blend well.

4. Open the dates or prunes and stuff each one with about ½ teaspoon of the almond-rice mixture. If the dates are small, push two together to form a "sandwich."

5. Sew the opening of the fish three-quarters of the way, then fill the stomach cavity with as many stuffed fruits as possible. Complete the sewing up.

6. Preheat the oven to 350°. Butter the ovenproof dish and place the stuffed fish on its side. Pour ½ cup water over, then sprinkle with salt and pepper and a little ginger. Add the chopped onion and the remaining stuffed fruit and dot the fish with the remaining 5 tablespoons butter.

7. Bake for 45 minutes on the middle shelf of oven, basting frequently.

8. Remove the fish from the oven, then raise the oven heat to highest setting. Untie the thread, pull out the stuffed fruit from the fish's cavity, and place it around the fish. Sprinkle both fish and fruit with ½ to 1 teaspoon ground cinnamon and the remaining 2 tablespoons ground almonds. Set the baking dish on the highest rack of the oven and bake until golden brown and crusty, about 15 minutes. Serve at once.

Note: One-half cup cooked rice can be substituted for the granulated rice, but the creamy texture of the stuffing will be affected.

Fish Baked with Almond Paste (*Hut Benoua*)

This dish, which comes from the fishing city of Safi, was served often at the New York home of a great Moroccan family, where its marvelous flavor never failed to create a sensation. My recipe is adapted from A *Quintet of Cuisines*, one of the Time-Life "Foods of the World" series.

INGREDIENTS

- 1 red snapper, sea bass, or striped bass (3 pounds), cleaned and scaled but with head and tail intact
  Salt
- ¼ cup salad oil
- ½ pound whole, blanched almonds (1½ cups)
- 4 to 5 tablespoons sweet butter, softened
- 1 tablespoon orange flower water
- 1 teaspoon ground cinnamon
- 1 cup confectioners' sugar, or more to taste
- 1 cup minced onion
- 1 tablespoon saffron water (page 21) or ⅛ teaspoon pulverized saffron
- ¼ teaspoon freshly ground black pepper

EQUIPMENT

Paper towels
10-inch skillet
Electric blender or nut grinder
Shallow 2-quart ovenproof serving dish (preferably earthenware)
Spatula

Working time: 30 minutes
Baking time: 40 to 45 minutes
Serves: 4

1. Rinse the fish under running water and rub it inside and out with 2 teaspoons salt. Let stand 10 minutes. Rinse again and pat dry with paper towels.

2. Heat the oil in a skillet and fry the almonds, stirring continuously with the spoon until just golden. Cool on paper towels.

3. Pulverize the almonds in an electric blender, then add 2 tablespoons of the softened butter, the orange flower water, cinnamon, sugar, and 3 tablespoons (or more) water and blend to make a smooth paste. Set aside.

4. Preheat the oven to 375°.

5. Stuff the belly of the fish with half the almond paste. Use 1 tablespoon of the butter to butter the ovenproof serving dish, then add the minced onion, ¼ cup water, and the saffron water and mix. Sprinkle with salt and ¼ teaspoon black pepper. Place the fish over the onion bed. Use a spatula to spread the remaining almond paste over the fish, forming a ripple design.

6. Melt the remaining 1 to 2 tablespoons butter and dribble it over the fish. Bake 45 minutes, or until the fish is completely cooked and the almond paste is crusty yet soft—just beginning to fall into the onion sauce. Serve hot, with Moroccan Bread (page 51) or *pita*.

Eel with Raisins and Onions (*Tasira*)

I learned this dish, a great Safi specialty, from an old cook reputed to be the best in her town. She was short and black, with a large growth on one of her cheeks, and unlike all the great Moroccan cooks I've met, she rarely cracked a smile. She worked in the steady, effortless manner of a natural-born chef, completing three perfect dishes with the simplest cooking equipment in a kitchen that had been converted from a garage one hour before.

INGREDIENTS

2 to 3 pounds conger or sea eel, cut into 6 large pieces
1 pound red onions, sliced
⅓ cup black or white raisins
1 good pinch pulverized saffron
1 heaping teaspoon ground cinnamon
½ teaspoon freshly ground black pepper
    Salt
½ cup granulated sugar
½ cup salad oil
2 tablespoons orange flower water

EQUIPMENT

Large saucepan
Thin-bladed knife
2½- to 3-quart heatproof baking dish
Medium-sized mixing bowl

Working time: 20 minutes
Cooking time: 1½ hours
Serves: 6

1. Wash the fish and drop into boiling water. Remove after 2 minutes and scrape off the skin with a thin-bladed knife. Remove the large center bone.

2. Spread the onions out in the baking dish. Sprinkle with the raisins. In the mixing bowl blend the spices, salt, and half the sugar with a little water. Coat each piece of fish with the mixture and place on the onion bed. Pour in the oil and a few tablespoons water. Bake in a preheated 400° oven, covered, 1 hour. (Moroccans cook fish far beyond the moment the flesh "flakes." They prefer to let the spices penetrate the fish entirely and then let the fish crumble, thus making a richer tasting sauce.)

3. Transfer to the top of the stove and boil down the sauce to a thick gravy, adding the remaining sugar and the orange flower water at the same time. Just before serving, run the fish and sauce under a hot broiler to glaze.

Fish Tagine with Tomatoes, Potatoes, and Green Peppers
(*Hut Tungera*)

Except for stuffed fish dishes and certain regional specialties, Moroccans cook fish with a marinade called *charmoula*. *Charmoula* is used throughout Morocco and invariably contains paprika, garlic, cumin, and green coriander, as well as such things as ginger in Marrakesh and red pepper oil in Tangier and Tetuán. The *charmoula* for this dish is fairly standard and can be used in the variations that follow; if you want to make it stronger you can add a few pinches of powdered cayenne.

Any of the following firm white-fleshed fish can be used in this and the following *tagines*: sea or striped bass; red snapper; porgy; or steaks of halibut, cod, haddock, or pollack.

When the Moroccans make fish *tagines* they almost always first arrange pieces of bamboo cane (or carrots or celery sticks) in a crisscross pattern in the earthenware *tagine slaoui*. This becomes a sort of a bed for the fish, keeping it from sticking to the bottom and assuring that there is always sauce underneath to give it flavor and keep it moist.

1 striped bass, 2 red snappers, or any large, firm white fish (4½ to 5 pounds), head and tail removed, scaled, and cleaned
Lemon juice (optional)
Salt
Charmoula (page 175)
3 large potatoes
3 red, ripe tomatoes
3 sweet green peppers
1 to 2 cloves garlic, peeled
1½ tablespoons tomato paste
⅓ cup lemon juice
¼ cup salad oil

Paper towels
Vegetable peeler
Paring knife
Large, shallow ovenproof serving dish (preferably earthenware)
6 six-inch pieces of cane or 6 bamboo chopsticks
Aluminum foil

Working time: 30 minutes
Cooking time: 60 minutes
Serves: 6

1. Early in the day, wash the fish. (If it smells "fishy," rub it with lemon juice and rinse.) Rub with salt and let stand 10 minutes. Rinse again and drain. Pat dry with paper towels.

2. Slice the fish crosswise into 5 or 6 large pieces. Rub in some of the *charmoula* and let stand at least 30 minutes (the longer the better) so that the spices can penetrate the fish.

3. *One and one-half hours before serving,* peel the potatoes and slice thinly. Slice the tomatoes crosswise. Halve the green peppers and remove seeds.

4. Preheat oven to 400°.

5. Make a lattice pattern in the bottom of the baking dish by crisscrossing the canes. Arrange the fish slices over canes. Dip the sliced potatoes in *charmoula* and spread over the fish. Repeat with the tomatoes and green peppers. Chop the garlic and sprinkle over the vegetables.

6. Mix the remaining *charmoula* with the tomato paste, lemon juice, oil, and ½ cup water. Pour this sauce over the fish. Cover with aluminum foil and bake 35 minutes. Remove cover. Raise the oven heat to the highest setting and move the baking dish to the uppermost shelf of the oven. Bake 20 minutes, or until the fish is cooked and a nice crust has formed over the vegetables. Serve warm, not hot.

Charmoula

½ cup green coriander leaves, coarsely chopped

½ cup parsley leaves, coarsely chopped

4 to 5 cloves garlic, peeled

2 tablespoons vinegar, preferably mild

⅓ cup lemon juice

1½ teaspoons salt

1 heaping teaspoon paprika

¼ teaspoon cumin

Cayenne to taste (optional)

EQUIPMENT

Mortar and pestle

Mixing bowl

Working time: 5 minutes

Makes: enough to marinate a 5-pound fish, or enough sauce for 6 people

Blend the herbs with the garlic and vinegar until pasty. Dump into the mixing bowl. Stir in lemon juice, salt, and spices.

Tagra

This Tangier variation, which is named after the casserole it is cooked in (see note below), is cooked precisely the same as the preceding recipe. The only difference is in the preparation of the *charmoula* and in the absence of the canes. Instead of adding paprika powder directly to the marinade, the paprika is added in the refined form of paprika oil, which is made as follows:

Boil ¼ cup salad oil in a small skillet; add 2 teaspoons paprika and ¼ cup water; boil for 10 minutes; allow to cool. The oil that rises is added to the *charmoula*; the paprika sediment is thrown away.

Note: The *tagra* is an unglazed peaches-and-cream-colored pottery bowl found in Tangier, Tetuán, Chaouen, and surrounding countryside. Before it can be used, it must be seasoned with grated onion, oil, and salt, then left to bake in a hot oven until the seasoning turns black. Then the pot is allowed to cool slowly in a turned-off oven. When cold, it is washed well and left to dry. The pot is then ready for fish cookery, either over charcoal or in the oven. They are never used over a gas flame or an electric range.

Fish Tagine with Olives (*Hut Bil Zeetoon*)

INGREDIENTS

1 pound green, cracked olives (preferably Greek, packed in brine)
1 fish, preferably carp (4 pounds), scaled, cleaned, belly opened, head removed
Charmoula (page 175)
2 lemons, peeled and sliced
¼ cup salad oil
3 to 4 tablespoons lemon juice

EQUIPMENT

3-quart saucepan
6 six-inch pieces of cane or 6 bamboo chopsticks
Ovenproof baking dish (preferably earthenware)
Aluminum foil

Working time: 30 minutes
Baking time: 1 hour
Serves: 6 to 8

1. Boil the olives three times, changing the water each time, to rid them of their bitterness (see page 195).

2. Follow steps 1 and 2 on page 174, but do not slice the fish. Mix half the *charmoula* with the olives; rub the remaining *charmoula* into the fish. Let stand 30 minutes. Preheat the oven to 400°.

3. Make a lattice pattern in the bottom of the baking dish by crisscrossing the canes, then arrange the whole fish over the cane. Spread the lemon slices over the fish and cover with the olives and *charmoula*, ⅓ cup water, and the oil. Cover with the aluminum foil and bake 45 minutes, then remove the cover, raise the oven heat to the highest setting and bake 15 minutes longer. Sprinkle with lemon juice and serve warm.

Shad Roe Tagine (*Tagine Beid Sherbel*)

INGREDIENTS

1 pound shad roe
1 onion, chopped
1 pound potatoes, peeled and sliced very thin
6 red, ripe tomatoes, peeled and sliced
½ recipe Charmoula (page 175) doubling the amount of cumin and paprika and omitting the lemon juice and vinegar
2 lemons, one sliced crosswise and the other cut into wedges

EQUIPMENT

Ovenproof serving dish
Mortar and pestle

Working time: 20 minutes
Baking time: 30 minutes
Serves: 4

1. Rinse the shad roe under slow running water. Leave to soak 15 minutes, then drain.

2. Preheat the oven to 400°.

3. Arrange the onions and half the potato slices in the bottom of the oiled baking dish and sprinkle them with some of the *charmoula*. Cover with half the tomatoes. Repeat the layers, then place the roes on top. Cover with the *charmoula* and place the lemon slices on top. Bake, uncovered, 30 minutes. Serve with lemon wedges.

Fish Tagine with Celery in the Style of Safi (*Hut Bil Karfas*)

For this fish *tagine* from Safi the bamboo canes in the bottom of the casserole are replaced by fresh celery ribs.

INGREDIENTS

1 striped bass or red snapper (4 pounds), cleaned and scaled, with head and tail left on
Lemon juice
Salt
½ cup chopped mixed fresh herbs (parsley and green coriander)
1½ teaspoons ground cumin
1 tablespoon sweet paprika
⅛ to ¼ teaspoon cayenne
Pinch of pulverized saffron
3 cloves garlic, peeled
¼ cup salad oil
2 large bunches celery (1½ pounds)
1 pound tomatoes (fresh or canned), peeled, seeded and chopped (see page 71)

EQUIPMENT

Paper towels
Mixing bowl
Shallow glass dish for marinating
Small paring knife
Large, shallow ovenproof serving dish (preferably earthenware)
Aluminum foil

Working time: 45 minutes
Baking time: 1 hour
Serves: 6 to 8

½ preserved lemon (see page 30)
1 teaspoon chopped parsley

1. Early in the day, wash the fish. If it smells "fishy," rub the flesh with lemon juice and rinse off at once. Rub inside and out with some salt, then let stand 10 minutes. Rinse and pat dry with paper towels. Score the fish at 1½-inch intervals.

2. Blend the herbs, spices, 1 teaspoon salt, the garlic, oil, and ¼ cup lemon juice into a *charmoula*. Turn the fish in the *charmoula* to coat evenly, then rub it into the cavity. Let stand *at least* 30 minutes or longer, so that the spices penetrate the fish.

3. Meanwhile, separate the celery ribs, cut away the leaves, and wash well. With a sharp paring knife, scrape off the strings from the back of each rib. Cut lengthwise down the middle, then cut crosswise into 2-inch pieces. Set the celery pieces aside.

4. Preheat the oven to 400°.

5. Arrange the celery pieces, in one layer, in the baking dish. Lay the fish over celery and pour the *charmoula* over the fish. Add the chopped tomatoes. Wash the preserved lemon, remove the pulp, and chop the peel into dice. Sprinkle the lemon peel and chopped parsley over the fish. Cover with aluminum foil and bake 40 minutes.

6. Remove the foil and spoon the sauce over the fish to moisten. Raise the oven heat to the highest setting and continue baking the fish, uncovered, on the upper shelf of the oven for 20 minutes. Taste for seasoning—the dish should be slightly peppery—and add salt, if necessary. Serve at once or cool, cover, refrigerate, and reheat before serving.

Fish Tagine with Carrots (*Hut Bil Kreezo*)

For a variation in the Casablanca manner, prepare Fish Tagine with Celery in the Style of Safi (page 178) but substitute carrots for the celery and decorate with thrice-blanched green, cracked olives (page 195).

Fish Stuffed with Eggs, Onions, and Preserved Lemons

A good Tetuán dish.

INGREDIENTS

1 firm, white, lean fish, such as red snapper, sea bass, halibut, or grouper (4 to 5 pounds) or 3½ pounds fish fillets

4 cups chopped red onions

   Pinch of pulverized saffron

   Salt to taste

¼ teaspoon freshly ground black pepper

⅔ cup salad oil

¾ cup chopped parsley

6 tablespoons sweet butter

3 eggs

1½ preserved lemons (see page 30)

EQUIPMENT

Boning knife

3-quart saucepan

Large and small skillets

Paring knife

2½-quart baking dish

Working time: 30 minutes

Baking time: 1 hour

Serves: 6 to 8

1. Wash the fish as directed in step 1 on page 174, slit open the belly and clean well. Dry fish with a damp cloth.

2. Rinse the onions well under running water (to rid them of sharpness), then drain. Mix the onions, saffron, salt, pepper, half the oil, parsley, and 2

tablespoons of the butter. Cook 15 minutes, until the onions are soft and transparent.

3. Meanwhile, fry 3 eggs in 2 tablespoons butter. When almost set scramble them until firm. Remove from the heat and stir into onion mixture. Rinse the preserved lemon and remove and discard the pulp. Sliver the peel and add to the onions. Stuff the fish with half the onion mixture. Place the fish in the oiled baking dish and cover with the remaining onion mixture.

4. Preheat the oven to 400°.

5. Sprinkle the fish and onions with remaining oil and butter. Pour in ½ cup water, cover, and bake 1 hour.

6. Just before serving, run the fish under a hot broiler to glaze.

Baked Fish with Rice

A savory fish dish from Safi.

INGREDIENTS	EQUIPMENT
½ pound raw rice, well washed	*Couscousiere*
⅓ cup chopped parsley	Cheesecloth
Salt to taste	Small mixing bowl
Freshly ground black pepper	Shallow 2½-quart baking
2 pinches pulverized saffron	dish
¼ cup sweet butter	Aluminum foil
3 tablespoons lemon juice	
¼ cup plus 1 tablespoon grated onion	*Working time:* 30 minutes
2 hard-boiled eggs, shelled and chopped	*Cooking time:* 1 hour for the
½ cup peanut oil	rice, 1½ hours (approxi-
1 fish (5 pounds), washed and cleaned, belly	mately) for the fish
slit, head and tail left on	*Serves:* 6 to 8

1. Bring plenty of water to a rolling boil in the bottom of a *couscousiere.* Fasten the perforated top on securely, as described on page 136, and steam the

rice in the top, covered with a cloth and lid, for 20 minutes. Remove, stir, and moisten the rice with 2 cups boiling water. Drain, then return the rice to steam again, *covered*, 20 minutes. Repeat the process, moistening, draining, and steaming a third time.

2. Mix the parsley, salt, ¼ teaspoon pepper, a pinch of saffron, the butter, and lemon juice. Stir in the 1 tablespoon grated onion and the eggs.

3. Preheat the oven to 400°.

4. Wash the fish as directed in step 1 on page 174. Stuff with the egg-rice mixture. Rub the fish all over with a little saffron until brilliant yellow. Place the fish in the oiled baking dish. Sprinkle with the remaining grated onion, the oil, and a little salt and pepper. Cover with the foil and bake 1¼ hours. Remove the cover and continue baking until the skin is crisp.

REGIONAL FISH SPECIALTIES

———◆———

There are many regional fish dishes that taste better on Moroccan soil, and you should try them if you visit any of the following towns.

RABAT: Shad prepared whole in a *tagine*. The fish is stewed on a bed of finely minced onions, seasoned with saffron, sugar, and cinnamon, and surrounded by a layer of white raisins. It turns crusty and golden, the raisins caramelize, and the result is delicious. It is similar to the eel dish of safi called *tasira* (Eel with Raisins and Onions, page 172).

SAFI: You will always find a certain *finesse* in Safi cookery. For example, the *smen* here is washed with herbs and spices, and not just *za'atar*; the *charmoula* for fish is more aromatic here than elsewhere, no doubt on account of the addition of pure saffron. Other Safi specialties than those recorded in this book are fish with lemon and olives; fish with butter, cumin and onions; fish with tomatoes and fennel stalks; and fish stuffed with freshly chopped tomatoes, rice, and plenty of herbs.

FEZ: This is, of course, an inland city, where fish dishes tend to be built around the Sebou shad and trout. In addition to Fish Baked with Stuffed Fruit (page 169) there are a number of shad *tagines* definitely worth looking for: shad with the wild artichokes called *coques*, shad with fava beans, shad with hot or sweet green peppers, and shad roe fried and served with *charmoula* sauce.

TANGIER: Two variations of *Hut tungera* (Fish Tagine with Tomatoes, Potatoes, and Green Peppers, page 173), one substituting chopped Swiss chard and the other the wild greens called *gurneen*.

TETUÁN: The fish specialties here have mostly to do with stuffings, though the *tagine* of anchovies in garlic sauce is not to be missed, and the Tetuanese are renowned for their skill in the making of fish omelets.

Among the great stuffings for fish are: tomatoes, rice, onion, olives, and preserved lemons; onion and eggs flavored with lemon and cinnamon; a thick, rich jam made of sweet green peppers and tomatoes cooked down with spices; and other "Andalusian-type" mixtures.

ESSAOUIRA: This is the city where the word "spicy" begins to have meaning. Here the cooks create a fish *couscous* that is extraordinary, as well as the esoteric *teegree*—sun-dried mussels cooked with olives and hot peppers and served as a first course in "salad" form.

Here also you will find squid stuffed with rice, tomatoes, and *charmoula*, and such Jewish specialties as fish balls poached in tomato sauce or stuffed inside pastry leaves and fried, and whole fish baked after being coated with cumin paste. There is also a scrumptious sardine *tagine* made with *charmoula* and wild greens from the nearby hills.

IN ALL CITIES: *Hut makalli*, or "fried fish," is a sort of street food that varies slightly from place to place. Basically, the fish is dusted in semolina flour before being fried, which gives it a fine crust, and often it is served—hot, warm, or cold—with *charmoula* as an accompanying sauce.

NINE

Poultry

Mr. Mehdi Bennouna, chief of the Agence Mahgreb Arabe Presse in Rabat, told me a story about chicken that is absolutely true. During the period of struggle against the French, he and several friends who were members of the Istiqlal (Independence party) used to meet once a week in Tangier to discuss politics, play cards, and enjoy each other's company. Each would bring a *tagine* from home, and when it was time for lunch would share it with his friends.

One of the men, like Mr. Bennouna, was from the city of Tetuán. One day he told the others that in Tetuán there were fifty ways to prepare chicken, each different and each delicious. Those who were not from Tetuán laughed, an argument broke out, and finally bets were laid down.

Once a week, over the next year, the man brought a different Tetuán-style chicken dish to the meetings. As each week passed he amazed and astounded his friends with increasingly interesting and delicious variations. Anticipation mounted, and a list of the dishes was compiled. On the fiftieth week they assembled, eager to taste the final pièce de résistance. The man arrived with the same pot that had offered up so many great chicken preparations, opened it, reached inside, and pulled out a whole uncooked chicken.

"What's this?" asked his friends.

"Chicken with feathers," he answered, and then with a smile: "Why not? It comes naturally that way."

He won the bet.

After he told me this story I asked Mr. Bennouna if he could remember any of the other dishes. In an incredible tour de force he rattled off all but two of them. Here is that list, in the order in which Mr. Bennouna gave it to me:

1. Chicken braised and fried (*mahammer*)
2. Chicken in highly spiced sauce with lemon and olives (*emshmel*)
3. Chicken in ginger sauce with lemon and olives (*makalli*)
4. Chicken stuffed with rice and tomatoes, steamed
5. Chicken stuffed with sweet *couscous*, served with sweet sauce
6. Chicken stuffed with salted *couscous*, served with brown sauce
7. Chicken stuffed with *sheriya*, fried in oil or roasted
8. Chicken stuffed with ground almonds, fried in oil or roasted
9. Chicken stuffed with celery and onions, served with savory sauce
10. Chicken stuffed with giblets
11. Chicken stuffed with *bakoola* (a wild herb) and garlic, steamed
12. Chicken stuffed with diced vegetables (artichokes, peas, carrots, and so on)
13. Steamed chicken served with cumin and salt
14. Chicken with layers of onions and tomatoes (*kammamma*)
15. Chicken with coriander, onions, fried almonds, and eggs (*tafaya*)
16. Chicken, Fez style, with *smen*, parsley, and sliced hard-boiled eggs
17. Chicken smothered in sweet tomato jam (*matisha mesla*)
18. Chicken smothered with green olives (*meslalla*)
19. Chicken with lemon and eggs (*masquid bil beid*)
20. Chicken, braised, fried, and coated with spicy eggs (*mefenned*)
21. Chicken with *smen*, chick-peas, and almonds (*kdra touimiya*)
22. Chicken with *smen*, rice, almonds, and parsley
23. Barbecued chicken (*mechoui*)
24. Boiled chicken (*mafooar*)
25. *Bisteeya,* Tetuán style, with plenty of lemons
26. *Couscous* with bite-sized pieces of chicken in a cinnamon-flavored sauce (*seffa merdurma*)
27. Chicken *couscous* with vegetables
28. Chicken with pastry leaves (*trid*)

29. Chicken with quince, honey, *amber*, and aga wood*
30. Chicken with quince and onions
31. Boned chicken wrapped in an omelet made with peas
32. Chicken in *tagine* with a vegetable (string beans, fennel, carrots, etc.)
33. Chicken simmered in *smen*
34. Chicken with prunes and almonds in honey sauce
35. Chicken with raisins
36. Chicken with fried eggplant (*derbel*)
37. Chicken with fried zucchini
38. Chicken with fried pumpkin, sweetened
39. Chicken cooked with spices (cumin and coriander seeds) to make *khelea* (preserved meat)
40. Sweet chicken *couscous* with onions, raisins, and chick-peas
41. Chicken served with giblet sauce, onions, chopped olives, and lemons
42. Chicken stuffed with mint
43. Chicken stuffed with *kefta* (chopped spiced lamb or beef)
44. Chicken cooked with the spices used for fish (the marinade *charmoula*)
45. Chicken with fried almonds
46. Roast chicken
47. Chicken with raisins, chick-peas, and onions
48. "Can't remember."
49. "Can't remember."
50. Chicken with feathers!

Tetuán is just *one* of the great gastronomic centers of Morocco. Think of the chicken dishes invented by the cooks of Fez, Marrakesh, and other cities and regions! Of all the poultry dishes I have learned, I have selected more than twenty recipes that I think are extraordinary.

* Aga wood is *oud kamerie* in Arabic, a hard, fragrant brown substance that is easily pounded to power. *Amber* is Arabic for ambergris—not the fossilized yellow amber worn by Berber women on necklaces, nor the gray-brown aromatic called ambrette that is used in coffee, in *tagines*, in *ras el hanout* and is called "the herb from Cyprus" when *amber* is not available. True ambergris until recently arrived in Morocco in caravans from Timbuctoo or was found washed up on the southwestern shores of Morocco (near Tiznit) after having been ejected by sperm whales. Soft and waxy, it is used to perfume food by many peoples, including the Chinese, who call it "dragon's saliva"; in the Middle Ages it was used to perfume sherbets and tea. Its aromatic properties were evidently highly potent. Alexander Dumas Père invented a tonic of ambergris, chicken stock, and sugar to invigorate tired middle-aged husbands.

Basic Method for Preparing Poultry

For most of the recipes in this chapter, prepare poultry as indicated below—the timings in the recipes include these steps:

1. Wash the chickens or other poultry in salted water and drain. Pound 4 cloves garlic and 2 tablespoons salt into a paste. Rub the paste into the cavity and flesh of the poultry, at the same time pulling out excess fat from under the skin and from the neck and rump ends. Pull out the thin translucent membrane from under the skin of the breast. Rinse the poultry well under running water until it no longer smells of garlic. (The garlic is used to rid the poultry of any bitterness that might spoil a sauce; it also acts to bring out its flavor, much like MSG.) Drain the poultry well.

2. If you suspect that your poultry is tasteless on account of "scientific breeding," use a method invented by Janet Jaidi to improve its taste: Rub it with the spices to be used in the recipe, a little butter or oil, and marinate it overnight. (If you do this, remember that you may have to readjust the spicing of your sauce at the end.)

3. If you are using whole poultry, it must be trussed. Trussing poultry is easy: clip off the wing tips and discard; slip the ends of the legs into a horizontal incision made just above the rump (turkeys often come this way), or slip the legs into incisions made on the lower sides of the breast.

Note: When stuffing turkeys or squabs or chickens, do not wash with garlic or salt.

FOUR DIFFERENT WAYS TO MAKE CHICKEN
WITH LEMON AND OLIVES

———◆———

Chicken with lemon and olives is one of the great combinations in Moroccan cookery, the dish that most often seduces foreigners and turns them into devotees of Moroccan *tagines*. There are numerous variations on this exquisite theme; I have included four, each one delicious, each one unique: *Djej masquid bil beid*—a glorious variation enriched by the addition of whipped and baked eggs; *Djej emshmel*—a multispiced classic served in a plentiful onion-based sauce; *Djej bil zeetoon meslalla*—a tangy variation literally smothered with whole or cracked green olives; and *Djej makalli*—a more subtle though no less delicious variation, flavored with ginger and saffron and served with a thick sauce enriched by additional mashed chicken livers. I recommend that you try them all.

Before the recipes, however, a few words about lemons and olives. I could barely contain my rage and my scorn when I read the following paragraph in an American women's magazine: "You needn't brine your lemons in order to taste a close reproduction of the Moroccan lemon chicken; fresh lemons do very well as a substitute. What you miss by making it with fresh lemons is the 'preserved' flavor (much like bottled lime juice)." This same writer then described the olives in her recipe as, simply, "green."

There is, and I cannot emphasize this enough, *no substitute for preserved lemons* in Moroccan food. (There is also not much similarity between the taste of preserved lemons and the taste of bottled lime juice, and, of course, no similarity as far as texture is concerned.) To not use preserved lemons is to completely miss the point, and also to miss a whole dimension of culinary experience. Preserved lemons are easy to make (page 30), and if carefully put up they will keep almost a year.

As for olives, I have written about them at length on pages 33–34. One does use "green olives" to smother *Djej bil zeetoon meslalla*—not California or Spanish ones, but unripened ones cracked and soaked in brine. (If you cannot get Moroccan olives, buy Greek ones and prepare as directed on page 195.)

For the other three recipes the classic olive to use is the ripe reddish-brown Moroccan *mchqouq* perfumed with citrus juice. When they are not available I have had excellent luck with Gaetas from Italy, Kalamatas from Greece, and also Greek Royal-Victorias that have been rinsed to rid them of bitterness.

Chicken with Eggs, Lemons, and Olives *(Djej Masquid Bil Beid)*

This is one of my favorite Moroccan dishes.

INGREDIENTS

2 chickens, cut up and prepared as directed on page 188
1 cup chopped parsley
3 cloves garlic, peeled and chopped
¾ cup grated Spanish onion
Salt to taste
½ rounded teaspoon ground ginger
Pinch of pulverized saffron
¾ teaspoon freshly ground black pepper
¼ cup sweet butter, melted
3 large or 6 small cinnamon sticks
10 eggs
2 preserved lemons (see page 30)
8 "red-brown" olives, such as Kalamatas, pitted and chopped
½ cup lemon juice

EQUIPMENT

5½-quart casserole with cover
Shallow, 2½-quart ovenproof serving dish
Mixing bowl
Whisk
Chopping knife
Aluminum foil

Working time: 30 minutes
Cooking time: 1 hour 30 minutes
Serves: 6

1. Place the cleaned chicken in the casserole. Add ⅔ cup of the chopped parsley, the chopped garlic, grated onion, salt, spices, half the butter, and the cinnamon sticks. Add 2 cups water and bring to a boil. Simmer, covered, about 1 hour or until the chickens are *very* tender and the flesh is almost falling off the bone. (During the cooking you may need to add more water.)

2. Preheat oven to 350°.

3. Transfer the chickens (but not the sauce) to the serving dish. Remove any loose bones and cinnamon sticks from the sauce in the casserole and, by boiling rapidly, uncovered, reduce to 2 cups of thick, rich sauce. Pour over the chickens.

4. Beat the eggs to a froth with the remaining parsley. Rinse and dice the preserved lemons, using the pulp if desired. Stir the lemons and chopped olives into the eggs and pour the egg mixture over the chickens. Cover the dish with aluminum foil and bake on the middle shelf of the oven for 20 minutes. Raise the oven heat to highest setting, remove the aluminum cover, and dot the eggs with the remaining melted butter. Transfer the dish to the upper shelf of the oven and bake 10 minutes more, or until the eggs are completely set and the chickens have browned slightly. Sprinkle with lemon juice and serve at once.

Note: Six Moroccan pigeons or 3 squabs may be substituted for the chickens, in which case the dish is called *Frach masquid bil beid*.

Chicken with Lemons and Olives Emshmel (*Djej Emshmel*)

I first ate this dish in a home in the city of Meknes, sometimes called the City of Olives. *Djej emshmel* (pronounced *meshmel* or *emsharmel*) is a classic Moroccan dish—chicken served in an intricately spiced, creamy, lemony, and sublime sauce with a scattering of pale-hued olives.

INGREDIENTS

2 to 3 chickens, whole or quartered, with their livers
6 cloves garlic, peeled
Salt
1 teaspoon ground ginger
1 teaspoon sweet paprika
¼ teaspoon ground cumin
¼ teaspoon ground black pepper
¼ cup salad oil
2½ cups grated onion, drained
¼ teaspoon pulverized saffron (mixed with turmeric, if desired)
½ cup mixed, chopped fresh herbs (green coriander and parsley)
1½ cups ripe "green-brown" olives, such as Royal-Victorias
2 preserved lemons (see page 30)
2 to 3 fresh lemons

EQUIPMENT

Large bowl
Paring knife
6-quart casserole with cover
Strainer, if necessary
Small mixing bowl

Working time: 30 minutes
Cooking time: 1 hour (approximately)
Serves: 8

1. The day before, using 4 cloves of the garlic and 2 tablespoons salt prepare the chickens as directed on page 188, then marinate both chickens and livers in 1 teaspoon salt, the remaining 2 cloves of garlic, sliced thin, the spices, and the oil. Refrigerate, covered.

2. The next day, place the chickens, livers, and marinade in the casserole.

Add ½ cup of the grated onion, the saffron, herbs, and 2 cups water. Bring to a boil, cover, and simmer 30 minutes, turning the chickens often in the sauce.

3. While the chickens are cooking, rinse and pit the olives. (If they seem a little bitter, cover with cold water, bring to a boil, and drain.) Set aside.

4. Remove the chicken livers from the casserole and mash them fine. Return to the casserole with the remaining grated, drained onions. (This will give a good deal of heftiness to the sauce.) Add water, if necessary. Continue cooking 20 minutes, partially covered.

5. Rinse the preserved lemons (discarding the pulp, if desired) and quarter. Add the olives and preserved lemon quarters to the sauce when the chickens are very tender and the flesh falls easily from the bone. Continue cooking 5 to 10 minutes, uncovered.

6. Transfer the chickens to a serving dish and spoon the olives and lemons around them. Cover and keep warm. By boiling rapidly, uncovered, reduce the sauce to 1½ cups. Add the juice of 2 fresh lemons to the sauce in the pan. Add more salt (and more lemon juice, if desired) to taste. Pour the sauce over chickens and serve at once.

Chicken Smothered with Green, Cracked Olives
(Djej Bil Zeetoon Meslalla)

For this recipe you can use the bitter green olives often sold "cracked" and packed in brine in Greek specialty stores; to get rid of the bitterness boil them three times. When I first learned this dish in Morocco I wondered how the olives were going to be pitted, since they were already cracked on one side. The Moroccans had a solution—they put them on the stone floor of the kitchen, tapped each of them smartly with a smooth stone, and the pits popped right out. I have often served this dish with uncracked Moroccan green olives, with great success.

INGREDIENTS

2 chickens, whole or cut up, with giblets, pre-pared as directed on page 188
1 teaspoon ground ginger
1 teaspoon freshly ground black pepper
¼ teaspoon pulverized saffron (mixed with turmeric, if desired)
1 tablespoon finely chopped garlic
¾ cup grated onion, drained
1 cup finely chopped mixed herbs (parsley and green coriander)
⅓ cup salad oil
½ teaspoon ground cumin
½ teaspoon sweet paprika
    Salt to taste
4 cups green olives (2 pounds), preferably Agrinon or Nafpiou
½ cup lemon juice, or more to taste

EQUIPMENT

5½-quart casserole with cover
Paring knife or smooth stone
1½-quart saucepan
Sieve
Large serving platter

Working time: **45 minutes**
Cooking time: **1 hour (approximately)**
Serves: 6 to 8

1. Place the prepared chickens in the casserole with all the ingredients except the olives and lemon juice. Cover with 4 cups water and bring to a boil, then reduce the heat, cover, and simmer 30 minutes, turning the chickens often in the sauce.

2. Meanwhile, pit the olives, using a paring knife or just smashing each one with a smooth stone. Cover the olives with water, bring to boil, and boil 5 minutes. Drain, cover with fresh water, bring to a boil, and boil 5 more minutes. Repeat the procedure one more time. Taste olives—they should no longer be bitter: if they are, boil them again. Drain and add to the casserole after the chicken has cooked 30 minutes.

3. Pour in the lemon juice and continue cooking until the chickens are very tender and the sauce is thick. Transfer the chickens to an ovenproof serving platter and place in a hot oven to brown. Reduce the liquid in the casserole to a thick gravy and adjust salt and lemon juice to taste.

4. To serve, cover the chickens completely with olives. Pour the sauce over and serve at once.

Chicken with Lemon and Olives, Makalli (*Djej Makalli*)

INGREDIENTS

1 chicken, cut in 6 pieces, with 2 chicken livers

6 to 7 cloves garlic, peeled

Salt

1 teaspoon ground ginger

¼ teaspoon freshly ground black pepper

1 preserved lemon, rinsed

¼ cup salad oil

¼ teaspoon pulverized saffron (mixed with turmeric)

½ cup grated onion, drained

6 sprigs green coriander, tied together with a thread

½ cup "red-brown" olives, such as Kalamatas or Gaetas

EQUIPMENT

Electric blender

Large bowl

Plastic wrap

4½-quart casserole with cover

Small mixing bowl

Olive pitter or paring knife (optional)

Working time: 30 minutes

Cooking time: 45 to 50 minutes

Serves: 4

1. The day before, using 4 cloves of the garlic and 2 tablespoons salt, prepare the chicken as directed on page 188. (Be sure to rinse well after rubbing with the garlic and salt.) Using the blender, combine the ginger, a little salt, the pepper, 2 to 3 cloves garlic, the pulp only of the preserved lemon (reserving the peel), and the oil into a sauce. Rub the sauce over the pieces of chicken and the livers. Cover with plastic wrap and refrigerate overnight.

2. The next day, place the chickens, livers, and sauce in the casserole. Add the saffron, onion, bundle of green coriander sprigs, and 2½ cups water. Stir and bring to a boil. Partially cover and simmer gently 30 minutes. Turn and baste the chickens often.

3. Remove the livers and mash, then return to the sauce. Rinse the olives and pit them, if desired. Add the quartered preserved lemon peel and olives for the final 15 minutes' cooking. Transfer the chicken to a hot oven to brown.

By boiling rapidly, uncovered, reduce the sauce to a very thick gravy, about ¾ cup. Remove the coriander sprigs. Spoon the sauce over the chicken, decorate with the lemon peel and olives, and serve at once.

———————————•◆•———————————

In *The Moors*, by the British adventurer Budgett Meakin, there is a recipe for chicken with olives that is fascinating and extremely esoteric. He describes a dish made with olives *and* raisins and flavored with grated nutmeg and allspice! I wish he had mentioned where he found it; I can find no traces of such a style of seasoning, and suspect it has been lost in the last seventy years.

CHICKEN KDRAS
————•————

A *kdra* is a certain type of *tagine,* cooked with the strong Moroccan butter called *smen,* a lot of onions reduced to butter softness, spiced with pepper and saffron, and usually "cut" at the end with a dash of lemon juice. The stews of many *couscous* dishes are based on the principles of the *kdra* sauce, as are some of the most famous dishes in the Moroccan repertory: *Djej bil hamus* (Chicken Tagine with Chick-Peas, page 203), *Djej kdra bil looz* (Chicken Kdra with Almonds, page 199), and Chicken Simmered in Smen (page 205).

Kdras are delicious and rich, and if they have a failing it is their somewhat unattractive, pale yellow look. To make them appear more appetizing Moroccans sometimes add an extra pinch of saffron at the end to make a yellower sauce. You can brown the chickens in a hot oven while preparing the sauce, though this is not done in classic *kdra* cooking.

In Fez *kdras* are always made without ginger, but in Rabat and Marrakesh and in the north this strict constructionist view is usually ignored; use ginger if you wish, but, if you are entertaining Fassis, do so with the knowledge that they will smile behind your back.

Chicken Kdra with Almonds and Chick-Peas (*Djej Kdra Touimiya*)

In one of the most famous *kdras* the chicken is accompanied by almonds as well as chick-peas. You might think that crisp almonds would go well with chicken, but, in fact, the almonds should be soft. If they are old it can sometimes take as long as two hours to transform them to this state.

INGREDIENTS

1 cup blanched whole almonds
½ cup dried chick-peas, soaked overnight, or ½ twenty-ounce can cooked chick-peas
¼ teaspoon pulverized saffron (mixed with a little turmeric)
   Salt to taste
1 teaspoon ground white pepper
½ teaspoon ground ginger
1 large cinnamon stick
3 tablespoons butter or 2 tablespoons *smen* (Cooked and Salted Butter, page 39)
1 chicken (3 to 3½ pounds), quartered, or 2 sets of chicken legs and thighs, or 3 squabs, or 6 Moroccan pigeons, prepared as directed on page 188
2 Spanish onions, quartered lengthwise and finely sliced
4 cups chicken stock or water, more if necessary
¼ cup chopped parsley
   Juice of 1 lemon, or to taste

EQUIPMENT

1-quart saucepan
2-quart saucepan
5½-quart casserole with cover
Chopping knife
Large, warm serving platter
Sieve

Working time: 35 minutes
Cooking time: 2 hours for the almonds, 1 hour or less for the chicken
Serves: 4 to 5

1. Cover the almonds with cold water and simmer, covered, at least 2 hours. (The cooking time is approximate—it depends upon the freshness of the almonds.)

2. In a separate saucepan, cover the soaked and drained chick-peas with fresh cold water, bring to boil, reduce the heat, and simmer, covered, 1 hour. Drain and submerge in a bowl of cold water. Rub the chick-peas to remove their skins. The skins will rise to the surface. Discard them. (If you are using canned chick-peas, rinse, drain, and skin them, and set them aside.)

3. In the casserole combine half the saffron, salt, the spices, butter or *smen*, and the prepared poultry. Cook over low heat, without browning, for 2 to 3 minutes. Chop 4 or 5 slices of onion fine, and add to the casserole with the 4 cups stock. Bring to a boil, add the drained, skinned chick-peas, and simmer 30 minutes, covered. (Do not add the canned chick-peas until the poultry has finished cooking.)

4. Add the remaining sliced onions and chopped parsley and continue cooking 30 minutes more, or until the poultry is very tender (the flesh almost falling off the bone). Transfer the poultry to the warm serving platter. Add the canned chick-peas to the sauce. By boiling rapidly, uncovered, reduce the sauce in the casserole to a thick gravy.

5. Drain the almonds and add to the sauce, along with remaining saffron. Cook together 1 or 2 minutes and spoon over the poultry. Sprinkle with lemon juice to cut the richness of the sauce. Serve hot.

VARIATION:

Chicken Kdra with Almonds (*Djej Kdra Bil Looz*)

This is simply a variation on the preceding recipe. Make it precisely the same way but omit the chick-peas and double the amount of almonds.

Chicken Kdra with Almonds and Rice (*Djej Kdra Bil Looz Bil Roz*)

For this *kdra* I advise you to use *smen* and not substitute butter, because *smen* goes so beautifully with rice (as it does with *couscous*). If you haven't any *smen* on hand, I suggest that you make some (see Cooked and Salted Butter, page 39) and return to this recipe when the *smen* is ready. In the meantime, you might as well sew up a cheesecloth bag for the rice. The principle behind poaching a bag of rice in the sauce is quite ingenious: the rice captures the flavor of the sauce, stays intact, and does not stick to the bottom of the pan.

INGREDIENTS

Same as in *djej kdra touimiya* (Chicken Kdra with Almonds and Chick-Peas, page 198), but omit the cinnamon stick and substitute 1 cup of rice for the chick-peas

EQUIPMENT

Same as for *djej kdra toui-miya*

plus

Cheesecloth bag for the rice

Working time: 45 minutes
Cooking time: 2 hours for the almonds, 1 hour or less for the chicken
Serves: 4 to 5

1. Follow step 1 (preparation of almonds) on page 198.
2. Follow step 3 (preparation and cooking of poultry) on page 199.
3. Fold a piece of cheesecloth in half and sew up two of the sides. Spoon in the dry rice and sew up the remaining opening. Make the bag large enough so the rice has room to expand (a capacity of 3 cups).
4. After the poultry has simmered 30 minutes, add the remaining onions, parsley, the bag of rice, and more water if necessary. (Be sure there is enough liquid in the pan both for the rice and for the sauce.) Poach the rice 20 to 25 minutes in the sauce, then remove the bag. Remove the poultry, when very tender, falling off the bones. Keep the rice and poultry warm.

5. Drain the almonds and add to the remaining sauce. Add the remaining saffron, and a little water if necessary. Cook together 5 minutes.

6. Meanwhile, open the bag of rice and form a pyramid in the center of the serving dish. Arrange the pieces of poultry around the rice. Add lemon juice to the sauce, then taste for seasoning and readjust. Spoon the almonds and sauce over the chicken. Serve at once.

Chicken Kdra with Turnips and Chick-Peas

I will never forget making a soup of young turnips from a French recipe of Elizabeth David's and discovering how delicious this vegetable can be. The turnips in Morocco are especially tender, and when I first began to cook Moroccan food I discovered there was hardly a *couscous* that didn't contain them. For this *kdra* try to use turnips that are young and freshly picked and that still retain their stalks and leaves. It's the stalks that "make" this dish. I have been told that fresh spinach leaves can be substituted if necessary.

INGREDIENTS

½ cup dried chick-peas, soaked overnight, or ½ twenty-ounce can cooked chick-peas
2 onions, quartered and sliced lengthwise
1 teaspoon white pepper
¼ teaspoon ground ginger
Pinch of pulverized saffron
½ teaspoon turmeric
Salt
4 tablespoons sweet butter or 2 tablespoons *smen* (page 38 or 39)
1 chicken (3 to 3½ pounds), quartered and prepared as directed on page 188
6 cups chicken stock or water
2 pounds young turnips, in 1½-inch cubes

EQUIPMENT

2-quart saucepan
5½-quart casserole with cover

Working time: 30 minutes
Cooking time: 2 hours
Serves: 4

(continued)

1 cup tender turnip leaves, finely chopped
¾ cup turnip stalks, finely chopped
   Juice of ½ to 1 lemon
   Chopped parsley

1. Cover the soaked and drained chick-peas with fresh cold water, bring to a boil, reduce the heat, and simmer, covered, 1 hour. Drain and submerge in a bowl of cold water. Rub the chick-peas to remove their skins. The skins will rise to the surface. Discard them. (If you are using canned chick-peas, rinse, drain, and skin them, and set them aside.)

2. Combine the onions, the spices, a teaspoon of salt, and butter or *smen* with the prepared chicken in the casserole. Pour in the chicken stock or water and bring to a boil. Add the drained, skinned chick-peas, turnips, turnip leaves, and turnip stalks. Cover and cook 40 minutes, then remove chicken and turnips and keep warm.

3. Continue cooking the sauce until it has reduced to a thick gravy and the chick-peas are soft. Add the juice of half a lemon, then taste the sauce for seasoning and adjust with salt and more lemon juice, if desired.

4. Place chicken and turnips (and canned chick-peas, if using them) in the sauce to reheat. Serve with a sprinkling of parsley.

Chicken Tagine with Chick-Peas (*Djej Bil Hamus*)

A sweet and spicy-sharp ginger-flavored chicken stew that comes to the table bright yellow and fragrant. Strictly speaking it is not a *kdra*, but a modern variation of a classic dish.

INGREDIENTS

- 1 pound dried chick-peas or 2 twenty-ounce cans cooked chick-peas
- 2 chickens, whole or quartered
- 5 cloves garlic, peeled
- Salt
- 1 teaspoon ground ginger
- 1 rounded teaspoon freshly ground black pepper
- Pinch of pulverized saffron
- 1 teaspoon turmeric
- ¼ cup finely chopped parsley
- 1 cinnamon stick
- ½ cup chopped scallions, white part only
- 5 tablespoons sweet butter
- 1 Spanish onion, sliced very thin
- ⅓ cup black raisins (optional)

EQUIPMENT

Mixing bowls
Large glass or stainless steel bowl
4-quart saucepan
5½-quart casserole with cover
Deep serving dish

Working time: 30 minutes
Cooking time: 1½ hours
Serves: 6 to 8

1. The day before, soak the dried chick-peas in water to cover. Using 4 cloves of the garlic and 2 tablespoons salt, prepare the chickens as directed on page 188. Then blend 1 teaspoon salt, the ginger, pepper, and the remaining clove garlic, crushed, with 2 tablespoons water and rub into the flesh of the chickens. Place in the large glass or stainless steel bowl, cover and let stand overnight in the refrigerator.

2. The next day, drain the chick-peas, place in the saucepan, cover with fresh water, and cook, covered, 1 hour. Drain and submerge in a bowl of cold water. Rub the chick-peas to remove their skins. The skins will rise to the

surface. Discard them. (If you are using canned chick-peas, rinse, drain, and skin them, and set them aside.)

3. Transfer the chickens and any juices in the bowl to the casserole. Add a pinch of saffron, the turmeric, parsley, cinnamon stick, scallions, and butter. Pour in 5 cups water and bring to a boil. Reduce the heat, cover, and simmer 1 hour, turning the chickens frequently in the sauce. When the chickens are very tender, remove and keep warm.

4. Add the finely sliced onions, freshly cooked chick-peas, and raisins to the sauce and cook until the onions are very soft and the sauce has reduced to a thick gravy. Return the chickens to the sauce to reheat. (If you are using canned chick-peas, add them now.) Taste the sauce for salt, and add a pinch of pulverized saffron for a good yellow color.

5. To serve, place the chicken parts in the deep serving dish, forming them into a mound. Spoon over the onion-chick-pea-raisin sauce. Serve hot with plenty of Moroccan Bread (page 51) or *pita*.

Chicken Simmered in Smen

This classic dish of Fez is like a *kdra*, except that it calls for less than the usual amount of onions. Rich Fassis (people from Fez) put up pounds of butter in airtight earthenware jugs and store it for years. When they want to impress a visitor they bring out some of their treasured *smen* and allow him a few sniffs. If they are feeling particularly gracious they may serve him *smen* in a dish like this, which, even when made with my "young" *smen*, is bound to make you feel as prosperous as a Fassi with a cellarful of it.

INGREDIENTS

1 chicken (3 pounds), quartered and prepared as directed on page 188, with 2 livers
¾ cup minced onion
¼ teaspoon pulverized saffron threads (mixed with turmeric)
½ teaspoon ground black pepper
Salt
¼ cup roughly chopped parsley
2–3 tablespoons *smen* (Cooked and Salted Butter, page 39)
2 tablespoons fresh sweet butter
½ preserved lemon (see page 30)
2 tablespoons fresh lemon juice

EQUIPMENT

5½-quart casserole with cover
Electric blender
Colander
Skillet
Flameproof serving dish
Chopping knife

Working time: 30 minutes
Cooking time: 1½ hours
Serves: 4

1. Place the prepared chicken in the casserole with the livers and minced onion. Sprinkle with the spices and 1 teaspoon salt. Toss to coat evenly.

2. Puree the parsley in the blender with ¼ cup water. Add half the "parsley water" and all the *smen* to the casserole. Pour in 1 cup water and bring to a boil. Reduce the heat and simmer, covered, 1 hour, adding more water if necessary. Remove the chicken to the colander when very tender and keep warm while the sauce simmers 1 full hour.

3. Heat the 2 tablespoons sweet butter in the skillet and gently brown the drained chicken quarters. Transfer to the flameproof serving dish, cover, and keep warm.

4. Meanwhile, add the remaining "parsley water" to the sauce in the casserole and, by boiling rapidly, uncovered, reduce to 1½ cups. Dump the sauce, livers, and odd bits of skin and bits in the blender jar. Whirl until the sauce is smooth. Pour over the chicken and reheat.

5. Discard the pulp from the preserved lemon and dice the peel. Sprinkle the diced lemon peel over the chicken. Simmer 5 minutes, taste for seasoning, and add additional salt if necessary. Sprinkle with lemon juice and serve at once.

THREE UNUSUAL CHICKEN TAGINES

In addition to the chicken with lemon and olives dishes, and the *kdras*, there are literally dozens of other chicken *tagines*. Here are three that have struck me as unusual: *djej matisha mesla*, an extraordinary delicious *tagine* of chicken cooked with a sweet tomato jam; *djej bisla*, a *tagine* of chicken smothered in small white onions and perfumed with gum arabic, and *djej bil babcock*, a robust *tagine* of chicken with prunes as prepared in the Rif Mountains.

Chickens Cooked with Sweet Tomato Jam (*Djej Matisha Mesla*)

One of the best combinations of Moroccan cookery is the use of honey to bring out the flavor of tomatoes. The tomatoes are slowly simmered, then rapidly reduced of liquid, and finally slow-fried with the honey in the released oil. You can cut corners by using sugar in place of honey, but you will lose some of the fineness. Although you can make this dish with canned tomato paste, I don't recommend it—the glory of *djej matisha mesla* is in the incredible richness of the tomato jam made from five pounds (!) of raw, fat, red, vine-ripened tomatoes. Of course it's expensive to buy that many tomatoes, but in my opinion it's worth every penny.

INGREDIENTS	EQUIPMENT
2 chickens (3 to 3½ pounds), quartered	Large mixing bowl
4 cloves garlic, peeled	Paring knife
Salt	5½-quart casserole
Pinch of pulverized saffron	Large, warm serving dish
¼ teaspoon ground ginger	
½ teaspoon freshly ground black pepper	*Working time:* 40 minutes
1 teaspoon chopped garlic	*Cooking time:* 1½ hours
¼ cup salad oil	*Serves:* 6 to 8
5 pounds fresh red ripe tomatoes	
⅓ cup grated onion	
¼ cup "coriander water" (see page 28) (optional)	
2 teaspoons ground cinnamon	
2 tablespoons tomato paste	
4 tablespoons thick, dark honey such as Greek Mount Hymettus	
2 tablespoons sesame seeds, toasted to golden brown in the oven	

1. The day before, using the 4 cloves garlic and 2 tablespoons salt, prepare the chickens as directed on page 188. Mix the spices, salt, chopped garlic, and oil and rub into the flesh of the chickens. Let stand, covered, in the refrigerator overnight.

2. Also the day before, peel, seed, and coarsely chop the tomatoes (see page 71) and refrigerate overnight.

3. The next day, place the chickens, with the marinade, in the casserole. Add 2 cups water, the grated onion, coriander water, salt, and 1 teaspoon of

the cinnamon. Bring to a boil, reduce the heat, and simmer, uncovered, 20 minutes.

4. Add the tomatoes, tomato paste, and a little sprinkle of salt. Cook over brisk heat, turning the chicken often in the sauce, until very tender. Remove chicken and keep warm while preparing the sauce.

5. Let the tomatoes cook down rapidly until all the water is completely evaporated (about 1 hour over high heat), stirring occasionally to avoid scorching and continuously the last 15 minutes. When all the water evaporates away the oil from the marinade will be released; the tomatoes will begin to fry in it, and will start to thicken considerably. Add the honey and the remaining teaspoon cinnamon and cook a few minutes to bring out their flavors. Reheat the chicken quarters in the sauce, rolling them around to coat them evenly. Transfer to the warm serving dish, sprinkle with the sesame seeds, and serve hot or warm.

VARIATION

An inexpensive Tetuanese version of this dish is done with 2 chickens cooked in a broth made with ½ teaspoon freshly ground black pepper and turmeric, salt, ½ cup butter, and 2 cups water. After 15 minutes three-quarters of the broth is transferred to another pan while the chickens continue to cook and brown slowly in the remaining fat. Meanwhile, the poured-off broth is used to cook 2 pounds peeled, seeded, and chopped tomatoes (see page 71) until no water is left in the pan. Then ½ cup granulated sugar, ¼ cup orange flower water, and 1 teaspoon cinnamon is added to the tomatoes and they are reduced again until they become a thick dark jam. One-quarter pound toasted blanched almonds and 1 tablespoon toasted sesame seeds are used to decorate the dish just before serving.

Chicken with Onions (*Djej Bisla*)

The aromatic gum arabic is most often used in Middle Eastern sweet desserts; here it gives a chicken *tagine* a mysterious flavor.

INGREDIENTS

2 chickens (3 pounds), whole or quartered, prepared as directed on page 188
¼ teaspoon black peppercorns
½ rounded teaspoon ground ginger
6 tablespoons butter
½ teaspoon pulverized saffron mixed with turmeric
1 or 2 grains gum arabic, pulverized
¾ cup grated onion
1 tablespoon whole cumin seeds wrapped in a cheesecloth bag
2 two-inch cinnamon sticks
2 pounds whole white onions, peeled

EQUIPMENT

5½-quart casserole

Working time: 30 minutes
Cooking time: 1½ hours
Serves: 6 to 8

1. Place all ingredients except the whole white onions in the casserole. Cover with 3 cups water and bring to a boil. Cover and simmer 1 hour, turning the chickens often in the cooking liquid, adding water whenever necessary. Remove chickens when very tender and, if desired, brown in a hot oven.

2. Meanwhile, add the onions to the casserole and boil quickly until they are tender and the sauce is well reduced. Serve all together, at once.

Chicken with Prunes, Rif Style (*Djej Bil Babcock*)

I heard about this dish from many people in Tangier, who told me the Moroccan writer Mohammed Mrabet had cooked it for them. Despite all the descriptions, I couldn't figure out the recipe. On a recent trip to Morocco I went to see Paul Bowles, who had discovered and translated Mrabet, and he recalled the measurements from memory. Back in New York I tested it, and it came out well. In the Rif Mountains, which rise from the Mediterranean coast, the people are individualistic and do things their own way—for example, they rub cumin into the flesh of chickens, which is unknown in other parts of the country.

INGREDIENTS

1 chicken (3½ pounds), prepared as described on page 188, with giblets
Salt to taste
Freshly ground black pepper
2 teaspoons ground cumin, or more to taste
¾ pound prunes, pitted
2 to 3 teaspoons ground cinnamon
2 large Spanish onions, sliced lengthwise
1 teaspoon turmeric
1 teaspoon ground ginger
1 cup whole, blanched almonds
Vegetable oil for frying

EQUIPMENT

2-quart saucepan
5½-quart casserole with
   cover
Skillet
Perforated spoon
Paper towels
Large serving dish

Working time: 30 minutes
Cooking time: 1 hour
Serves: 4

1. Cut off the wings and legs from the prepared chicken, leaving the breast in one piece. Rub all the pieces with salt, pepper, and cumin. Let stand 1 hour.
2. In a separate saucepan, cover the prunes with cold water and add the cinnamon. Bring to a boil, reduce the heat, and simmer 30 minutes. (If the prunes are excessively dry, you will need to soak them for at least 1 hour beforehand and cook them a bit longer, until tender.)

3. Steam the sliced onions in the casserole with the turmeric, ginger, salt, pepper and ¼ cup water for 15 minutes.

4. Meanwhile, brown the almonds in the oil, remove with the perforated spoon, and drain on paper towels. Brown the chicken evenly on all sides in the same oil, then transfer to the steamed onions with 1 cup water. Cover and simmer 30 minutes.

5. Add the cooked prunes and some of the prune water to the casserole and continue cooking until the chicken and prunes are very tender.

6. To serve, arrange the chicken breast in the center of the serving dish, place the legs and wings around, and cover all with prunes and sauce. Sprinkle with the almonds and serve at once.

One day, when all the birds had gathered to make their final arrangements before beginning a pilgrimage to Mecca, they passed a resolution: "If God wills we will start tomorrow." But the hens and chickens cried out: "Even if God does not will it we will start tomorrow." When the time came to start they were punished for these irreverent words—they could not fly. The other birds cursed them and cried: "The traitors shall stay at home!" Ever since that time chickens have been confined to the poultry yard.

—A folktale, as related by Dr. Françoise Legey in *The Folklore of Morocco*

CHICKENS ROASTED, FRIED, OR STEAMED

Here are four marvelous ways to cook chicken, totally different from chicken *tagines*: *Djej mechoui*, chicken roasted in the style of Marrakesh; *djej mahammer*, braised and browned chicken (or turkey, or rabbit) prepared in a spicy sauce; *djej mefenned*, a variation on *djej mahammer*, in which the chicken is finally served in a coating of eggs—difficult to make but a tour de force—and *djej mafooar*, chicken steamed to a delectable silken texture.

Roasted Chicken (*Djej Mechoui*)

In one of the palaces of the royal family in Marrakesh there is a huge room set aside for the spit-roasting of chickens. At least a dozen spits are slanted diagonally across piles of burning hot coals, each attended by two men—one to crank the spit, the other to paint the roasting chickens with spiced butter.

INGREDIENTS

- 3 scallions, white part only, chopped
- 1 clove garlic, peeled (optional)
- 2 tablespoons roughly chopped mixed herbs (green coriander and parsley)
- 1 teaspoon salt
- 1½ teaspoons sweet paprika
  Pinch of cayenne
- 1½ teaspoons ground cumin
- ¼ cup softened sweet butter
- 2 broiler-fryers (2 pounds), whole, split, or quartered, prepared as directed on page 188

EQUIPMENT

Mortar and pestle
Outdoor barbecue or roasting pan for indoor grilling
Large spoon

Working time: 10 minutes
Grilling or broiling time: 25 minutes, approximately
Serves: 4

1. Pound the scallions in a mortar with the garlic, herbs, salt, and spices. Blend with the butter to make a paste. Rub the paste over the prepared chickens and into its cavities. Let stand at least 1 hour.

2. Heat charcoal in an outdoor grill or heat up the broiler.

3. Arrange the pieces of chicken skin side up over the coals or skin side down under the broiler. After 5 minutes turn and baste with any extra paste or the juices in the roasting pan. Continue turning and basting every 5 minutes until the chickens are done—depending on the heat of the coals.

Chicken Braised and Browned (*Djej Mahammer*)

This is a Rabat recipe for a dish that is cooked and served throughout Morocco. In Tangier some people add a little bit of hot red pepper to the sauce and eat the chicken with sautéed potatoes; in Fez they sprinkle it with buttered and browned almonds; and in Marrakesh, where it is served without accompaniment, the sauce is usually jazzed up with extra paprika, and sprigs of mint are added with the green coriander.

INGREDIENTS

⅛ teaspoon pulverized saffron soaked in ¼ cup hot water

1 teaspoon mashed garlic

¼ teaspoon ground turmeric

2 teaspoons paprika

¼ teaspoon ground cumin

Salt

2 chickens (3 pounds each), whole, prepared as directed on page 188, with 3 livers

¼ cup grated onion

¾ cup sweet butter

4 sprigs green coriander, pounded to a paste in a mortar

EQUIPMENT

Small mixing bowls

5½-quart casserole with cover

Large skillet (optional)

Large serving platter

Working time: 30 minutes

Cooking time: 1 hour 15 minutes

Serves: 8

1. Mix the saffron water with the garlic, spices, and salt. Rub into the prepared chickens and lay them on their sides in the casserole. Add the livers, onion, and half the butter. Pour in 3 cups water and bring to a boil. Add the coriander and simmer, covered, over moderately low heat 1 hour, turning the chickens from time to time.

2. Midway, remove and mash the livers, then return them to the sauce.

3. When very tender, remove the chickens and keep warm. Heat the remaining butter in the skillet and brown one chicken at a time until crusty all

over. Transfer to a serving platter and put in a warm oven while browning the second chicken. (They can also be browned in a very hot oven.)

4. Meanwhile, by boiling rapidly, uncovered, reduce the sauce to make about ¾ cup thick gravy. Serve the chickens with the sauce poured over.

VARIATION:

Turkey Braised and Browned (*Bibi Mahammer*)

This is a simple variation of *djej mahammer*: substitute an 8-pound turkey for the two chickens and increase the cooking time in step 1 by 1 hour. For the browning portion of this dish you will need a restaurant-size skillet; in Morocco they either use a huge pot, about 10 quarts capacity, or brown the turkey in a hot oven.

VARIATION:

Rabbit Braised and Browned (*Lernib Mahammer*)

Another variation of *djej mahammer* uses a 4-pound rabbit cut up into parts. Add 1 teaspoon *ras el hanout* (page 26) to the sauce, and, when the rabbit is browning (step 3), add ½ pound soaked and drained raisins to the sauce. In Fez this dish is always served with a good sprinkling of browned almonds.

Chicken Braised and Browned and Coated with Eggs
(*Djej Mefenned*)

This is yet another variation of djej mahammer, and one of the most difficult of all Moroccan chicken dishes to execute well. If the technique of
twirling the whole chicken in sizzling butter while basting it with seasoned
eggs seems too difficult, you can do it the Tetuánese way: quarter the
chicken, coat the pieces separately, and then fry them as one might fry
chicken in America.

James Skelton, an expatriate Australian who lives in a restored palace in
the *medina* in Marrakesh, told me about a version of this dish he ate years
ago at the Maison Arabe restaurant: the egg-coated chicken had been boned
and then stuffed with browned, chopped almonds and honey. Before so
awesome a feat of culinary skill even the tour de force of *djej mefenned* begins
to pale.

INGREDIENTS	EQUIPMENT
Same as for *djej mahammer* (Chicken Braised and Browned, page 213) plus	Same as for *djej mahammer* plus
8 eggs	String
½ cup finely chopped parsley	Whisk
½ heaping teaspoon paprika	Large shallow pan
¼ teaspoon ground cumin	
⅛ teaspoon salt	*Working time:* 45 minutes
½ cup sweet butter	*Cooking time:* 1½ hours
¼ cup lemon juice	*Serves:* 8

1. Follow steps 1, 2, 3 and up to the point of serving in step 4 on pages
213–214. Strain the fat from step 3 and reserve. Tie the chickens' feet together
with string.

2. Beat the eggs with the parsley, paprika, cumin, and salt to a good froth and transfer to a large shallow pan. Roll the first crusty chicken in the eggs until well coated.

3. Clean the skillet used in step 3 and return the reserved fat plus the ½ cup sweet butter. Heat the fat and butter, then add the first egg-coated chicken. As the egg coating browns, start spooning additional beaten eggs from the pan over the chicken. The eggs will slip over the chicken into the hot butter and begin to congeal. Immediately lift the congealing eggs with a spoon and apply them again to the body of the chicken, pressing lightly. As you do this, more and more of the egg mixture will adhere. (Regulate the heat as you work. It takes about 4 minutes to "do" each bird.) Continue to "patch" pieces of egg onto empty spaces and slowly turn the bird so the egg crust browns in the butter. (At the same time you can apply more egg coating to the other side of the bird.) Remove the first chicken carefully to the serving platter and keep warm in a slow oven, then continue with the next chicken. When both are ready, sprinkle them with the lemon juice. Heat the sauce, pour over the chickens, and serve at once.

Steamed Chicken (*Djej Mafooar*)

This dish is quite beautiful, in its simplicity. The chicken is rubbed with saffron, butter, and salt, then steamed above boiling water until very tender. Its skin becomes silken, and the whole chicken acquires a delicate taste.

In Tangier small white onions are placed inside the chicken along with a few sprigs of parsley. In Tetuán the chicken is stuffed with wild greens or rice, tomatoes, olives, and pickled lemons and is spiced with cayenne. Some people gently brown the chicken in butter after removing it from the steamer, but I think this method interferes with the delicacy.

One thing you should know is that a steamed chicken must be served at once if you want to eat it hot. It does not reheat well, but it is excellent served cold, accompanied, in the Tetuán style, by sliced raw onions and chopped parsley.

INGREDIENTS

2 good pinches pulverized saffron
1 teaspoon salt
¼ cup sweet butter, softened
1 whole chicken (3 pounds), prepared as directed on page 188
  Ground cumin
  Cayenne pepper (optional)

EQUIPMENT

Mortar and pestle
Couscousiere or steamer
  with tight-fitting lid
Cheesecloth

Working time: 10 minutes
Steaming time: 1 hour
Serves: 4

1. Pound the saffron with the salt and blend with the softened butter. Rub into the skin of the prepared chicken.

2. Fill the bottom of *couscousiere* (or steamer) with water and bring to a boil. Seal on the perforated top as directed in step 2 in the *couscous* master instructions (page 136). Place the chicken in the top container and cover with a double layer of cheesecloth. Close the lid tightly and steam 1 hour *without lifting the cover*. Serve at once, *as is,* with accompanying bowls of ground cumin and coarse salt, or, if desired, mix cumin and salt with a sprinkling of cayenne pepper.

Note: You can substitute a 6- or 7-pound turkey for the chicken, increasing the steaming time to 2 hours (and changing the name to *bibi mafooar*). Of course, you will need an enormous *couscousiere* to do the job!

STUFFED POULTRY

—◆—

When Moroccans describe feasts given by past sultans and pashas their eyes grow large as they speak of platters piled high with "mounds" of stuffed pigeons, each bird stuffed with a different substance. If these stories of boundless luxury are true (and they probably are), there are certainly enough stuffings in the Moroccan repertory to do the job: *couscous*; raisins and almonds; rice and almonds; almond paste; and an unlimited number of vegetable stuffings made of everything from celery, onions, and parsley to the bitter wild herb *bakoola*.

Stuffed Turkey (*Bibi Ma'amrra*)

I first had this dish at a luncheon in an orange grove outside of Rabat. After we had consumed one one-hundredth of a delicious *bisteeya* that was twenty-five inches in diameter, a servant brought out two young turkeys that had been braised in a huge vat. The stuffing was heavenly—almonds, spices, raisins, and steamed rice—and the outside of the turkey was coated in thick thyme-flavored country honey. Then came a forequarter of lamb heavily spiced with paprika and cumin, followed by a vegetable *couscous* and, last, two enormous platters of fresh fruits. After that feast I began to understand Moroccan hospitality. After all, we were only six for lunch!

1 cup raw rice

¼ cup blanched, slivered almonds

½ cup raisins

¾ cup almond meal (¼ pound almonds, pulverized)

Salt

1 teaspoon ground cinnamon

1 cup sweet butter

½ cup confectioners' sugar

1 turkey (6½ to 7 pounds)

1 lemon, halved

Pinch pulverized saffron

2 rounded teaspoons ground cinnamon

¼ rounded teaspoon ground ginger

¼ rounded teaspoon freshly ground black pepper

⅔ cup grated onion, drained

¾ to 1 cup dark honey, such as the Greek Mount Hymettus

Large saucepan

Couscousiere or small steamer

Mixing bowl

Large roasting pan with cover

Paper towels

Needle and strong thread

Large spoon

Warm serving platter

Working time: 1 hour 40 minutes

Cooking time: 2 hours (approximately)

Serves: 6 to 8

1. Bring plenty of water to a rolling boil in the large saucepan. Slowly sprinkle in the rice without losing the boil. Cook fast for 10 minutes, stirring once. Drain the rice in the oiled top container of the *couscousiere*. Toss with forks to break up the rice and sprinkle with ½ cup cold water. Toss again to separate the grains.

2. Bring plenty of water to a rolling boil in the bottom of the *couscousiere*. Set the container with rice on top and add the slivered almonds. Cover the container tightly and steam 10 minutes. Toss rice and almonds with two forks to separate the grains. Add the raisins, cover again, and steam another 10 minutes. Dump into the mixing bowl. Add the almond meal, salt, cinnamon, ¼ cup of the butter, and the sugar. Taste for seasoning and readjust. Set aside to cool.

3. Rub the turkey well with lemon and salt. Rinse, drain, and pat dry with paper towels.

4. Stuff the turkey at both ends with the rice-almond stuffing, packing it loosely. Sew the openings closed with strong thread. (Extra stuffing can be heated and served separately.) Tie the turkey's feet together and place the bird breast side up in the roasting pan.

5. Mix the saffron, cinnamon, ginger, and pepper with ⅓ cup water and rub over the turkey. Add 3 to 4 cups water, the grated onion, a sprinkling of salt, and half the remaining butter to the pan. Cover and cook over moderately high heat, adding water when necessary and basting the turkey frequently.

6. At the end of the first hour of braising add the honey to the juices in the pan. Continue cooking and basting the turkey until tender (approximately 2 hours; internal temperature 185°). Remove the cover, turn up the heat, and reduce the sauce until all the liquid in the pan has evaporated and the honey begins to caramelize, constantly turning the turkey in the glaze to coat evenly. Transfer the turkey to the warm serving platter and remove the string. Stir the remaining butter into honey in the pan to make a rich, thick sauce. Pour over the turkey and serve at once.

An Adventure in Marrakesh

Winter nights are cold in Marrakesh. I shivered as I moved through the narrow passageways of the *medina*, searching out the El Bahia Restaurant in the maze. Moorish restaurants are often built in old palaces with windows starting on the second floor—a type of architecture that reflects the Moroccan desire to shroud life in mystery and to hide secrets from prying eyes. My visit to the kitchen of a restaurant would be an unprecedented invasion into a world of jealousy and intrigue—a fact I did not know as I pounded on the wooden door.

An unveiled young girl wearing floppy pantaloons led me through the empty dining room, across an open courtyard, and into a white-tiled shed. This large, stark place was the kitchen. Four women, ranging in age from twenty-six to sixty, were waiting there, talking and laughing. When I came in they stopped and looked me up and down with a small measure of scorn. They had been informed of my request. They knew that a *nasrani* was coming, and, in fact, my list of requested dishes was posted on the wall.

Three of them gave me shy smiles, but one, who was huge, fat, and black, expressed her derision with an outraged sniff. It was she, the black Chleuh, who had the recipes, whispered the owner's wife—*she* who had once worked in the kitchens of El Glaoui, the pasha of Marrakesh. There was no doubt that *she* was the "Queen Bee" of the group. I gaped as she fluttered her elbows and batted her eyelids and ran a monologue in her native Berber dialect which neither I nor the owner's wife could understand.

Whatever she said seemed to embarrass the youngest of the cooks; she stole off to the far corner and began quietly to knead dough. The pastry cook, a short, fair Berber woman with enormous breasts, set to work frying almonds. She was helpful and answered all my questions, giving long descriptions of desserts she could make for me if I wished. From time to time she threw indecipherable cracks in Chleuh at the Queen Bee, who sat in the corner plunging a chicken, up and down like a Yo-yo, into boiling water. I felt that I had at least one friend in that kitchen, but I was hoping for a change in alliances. I knew—I could *feel*—that the Queen Bee was the best cook, and I wanted her to like me so she would tell me some of her culinary secrets.

At this precise moment one of the almonds popped out of the pan onto the floor. Suddenly all kitchen work came to a stop and everyone stared. I looked first at the pastry cook, but she turned hastily and avoided my eyes. Then the young one turned back to her dough. But the Queen Bee leered at me, and at that moment I knew what I had to do.

I bent down, retrieved the almond, sniffed it, and tossed it back into the pan. When I glanced again at Queen Bee, she gave me a mischievous smile. I had moved too quickly for her—she'd intended to return the almond herself, to show defiance of my American "hygiene." But I'd beaten her to the punch, and in some strange way this won her over. In her enthusiasm she revealed some of her recipes, including the following one, for chicken stuffed with rice and raisins. Then she stopped, as if realizing these secrets were *her* wealth. They say in Morocco, "What the tongue refuses, the eyes and hands can say." She smiled, squeezed my hand, and I knew the lesson was over.

Chicken Stuffed with Rice and Raisins, Marrakesh Style

INGREDIENTS

1 cup raw rice
¾ cup sweet butter
¾ cup raisins
6 tablespoons granulated sugar
1 teaspoon ground cinnamon
  Salt and freshly ground black pepper
½ teaspoon *ras el hanout* (page 26) (optional)
2 chickens (3 pounds each), ready to cook, with giblets and necks
2 pinches pulverized saffron

EQUIPMENT

3-quart saucepan
Couscousiere or steamer
Mixing bowl
Paper towels
Needle and heavy thread
5½-quart casserole

Working time: 1 hour
Cooking time: 1¾ hours
Serves: 6 to 8

1. Follow directions for handling rice in step 1 on page 219.
2. Bring plenty of water to a rolling boil in the bottom of the *couscousiere*. Set the container holding the rice on top and steam, covered, 10 minutes.
3. Stir in ¼ cup of the butter and the raisins. Toss with the rice and steam another 10 minutes. Dump into the mixing bowl and add ¼ cup of the sugar, half the cinnamon, salt and pepper to taste, and *ras el hanout*, if desired. Set aside to cool.
4. Wash the chickens well under running water. Salt them. Remove and discard as much fat as possible, but avoid tearing the skin. Rinse off the salt and drain. Pat dry with paper towels.
5. Stuff the chickens with the cooled rice, then close the openings at neck and rump, sewing securely with heavy thread. Blend ¼ cup of the butter with the saffron and a little salt. Rub over the chickens.
6. Boil 3 cups water in the casserole and carefully slip in the two chickens. Add the remaining sugar, giblets, and necks, and simmer, covered, over moderately low heat 1½ hours, turning the chickens frequently in the sauce. When they are very tender, remove from the casserole and keep warm. Reduce the sauce over high heat until the sugar begins to caramelize. Stir the remain-

ing ¼ cup butter into the sauce and combine well. Return the chickens and brown carefully on all sides. Remove the thread and serve hot with the sauce.

Note: The chicken can be browned in a hot oven.

VARIATION:

Pigeons Stuffed with Couscous (*Frach Ma'amrra*)

In this luxurious variation on the preceding recipe, the chicken is replaced by 6 Moroccan pigeons or 3 squabs; *couscous* is substituted in the stuffing for rice.

INGREDIENTS

 6 pigeons, or 3 squabs, or 1 chicken
   Salt and freshly ground black pepper
½ cup uncooked *couscous*
⅓ cup tightly packed raisins
⅓ cup whole, blanched almonds
½ cup sweet butter, more if necessary
   Ground cinnamon
 2 pinches pulverized saffron
 3 tablespoons dark honey, such as the Greek
    Mount Hymettus
   Pinch to ½ teaspoon *ras el hanout* (page 26)
½ cup grated onion
 1 cinnamon stick

EQUIPMENT

Paper towels
Large, shallow pan
Mixing bowls
Couscousiere or steamer
Baking sheet
Chopping knife
Needle and thread
5½-quart casserole with
  cover
Large spoon
Large, warm serving platter

Working time: 1 hour
Cooking time: 1¼ hours,
  approximately
Serves: 4 to 6 (as part of a
  Moroccan dinner)

1. Wash the poultry under running cold water and pat dry with paper towels. Rub cavities with salt and pepper. Set aside.

2. Follow steps 1 and 2 of the master *couscous* instructions on page 136. Steam the *couscous* 10 minutes, then turn out and let dry, as directed in step 3 (page 136), for 20 minutes.

3. Meanwhile, soak the raisins in hot water. Brown the almonds in a 250° oven until golden brown. When cool, chop coarsely.

4. Steam the *couscous* a second time for 15 minutes, adding 2 tablespoons of the sweet butter to the grains. Toss lightly.

5. Dump the *couscous* into a mixing bowl and add the chopped almonds, drained raisins, ¼ teaspoon cinnamon, ¼ teaspoon black pepper, and 1 pinch of the pulverized saffron. Mix well and add 1 tablespoon of the honey and *ras el hanout* to taste. Mix well with two forks.

6. Stuff the poultry and sew up securely with thread. Blend 2 tablespoons of the butter with a pinch of saffron and a little salt. Rub over the poultry, then place in the casserole, breast side up, on a bed of grated onion. Add the cinnamon stick, a little salt, the remaining butter, ¾ teaspoon pepper, and 2 cups water. Bring to a boil, reduce the heat, and simmer, covered, 30 minutes, basting the squabs from time to time. Continue cooking, uncovered, until the birds are fully cooked (i.e., when juices run yellow at the piercing of the thighs). Turn the poultry often in the liquid and add water, if necessary, to avoid scorching.

7. Remove the poultry and, by boiling rapidly, reduce the cooking liquid to 1 cup. Add the remaining honey and 1 scant teaspoon cinnamon to the sauce. Stir to blend well. Return the birds to the thick sauce and glaze them by turning gently as the sauce reduces. (It may be necessary to add more butter during the glazing period.)

8. Transfer the poultry to the warm serving platter. Remove the threads. With a wooden spoon, swirl the sauce to combine. Add a little butter, taste for salt, pepper, cinnamon, and sweetness, and readjust to taste. Pour the sauce around the birds and serve at once.

Note: One-half teaspoon ground ginger is sometimes substituted for the ¾ teaspoon black pepper.

Chicken Stuffed with Almond Paste (*Djej Mashee Bil Looz*)

This dish is a specialty of Safi, a town about a hundred miles down the coast from Casablanca famous for its glazed pottery. *Djej mashee bil looz* is extremely sweet: when I taught it some of my students were skeptical, but a Hungarian importer who eats *lekvar* (a Hungarian sweet prune butter) every morning of his life told me it was the most delicious chicken he had ever tasted.

INGREDIENTS

   2 chickens, ready to cook
     Salt and freshly ground pepper
   2 pinches pulverized saffron
1¼ teaspoons ground cinnamon
   ¼ teaspoon ground ginger
1½ cups minced onions
   6 tablespoons sweet butter
     Salad oil for frying
1½ cups whole, blanched almonds
   1 cup confectioners' sugar
   1 tablespoon orange flower water

EQUIPMENT

5½-quart casserole
Large spoon
Skillet
Electric blender or nut
   grinder
Mixing bowl
Shallow ovenproof serving
   dish
Small saucepan

Working time: 30 minutes
Cooking time: 30 minutes
Baking or roasting time: 20
   minutes
Serves: 6 to 8

1. Prepare the chickens as directed on page 188, but instead of garlic and salt, rub with salt and pepper.

2. Soak the saffron in 2 tablespoons hot water, mix with ¼ teaspoon of the cinnamon, the ginger, salt, and pepper. Rub over the chickens, then place the chickens in the casserole with the onions and ¼ cup of the butter. Pour in 1 cup water and bring to a boil. Reduce the heat and simmer 30 minutes,

basting the chickens from time to time and adding more water to the pan if necessary.

3. While the chickens are cooking, heat enough oil in the skillet to cover the bottom of the pan. Brown the almonds evenly, then drain on paper towels. When cool, pulverize them in a blender or pass them through a nut grinder. Mix with the sugar, the remaining 1 teaspoon cinnamon, the orange flower water, and just enough water to give the mixture the consistency of paste. Separate into two equal parts.

4. Preheat the oven to 400°.

5. Remove the chickens from the casserole and let drain. By boiling rapidly, uncovered, reduce the sauce to ¾ cup. Spoon into serving dish. Using half of the paste, stuff the cavity of each bird, then arrange the chickens in the serving dish and spread the remaining paste over the chickens, packing it gently against the contours of their bodies. Melt the remaining butter and use it to coat the chickens. Bake 10 to 20 minutes, or until the almond paste is midway between forming a crust and melting into the sauce. Serve at once.

Chicken Stuffed with Eggs, Onions, and Parsley (*Lema Ma'amrra*)

This recipe is adapted from *Moorish Recipes*, collected and compiled by John, Fourth Marquis of Bute, K.T. Though Lord Bute (whose book is both charming and instructive) says that his recipes from the Mennebi Palace in Tangier "follow more closely the Marrakesh taste," this particular recipe is decidedly Tetuanese, with a strong Andalusian influence indicated by its egg crust.

INGREDIENTS

1 chicken (3 to 3½ pounds), with neck and
    giblets
4 cloves garlic, peeled
  Salt
½ teaspoon freshly ground black pepper
5 large eggs
2 tablespoons butter
¾ cup minced onion
¼ cup chopped parsley
1½ teaspoons turmeric
  Pinch of pulverized saffron
½ teaspoon ground ginger
3 tablespoons salad oil
2 cups chicken stock or water
2 cinnamon sticks

EQUIPMENT

Needle and thread
10-inch skillet
Mixing bowl
5½-quart casserole with
  cover
1½-quart shallow ovenproof
  serving dish

Working time: 30 minutes
Cooking time: 1 hour 15
  minutes
Serves: 4

1. Prepare the chicken as described on page 188, but do not truss. Sew up the neck opening securely. Rub the large cavity with salt and pepper.

2. Fry the eggs in the butter until almost set, then scramble. When firm, mix with the onion, salt, parsley, turmeric, saffron, black pepper, and ginger. Stuff the chicken with a little more than half this mixture, sew up the rump opening, and tie the feet together. Reserve the remaining egg mixture.

3. Place the chicken in the casserole, breast side up, with the neck, giblets, oil, and chicken stock. Bring to a boil. Add the cinnamon sticks and simmer, partially covered, for 1 hour, basting the chicken often and adding more stock or water if necessary. Remove the chicken when it is very tender and place in an ovenproof serving dish. Reduce sauce to a thick gravy, about ¾ cup. Discard the cinammon sticks.

4. Preheat the oven to the highest setting.

5. Spoon the remaining egg mixture over the chicken and surround with the gravy. Place in oven long enough to brown nicely, and serve at once.

Chicken Stuffed with Kefta and Eggs

Another version of stuffed chicken from the Tetuanese can be made with minced beef and eggs. It's equally good as a stuffing for Braewats (page 122) with a good sprinkling of ground cinnamon.

INGREDIENTS

1 cup grated onion
½ cup chopped parsley
¾ teaspoon freshly ground black pepper, or more to taste
¾ teaspoon turmeric
10 tablespoons butter
1 pound ground beef
8 to 10 eggs
½ cup lemon juice
Salt
3 whole chickens, prepared as directed on page 188
½ cup salad oil

EQUIPMENT

3-quart saucepan
Mixing bowl
Whisk
Needle and thread
6-quart casserole
Large ovenproof serving platter

Working time: 20 minutes
Cooking time: 1½ hours
Baking time: 10 minutes
Serves: 8 to 10

1. Cook the onion, parsley, ½ teaspoon each of the black pepper and turmeric, butter, and ground beef in the 3-quart saucepan over moderate heat for 3 to 4 minutes, stirring, then add a cup of water and bring to a boil. Stir to separate the meat and cook until the water has evaporated and the meat is lightly browned.

2. Beat the eggs and lemon juice and pour over the meat. Cook over low heat, stirring continuously, until the eggs set. Taste and adjust seasoning and allow to cool.

3. Stuff the three chickens with equal amounts of the stuffing and sew up carefully. Place the chickens in the large casserole with the remaining spices, a sprinkling of salt, the oil, and 1 cup water. Bring to a boil, cover, and cook for 1 hour or until the chickens are tender.

4. Place the chickens on the serving platter and brown in a hot oven. Meanwhile, reduce the cooking liquid to a rich gravy. Serve at once.

Chicken Stuffed with Mint

Still another Tetuanese dish, to be made with freshly chopped mint leaves and scrambled eggs. Unusual but pleasant.

INGREDIENTS

3 whole chickens, prepared as directed on page 188, but not trussed, with necks and giblets
Salt to taste
¼ teaspoon freshly ground black pepper
¼ teaspoon ground turmeric
⅔ cup butter
½ cup grated onion
3 cups chopped mint leaves, loosely packed
2 teaspoons lemon juice
6 eggs

EQUIPMENT

Needle and thread
6½-quart casserole with cover
Small saucepan
Skillet

Working time: 20 minutes
Cooking time: 1 hour
Serves: 8 to 10

1. Sew up neck openings of the chickens, then rub with salt, pepper, and turmeric. Place the chickens in the casserole, breast side up, with the necks, giblets, butter, onion, and 1 cup water. Bring to a boil, reduce the heat, and simmer, partially covered, for ¾ hour, or until tender.

2. Put the mint in a small saucepan and pour the remaining chicken gravy over, add the lemon juice and reduce until all the liquid has evaporated. Fry one-third of this mint mixture in a skillet with 2 of the eggs. When the eggs are almost set, break up the yolks and allow the mixture to "fluff," then stuff one chicken and sew up securely. Repeat with the remaining chickens. Brown in a hot oven and serve immediately.

TEN

———◆———

Meats

Moussems, the festivals and pilgrimages of the various Berber tribes, are marvelous occasions, a combination of religious celebration and folk festival in which whole cities of tents sprout up for several days in the mountains near the tombs of revered saints. Tradesmen appear with muleloads of goods, and there is much dancing and singing, often at night by the light of torches— and, always, plenty of food.

At some *moussems* there are secret rites, various forms of trance dancing and even religious-ecstatic mutilations. But most *moussems* are not like that— they are open to all, and the Moroccan government encourages foreign tourists to attend. Probably the most famous of these is the Festival of the Betrothed, held in late September every year near the tiny town of Imilchil, high in the Middle Atlas Mountains. The last time I went it was still a fabulous sight, those thousands of wool tents, those herds of goats and lambs and sheep, revealed through the mists at dawn nestled between barren and stony peaks.

The people of the Ait Hiddous tribe are sheepherders, and their women, who go about unveiled, are known to be generous, strong, proud, dignified, and equal to their husbands in every way. In fact there is an old Moroccan proverb: "A Berber woman is the ridgepole of the tent." A girl of the Ait Hiddous marries whomever she likes, and brings no dowry. She will work side by side with her husband, help him gather wood and tend the flocks, bear children, and cook the Berber specialties: *mrouzia, mechoui, begrir, tutlin,* and so on.

One of the purposes of the *moussem* of Imilchil is to provide an opportunity for widowed or divorced Berber women to find new husbands. They call these women *twindals,* and you will see them, if you go to Imilchil in September, standing about in groups of six or seven, wearing necklaces of egg-sized ambers, heavy silver bracelets, dark blue coats striped in red and green and white, and pointed headdresses held in place by multicolored ropes studded with sequins. They are waiting around, of course, to peruse and be perused by the men who have come to Imilchil to find a bride. There is much scouting and mutual eyeing of available mates, various forms of dalliance and flirtation with the eyes, and then proposals and acceptances that are resolved, on the last day of the festival, in a number of mass weddings.

Despite the tourists, Imilchil is still great—there is singing and dancing, the charming courtship rituals of the handsome young Berbers and the incredibly flirtatious *twindals,* and you can wander about from tent to tent, inhaling the aromas of marvelous Berber *tagines,* and, best of all, that great Berber specialty, *mechoui,* roasted lamb.

The Berbers claim to be first (vying with the Turks) to have figured out an excellent way of barbecuing lamb. Here they roast the animals on spits over pits of burning charcoal embers, basting them all the while with herbal butter, having rubbed the flesh first with garlic and spices. This way the whole animal becomes incredibly crisp on the outside while staying juicy and butter-tender underneath. It is so tender, in fact, that you can eat it with your fingers, which is how it is done—even though it burns.

I've had wonderful-tasting *mechouis,* not only at *moussems* in the Middle Atlas, but all through Morocco. Some of the best have been in the Moroccan Souss, where the lambs munch on wild herbs and acquire a strong flavor very much like the *pré salé* of Brittany in France. But in the town of Tineghir in the Sahara on the famous "Route of the Casbahs" near the beautiful Todra gorges, I ate a *mechoui* prepared in a totally different style.

The *caid* obtained the services of the "master butcher" of the town one November Sunday following the Day of Independence. Before slaughtering the lamb the butcher had prepared charcoal embers inside a huge earthen furnace built against a wall. The furnace was terrifically hot. After the lamb was killed and cleaned and prepared for roasting, he skewered it on a thick piece of green wood and then inserted it vertically into the furnace. No spices of any sort were rubbed into the flesh. His assistant slit the lamb's eviscerated stomach, which was filled with undigested grass. He mixed this with mud and used it to seal the iron cover on top of the oven. Three hours later the *mechoui* was completely done—meltingly tender, it was served with ground cumin and coarse salt. This style of cooking *mechoui* is Saharan.

Another big lamb-eating occasion for everyone in Morocco is the annual holiday called Aid el Kebir, the Festival of the Sacrifice of the Lamb, which occurs on the tenth day of the twelfth month of the Muslim calendar year and commemorates the sacrifice of Abraham. Every Moroccan tries to get hold of a sheep for Aid el Kebir; if he cannot get one he may settle for a kid or, if he is very poor, a fowl. The point is to make a sacrifice and then enjoy it.

The trick, as I found out, is to choose the best time to buy your lamb. It will be more expensive if you buy it early, but this gives you time to properly fatten it up. On the other hand, if you buy it at the last minute it will be very cheap, but scrawny and not likely to taste very good. So you balance the resources of your purse against the needs of your stomach, get help for the bargaining from a Moroccan friend, and buy sometime in the middle.

When the lamb is properly fat, you arrange with a slaughterer who will kill the lamb according to religious law. The meat is then hung in two halves, after which comes the portioning, which, for better or for worse, I always did myself, following a drawing in an old *House and Gardens* cookbook that showed me where everything was. Actually I had only moderate success as a meat cutter. The odds and ends, the pieces I didn't know what to do with, and the pieces I accidentally sliced wrong, went into what I used to call the "*kefta* pile," to be used for Moroccan ground-meat dishes. I confess that the first couple of years my "*kefta* pile" was very large.

As soon as the slaughterer left the house I would rush the lamb's liver into my freezer, and as soon as it was cool would rub it with a marinade and grill it on skewers over charcoal for the dish called *kouah*. The next day I would marinate the kidneys and heart in freshly chopped green coriander, grated onion, cumin, and salt and then grill them, too—they were always delicious.

The brains went for the salad called *mohk* (Brain Salads I and II, pages 86 and 87), the slaughterer took the trotters for a dish called *hergma* (simmered with chick-peas, red pepper, and onions), which I have never wanted to eat, and Moroccan friends made a *tagine* they liked very much of intestines and lungs. As for the head, minus the brains, it was steamed and served with cumin and salt. In Fez there is a special area where these steamed lambs' heads, called *raseem bahaar*, can be bought, and I am told they are a morning favorite of the kif smokers, who believe the head is the richest part of the body and will give them strength.

Aside from the meat dishes that are grilled and roasted, the dishes of lamb that are braised, browned or steamed, and all the delicious things you can do with *kefta*, most of the recipes in this chapter are for meat *tagines*, those marvelous, slowly simmered Moroccan stews in which the sauce is everything and the meat literally falls off the bones. A whole book could be written of recipes for meat *tagines*; there are endless variations, and, though the spicing may look the same, each dish has subtle differences and special proportions that make it unique. I have divided these *tagines* into "fragrant *tagines*," made with lemons and olives; "robust *tagines*," made with cumin and paprika; and "*tagines* of meat with fruit." Make them all, they are glorious—and like the numerous chicken *tagines* they form the backbone of the Moroccan diet.

LAMB GRILLED AND ROASTED

Roasted Lamb (*Mechoui*)

I am not going to suggest you spit-roast a whole lamb; I realize that for most readers that is out of the question. Instead I recommend that you make *mechoui* with a ten-pound forequarter. Though it may taste a little better if you can dig a pit, fill it with charcoal, and set up a roasting spit in your back yard, I guarantee that with this adaptation you will obtain good results in the oven of your home, be it country house or city apartment.

Actually, the same problem confronts the Moroccan city dweller. She knows that the best place to eat *mechoui* is in the *bled*, because if she cooks it in the city, where most people do not have a full-sized stove, she will have to send her meat to a community oven, and there the workers will be extremely casual about basting the lamb. The best Berber *mechoui*, you see, is swabbed down every ten minutes with butter and spices.

Fortunately, most Americans have large stoves in which a forequarter can easily be roasted, and are therefore in a better position to cook *mechoui* than the average person in Rabat or Casablanca. Buying a whole forequarter in America can, however, be an amusing experience.

The paste used to flavor the meat in this recipe is in the style of Rabat.

INGREDIENTS

    1 forequarter lamb (10 pounds)
1½ tablespoons ground coriander seed
4 to 5 cloves garlic, peeled and mashed
    2 teaspoons ground cumin
    1 teaspoon sweet paprika
    6 tablespoons sweet butter, softened
      Salt to taste

EQUIPMENT

Sharp paring knife
Roasting pan large enough
   to hold the lamb
Large spoon or bulb baster

Working time: 10 minutes
Roasting time: 3 hours
Serves: 8 (as part of a
   Moroccan dinner)

1. Carefully remove extraneous fat from the lamb, then make deep incisions under the foreleg bone along the breastplate. Blend all the other ingredients into a paste and rub into the meat. Let stand 10 minutes.

2. Preheat the oven to 475°.

3. Place the lamb, fatty side up, in a large roasting pan. Place on the middle shelf of the oven and roast 15 minutes. Reduce the heat to 350° and continue to roast for about 3 hours, or until the meat can easily be removed from the bones with your fingers. Baste every 15 minutes with the juices in the pan. Serve at once, while still burning hot. Eat with your fingers and have a bowl of ground cumin and salt ready for those who like to dip their meat.

(*continued*)

Note: The secret of a good *mechoui* is to obtain a crisp beautifully browned crust, while the meat inside is sweet, juicy, and meltingly tender. The lamb should not be pink, as the French like it, or tough and dried out, as it is so often served in the United States.

Skewered and Grilled Lamb (*Quodban*)

One of the most famous dishes of the Middle East and the Arab world is skewered lamb or beef, known variously as *shish kebab, shaslick,* brochettes, and so on. In some parts of Morocco these are eaten with a good sprinkling of hot spices, followed by a soothing glass of highly sweetened mint tea. On the road between Meknes and Rabat there is a small town called Khemisett, which specializes in serving spicy *quodban* to travelers. Here, the vendors of the many competing stalls grill the meat on skewers, then remove it and place the pieces within pieces of barley bread encrusted with salt crystals.

INGREDIENTS	EQUIPMENT
1½ pounds boned leg of lamb, cut into ¾-inch cubes	Shallow dish
	Broiler or outdoor grill
1 cup beef or mutton fat, cut into ¼-inch cubes	12 skewers
1 onion, grated	*Working time:* 10 minutes
¼ cup finely chopped parsley	*Marinating time:* 2 hours
Salt to taste	*Grilling time:* 5 to 8 minutes
½ teaspoon freshly ground black pepper	*Serves:* 6

1. Place the lamb in the shallow dish with the chunks of fat and all the other ingredients. Toss well and let stand for 2 hours.

2. Heat up the grill.

3. Thread the meat alternately with the fat chunks, pressing the pieces together. (There should be 6 to 8 small pieces of meat and 4 pieces of fat on

each skewer.) Broil the meat a few inches from the heat, then turn when well browned and grill the other side. (Moroccans usually grill the meat until well done.)

4. To serve, each guest slides the pieces of meat, one by one, into a wedge of Moroccan Bread (page 51), and then sprinkles on some cayenne, cumin, and salt, which are served in separate bowls, to taste.

Note: For a spicier *kebab*, add a scant teaspoon paprika and cumin. Also, 1½ pounds beef fillet can be substituted for the lamb.

VARIATION:

Skewered and Grilled Liver, Berber Style (*Kouah*)

INGREDIENTS

1 pound lamb's liver, in one piece
¼ pound mutton fat
Salt
½ teaspoon cumin
1½ teaspoons paprika
Pinches of cayenne to taste

EQUIPMENT

Griddle or wire rack for charcoal grilling or a seasoned skillet
Broiler or outdoor grill
12 skewers

Working time: 10 minutes
Grilling time: 5 to 7 minutes
Serves: 4 to 6 (as part of a Moroccan dinner)

1. Firm the lamb's liver by lightly searing on both sides on a hot griddle or in a well-seasoned skillet. Cut into smallish chunks. Cut the fat into smaller chunks.

2. Mix the liver and fat with salt and the spices and thread on skewers, beginning and ending with pieces of liver. Grill quickly on both sides and serve very hot, with Moroccan Bread (page 51). In Tangier thinned Harissa Sauce (page 30) is often served with *kouah*.

Skewered and Grilled Liver, Berber Style (*Tutlin*)

Substitute sheep's caul for mutton fat. The caul should cover the threaded meat entirely.

Seared Lamb Kebabs Cooked in Butter (*Tagine Kebab Meghdor*)

In Marrakesh, where this dish is most frequently served, it is known as the "ABC of Moroccan cooking." The A stands for the grilled *kebabs*, the aspect of Moroccan cooking usually first observed by a tourist in the Djemaa el Fna. The B is for the *tagine slaoui*, in which the seared lamb *kebabs* are next cooked. And the C is for the sauce, which, the tourist finally learns, is the whole point of Moroccan food. Therefore, if you eat *tagine kebab meghdor*, you will eat a dish that encompasses these ABCs, and you will then comprehend what Moroccan cooking is all about. (This not only tells you about *kebab meghdor*, but also gives you a taste of the Moroccan sense of humor.)

The Moroccans first grill the *kebabs* over charcoal before adding them to the *tagine*, but you can grill them on aluminum foil under the broiler, so long as the broiler is sufficiently well heated for the meat to sear fast. Though it is not obligatory, I like the traditional way of serving this dish, with eggs poached in the sauce with the meat in the final minutes of cooking. Americans sometimes have difficulty extracting the eggs neatly from a central serving dish–*tagine* pot, so if you like you can finish off *tagine kebab meghdor* in individual au gratin dishes, adding an egg to each, covering, then poaching the eggs in a preheated oven. Or you can serve them as I do, to be devoured communally from the same dish.

INGREDIENTS	EQUIPMENT
1½ pounds boned leg of lamb, trimmed of fat and cut into 1-inch pieces	Mixing bowl Aluminum foil or skewers

1 cup grated onion
Salt and freshly ground black pepper to taste
3 cloves garlic, peeled and crushed
¼ cup sweet butter
¼ cup mixed chopped herbs (fresh parsley and green coriander)
1 teaspoon ground cumin
1 rounded teaspoon sweet paprika
1 small cayenne pepper or ¼ teaspoon (or less) ground cayenne
1 cinnamon stick
Juice of 1 lemon
4 to 6 eggs

3½-quart casserole
Large ovenproof skillet, *tagine slaoui,* or electric skillet, with cover, or 4 to 6 au gratin dishes

Working time: 15 minutes
Ripening time: 1 hour (minimum)
Cooking time: 45 minutes
Serves: 4 to 6

1. Toss the lamb with half the grated onion, salt, pepper, and the crushed garlic. Let "ripen" at least 1 hour.

2. Turn the oven broiler on to the highest heat; arrange the lamb on aluminum foil, and when the broiler is very hot sear quickly on both sides. Or thread on skewers and grill over charcoal. Remove the lamb when seared (it need not be fully cooked).

3. Melt the butter in the casserole. Add the meat, the remaining onion, the herbs, and spices. Cook briefly, then add enough water to almost cover the meat. Bring to a boil, reduce the heat, and simmer, partially covered, 45 minutes, stirring from time to time and adding water if necessary to maintain about 1 cup sauce.

4. Transfer the meat and sauce to the ovenproof serving dish and sprinkle with the lemon juice. Break in the eggs carefully, cover the dish, and poach until the eggs are set, either in a hot oven or on top of the stove. (If using au gratin dishes to poach the eggs, divide the *tagine* into equal portions, drop one egg into each dish, cover each dish with foil, and bake 10 minutes in a preheated 375° oven.) Serve at once, with plenty of Arab bread or Moroccan Bread (page 51) for mopping up the sauce.

Tangia

On a recent trip I asked the Ministry of Tourism to find a woman who could teach me to prepare the great specialty of Marrakesh—*tangia*. When I arrived the tourist office was in a state of pandemonium. The local director was frantically telephoning all over town calling all the women he knew, sometimes using two phones at once. He was chain-smoking cigarettes, thrashing in his chair, buzzing his secretaries and giving embarrassed glances, because, as he finally explained, though everybody was quick to agree that *tangia* was *the* great Marrakesh dish, nobody was prepared to teach me how to make it.

Then, finally success! The director learned from one of his informants that *tangia* is a dish made by *men*—a dish of soldiers, sheepherders and others separated from women. He pushed a button on his desk. His chauffeur appeared at the door.

"Do you know how to make *tangia?*"

"Of course I do, sir," said the chauffeur.

"Then take this American woman and teach her how to make it!"

I was dumfounded, but I was also desperate and grateful. I had come a long way to learn to make *tangia*, had only a day for the task, and the hour was late.

The driver, Ahmed Labkar, was eager but stunned by the request. We drove first to a gate to the *medina* so he could retrieve his precious *tangia* pot from his house. As soon as I saw it my confidence was restored. It was shaped like a Grecian urn with a wide belly, narrow neck, and handles on both sides, and it bore the patina of heavy use. Ahmed handled it with great care—a well-seasoned *tangia* pot, he told me, was one of the keys to the success of good *tangia*—and he further informed me that the best pots for this Marrakesh specialty were to be bought in Rabat!

It was dark by the time we reached the Djemaa el Fna, parked the car and entered the *souks* to buy materials for the dish: 4½ pounds shoulder of lamb, a small amount of saffron threads and ground cumin, a head of garlic (he later used 8 cloves), a preserved lemon, a bottle of oil, salt and pepper.

Our next stop was the kitchen of the *maison d'accueil* directly beneath the Koutoubia Mosque, where Ahmed completed the entire preparation of the dish in less than 10 minutes. Aside from crushing the garlic and rinsing the lemon, his only chore was to stuff the ingredients into the pot and then cover the opening with parchment paper, tie it down with a string, and punch four holes in it with a pencil.

"*Voilà, Madame!* It is now ready to cook."

We next drove to a *hammam*—a bath house—walked around to the back and entered the furnace room area, or *femachie*. Here a number of old men were lying around on piles of broken nut shells, smoking pipes and tending the furnace that heated the stones in the baths. In exchange for one dirham (about 22 cents) our *tangia* pot was buried in hot ashes. Here it would cook, Ahmed explained, for a minimum of 16 hours. As we parted for the evening, his final words were: "I'm sorry we didn't make it with camel meat—it makes a better *tangia*."

The next morning I received word that the Khalifa of Marrakesh was waiting for me in the hotel lobby. Somehow during the night word of my mission had reached him.

Yes, he confirmed, indeed, *tangia* could only be made by a man, and it was also a dish that *must* be eaten out of doors. He had come to offer me the use of a pavilion in the Menara gardens for the midday tasting.

Around noon Ahmed and I fetched the *tangia* pot from the *femachie*, took it to the gardens and ate it upon an old Moroccan carpet that had been sent over for our use.

How did it taste? Very good, very good indeed.

LAMB BRAISED, BROWNED, OR STEAMED

◆

The trick in these dishes is to cook the lamb *beyond* the point of stringiness to the stage where the meat is butter-tender and very moist.

Lamb Braised and Browned (*El Lahm Mahammer*)

In this classic dish the lamb is first braised in a spicy sauce and then browned in butter in a skillet; when complete the dish should be a reddish color (from the paprika) and so tender the meat falls easily off its bones. I have found that the browning part is difficult to do when dealing with a large cut such as a shoulder or a leg; instead of frying I put the meat, just before serving, in a hot oven, from which it emerges crusty brown and delicious.

El lahm mahammer is traditionally served either with fried almonds or fried potatoes. I serve it with almonds if it is to be followed by a *couscous* with lots of vegetables; otherwise I offer potatoes.

INGREDIENTS

4 pounds shoulder or rack of lamb, cut into 4 parts
2 cloves garlic, peeled
Pinch pulverized saffron
¼ teaspoon turmeric
½ teaspoon ground ginger
1½ teaspoons paprika
1 teaspoon ground cumin
⅛ to ¼ teaspoon cayenne (optional)
2 tablespoons sweet butter
¼ cup grated onion
Salt to taste
5 sprigs green coriander, tied together with a thread
½ cup whole, blanched almonds
Vegetable oil for frying

EQUIPMENT

Paring knife
Small mixing bowl
5½-quart casserole with cover
Large spoon
Shallow ovenproof serving dish
Skillet
Paper towels
Chopping knife (optional)

Working time: 40 minutes
Cooking time: 3 hours (approximately)
Serves: 6 (as part of a Moroccan dinner)

1. Early in the day, trim the lamb of extraneous fat. Mash the garlic cloves with the spices and blend with the butter to make a paste. Rub well into the pieces of lamb and let stand 10 minutes or longer.

2. Place the meat in the casserole with onion, 2 cups water, and salt. Bring to a boil, reduce the heat, and simmer, covered, for 1 hour, turning and basting the lamb. Add the green coriander sprigs. Continue cooking the lamb, adding water if necessary, until the meat is very tender and almost falling off the bone. Cool, skim, and discard the fat (or save it to fry potatoes).

3. Thirty minutes before serving: preheat the oven to 450°. Transfer the lamb to the ovenproof serving dish. By boiling rapidly, uncovered, reduce the sauce to a thick gravy in the casserole. Spoon the gravy over lamb and brown in the oven.

4. Meanwhile, sauté the almonds in the oil until golden brown. Drain on paper towels and chop coarsely or leave whole. Sprinkle over the meat just before serving.

VARIATION:

Braised and Browned Leg of Lamb (*Risla Mahammer*)

Substitute a half leg of lamb for the shoulder or rack of lamb in the preceding recipe. Follow the directions exactly as given, or, if you wish to be traditional, in step 3 fry the meat in the fat skimmed in step 2—although leg of lamb tends to be a bit dry when prepared this way.

VARIATION:

Forequarter of Lamb Braised and Browned (*Delah Mahammer*)

In this variation of *el lahm mahammer*, substitute a 10-pound forequarter of lamb for the shoulder or rack.

Note: One rarely finds a pot large enough to do this in an American home. However in Morocco, where in a traditional household a huge number of relatives and servants must be fed, there will often be several pots sufficient to hold such an enormous piece of meat. When I helped make this dish in such a house it was cooked on a charcoal brazier, thank God, because otherwise it would have been very difficult to turn it over. As it was, it took three of us to brown it in an enormous pot: two to turn the meat and one to steady the one-foot-high brazier.

Steamed Lamb (*Baha*)

If you really love the taste of lamb you will love this dish. It's a pity that we Americans know so little about steaming meats; just as steamed vegetables keep their original flavors, so do steamed chickens and lamb.

If you don't have a steamer, use a *couscousiere* or a colander with a tight-fitting lid that fits snugly over a kettle.

Some people think that steamed lamb looks unattractive (though no one denies that it is incredibly good). If you feel this way you may brown the meat quickly in butter or oil at the end, or roast it at high heat until it browns.

Steamed food should be eaten the moment it is ready, when it is at its peak: if left too long, it will dry out.

INGREDIENTS	EQUIPMENT
5 to 5½ pounds shoulder and part of the rib section of young spring lamb	Paring knife
Pinch pulverized saffron	Steamer, or *couscousiere*, or colander over a kettle
Sweet butter, softened	Cheesecloth
1½ teaspoons coarse salt	Tight-fitting lid
½ teaspoon freshly ground black pepper	
1 bunch fresh parsley sprigs	*Working time:* 5 minutes
4 to 5 whole baby onions (optional)	*Steaming time:* 2 hours
Vegetable oil (optional)	*Serves:* 8 (as part of a Moroccan dinner)

1. Trim the lamb of excess fat: the thin fell can be left on. Blend the saffron with ¼ cup butter, salt, and pepper. Rub into the lamb flesh.

2. Bring plenty of water to a boil in the bottom of a steamer, kettle, or *couscousiere* (to borrow a trick from Diana Kennedy, author of *The Cuisines of Mexico*,* toss in a penny—when the penny stops clicking you need more water). Dampen a piece of cheesecloth and twist into a strip the length of the circumference of the kettle's rim. Use this strip to fasten the perforated top so that it fits snugly on top. Check all sides for effective sealing: steam should rise only through the holes. Make a bed of parsley over the holes and rest the shoulder of lamb on it. Surround with the onions, if used, and cover with a double layer of cheesecloth and then, tightly, with a lid. *Do not lift the lid during the first 1¾ hours* of steaming. Be very careful, and stand back when lifting the lid. If the lamb is tender and falling off the bone it is ready; if not, continue steaming 15 to 30 minutes longer.

3. If desired, brown in oil and butter or rub again with butter and brown in a very hot oven (highest setting). Serve with bowls of ground cumin and salt, to be used as a dip.

* New York: Harper & Row, 1972.

Lamb with Almonds and Hard-Boiled Eggs, Fez Style (*Tafaya*)

This dish, which is served throughout Morocco at weddings, circumcisions, and other important occasions, is made particularly well in Fez. It dates from the time of the Andaluz, when much cooking was done with oil.

Another way to prepare *tafaya* is to let all the liquid in the casserole evaporate, then add some oil, allow the meat to fry for a short time, add more water, let it evaporate again, and then fry again. If you do this the meat will be very crusty and brown and the only sauce will be oil. Not so with the following recipe which is updated and very good.

INGREDIENTS

3 pounds lamb shoulder, cut into 1½-inch chunks
Pinch of pulverized saffron
1 rounded teaspoon ground ginger
½ teaspoon freshly ground black pepper
Salt
3 cloves garlic, peeled and cut up
¼ teaspoon turmeric
8 sprigs green coriander, tied together
4 two-inch cinnamon sticks
¾ cup grated onion
¼ cup sweet butter or salad oil
¾ pound whole, blanched almonds
7 hard-boiled eggs

EQUIPMENT

4½-quart casserole with cover

Working time: 15 minutes
Cooking time: 2 hours
Serves: 4 to 6 (as part of a Moroccan dinner)

1. Place all the ingredients except the hard-boiled eggs in the casserole, cover with 3 cups water, and bring to a boil. Reduce the heat and simmer, covered, 2 hours, or until the meat is very tender and the sauce has reduced to 1½ cups. (You may need to add water during the cooking.)

2. Decorate with halved hard-boiled eggs just before serving.

Note: The almonds can be fried separately and sprinkled over the dish just before serving. Also, in some parts of the country the eggs are rolled first in saffron water (page 21) to color them bright yellow.

KEFTA

—◆—

Kefta is meat (lamb or beef) finely ground and liberally spiced. In traditional Moroccan homes I've seen it chopped by hand with a heavy steel knife and then kneaded with spices into a smooth paste. The Moroccans knead their ground meat with great effort so their meatballs will be smooth.

When I first lived in Morocco I bought ready-mixed *kefta* from my butcher. After a while I decided he used too much paprika, so I began to make my own. In America I buy ground or half-ground beef chuck and shoulder lamb chops, which I cube and then run through a meat grinder. Then I add herbs, spices, and grated onion in various proportions and combinations, depending on the dish, and sometimes a little *ras el hanout* when I want a particularly exotic flavor. The fact is that most Moroccan cooks make a variant of this recipe for *kefta,* learned from their mothers or typical of their hometowns; there is no wrong formula except a *kefta* that doesn't taste good.

Kefta is best when it is freshly ground, and when the meat contains enough fat so that it comes out moist. Anything less than one part fat to ten parts of meat is too lean. After being spiced *kefta* should be left to "ripen" for at least an hour.

Claudia Roden, in her excellent *Book of Middle Eastern Food,** tells of a way to knead the meat in an electric blender. She starts off with the onion, then adds the spices and herbs, and when that is all pureed she slowly adds the meat until she obtains a finely blended paste.

There are many things you can do with *kefta.* The easiest and most classic is to place the meat onto skewers in sausage shapes and then grill the

* New York: Alfred A. Knopf, 1972.

brochettes over charcoal or under a broiler. They make a marvelous first course when eaten with Moroccan bread, which your guests should use to slip the meat off the skewers. If you are driving around Morocco, you will see stands offering *kefta* grilled this way; don't hesitate to stop if you feel like a snack.

One of the most delicious *kefta* dishes, and one that will very cheaply serve an entire family well, is *kefta mkaouara* (Meatball, Tomato, and Egg Tagine, page 250), a stew of *kefta* balls served in a rich cinnamon-flavored tomato sauce, in which eggs, in the final few minutes before serving, are poached. The meat, the eggs, and the sauce should be served together in the shallow pot in which they were cooked, accompanied by real Moroccan bread. If you like, you can do this dish in an electric frying pan set on the table. *Tagine kefta emshmel* (Meatball Tagine with Spices and Lemon, page 251) and *kefta meghdor* are delicious variations on lamb dishes in which meatballs have been substituted for cubes of meat. *Kefta ma'ammra* (Stuffed Vegetable Tagine, page 252) is a marvelous *tagine* of tomatoes and zucchini stuffed with *kefta* and glazed over at the end with herbed eggs.

There are numerous other *kefta* dishes, including the Berber *bisteeya* called *tarkhdoult*, in which minced meat is substituted for chicken, and *kefta*-stuffed *braewats*, similar to the Turkish *burek* but garnished at the end with a sprinkling of cinnamon and sugar.

Kefta on Skewers

I've been making *kefta* this way for fourteen years, ever since I first read Z. Guinaudeau's *Fes vu par sa cuisine*. After trying numerous other formulae I've returned to this one, convinced it is the best. Actually I've slightly altered Mme. Guinaudeau's proportions to my own taste, and when *ras el hanout* is not available I've made a mini version of this exotic spice mixture out of pinches of ground allspice, cinnamon, ginger, nutmeg, ground cardamom, pepper, and cloves.

This is not a typical *kefta* recipe. If you buy *kefta* meat in the *souks*, raw or cooked on skewers, it is more likely to contain cumin, paprika, grated onion, salt, pepper, parsley, cayenne, and sometimes some minced green coriander.

INGREDIENTS

1½ pounds ground beef or lamb, or a mixture of
    the two, 10 percent of it fat
1 small onion, grated
⅓ cup finely chopped parsley, mixed with some
    chopped green coriander
2 large pinches dried mint or 4 pinches freshly
    chopped mint
1 large pinch dried marjoram or 2 pinches
    fresh marjoram
    Salt and freshly ground black pepper
½ teaspoon ground cumin
½ teaspoon *ras el hanout* (page 26, or see
    above) (optional)

EQUIPMENT

Mixing bowl
12 skewers

Working time: 10 minutes
Broiling or grilling time: 5
   to 10 minutes
Serves: 6

1. Combine all the ingredients and knead well. Let ripen at least 1 hour.

2. With wet hands, separate the meat mixture into 24 sausage shapes, packing them around the skewers, two on each one.

3. Grill rapidly on both sides, 2 to 3 inches from a broiler flame or over charcoal, until done to taste. (Moroccans prefer them well cooked.) Serve, hot, at once, with Arab bread such as *pita* or Moroccan Bread (page 51).

Meatball, Tomato, and Egg Tagine (*Kefta Mkaouara*)

One of the delights of Moroccan home cooking, a marvelous dish to serve with Moroccan Bread (page 51) or warmed-up *pita*.

INGREDIENTS

For the kefta:

- 1 pound finely ground lamb or beef
- 2 tablespoons chopped parsley
- 1 tablespoon chopped green coriander
- ½ teaspoon ground cumin
- 1 small onion, grated
- 1 to 2 good pinches cayenne
- Salt
- 2 tablespoons vegetable oil

For the sauce:

- 2 medium onions, chopped
- 1 small bunch parsley, chopped
- 2 pounds tomatoes, peeled, seeded, and chopped (see page 71) or 2-pound can imported tomatoes, drained and seeded
- 1 teaspoon ground cumin
- 1 teaspoon freshly ground black pepper
- 2 cloves garlic, peeled and chopped
- ½ teaspoon ground cinnamon
- ¼ teaspoon cayenne pepper
- 6 eggs

EQUIPMENT

Mixing bowl
Shallow heatproof serving dish or electric frying pan, with cover

Working time: 25 minutes
Cooking time: 45 minutes
Serves: 5 to 6 (as part of a Moroccan dinner)

1. Combine all the ingredients for the *kefta* except the oil. Form into 1-inch balls with wet hands and brown in the oil on all sides. Remove from pan and set aside, covered.

2. Add the remaining ingredients, except for the eggs, to the pan. Cook, uncovered, 30 minutes, or until the sauce has reduced to a thick gravy.

3. Return the *kefta* to the sauce and continue cooking together 10 minutes. Carefully break the eggs into the sauce and poach them until set. Serve at once, directly from the pan.

Meatball Tagine with Spices and Lemon (*Tagine Kefta Emshmel*)

INGREDIENTS

For the kefta:

- 1 pound ground lamb or beef
- 1 teaspoon salt
- ¼ teaspoon freshly ground black pepper
- 2 tablespoons grated onion, drained
- 1 tablespoon chopped parsley
  Cumin to taste
- 2 teaspoons sweet paprika

For the sauce:

- 3 tablespoons sweet butter
- ½ cup grated onion
- ¾ teaspoon ground ginger
- ¼ teaspoon freshly ground black pepper
- ¼ teaspoon pulverized saffron, mixed with some turmeric
  Cayenne to taste (see note)
  Salt to taste
- ¼ teaspoon ground cumin
- 1 teaspoon sweet paprika
- ½ cup chopped green coriander or parsley
  Juice of 1 lemon, or to taste

EQUIPMENT

Mixing bowl
Meat grinder
Large skillet with cover
Warm serving platter

Working time: 15 minutes
Cooking time: 30 minutes
Serves: 4–5

1. Mix all the ingredients for the *kefta* and run twice through a meat grinder. Knead well to a smooth paste, then shape into 1-inch meatballs.

2. Put all the ingredients for the sauce in the skillet except the lemon juice. Add 1½ cups water and bring to a boil. Reduce the heat, cover, and simmer 15 minutes. Add the *kefta* and poach in the sauce for 30 minutes. Add the lemon juice and serve at once, on a heated platter, with plenty of Moroccan Bread (page 51) for mopping up the thick sauce.

Note: In some Moroccan homes where fiery dishes are appreciated a whole dried red pepper is added to the sauce.

VARIATION:

Kefta Cooked in Butter (*Tagine Kefta Kebab*)

Prepare the *kefta* meat as described above. Brown in a skillet or under the broiler, then substitute for the lamb pieces in recipe for *tagine kebab meghdor* (Seared Lamb Kebabs Cooked in Butter, page 238). Serve with or without eggs poached in the sauce.

Stuffed Vegetable Tagine (*Kefta Ma'ammra*)

Stuffed vegetables are not often found in Morocco, though they are very popular in neighboring Algeria, where Ottoman cooking exerted a greater influence. However, in the cities of Tetuán and Rabat I have come across two *tagines* of stuffed vegetables that are quite unique. The Tetuanese one was served in a beautifully arranged *tagine slaoui* filled with four large, juicy stuffed tomatoes surrounded, around the rim, by zucchini shells, also stuffed. The whole was glazed with herbed eggs, and it was very good. In Rabat the dish was more robust in flavor, and looked more like an artist's palette. It consisted of hollowed-out carrots, potatoes, green peppers, Spanish onions, tomatoes, and zucchini, all stuffed with ground meat covered by a tomato sauce highly seasoned with paprika, cumin, and lemon juice. The Tetuán dish is presented here:

INGREDIENTS

5 or 6 medium zucchini (about 2 pounds)
4 or 5 large red, ripe tomatoes
    Salt
  ¾ pound ground beef or lamb
  ½ teaspoon freshly ground black pepper
  ½ teaspoon ground ginger
  1 two-inch cinnamon stick
  3 cloves garlic, peeled and crushed
  ¼ cup mixed chopped herbs (parsley and green coriander)
  ½ teaspoon dried mint
  ¼ cup raw rice
  1 cup grated onion
  ¼ cup sweet butter
2 to 3 tablespoons lemon juice
    Additional freshly ground black pepper
  2 tablespoons salad oil
  3 large eggs, well beaten

EQUIPMENT

Paring knife
Vegetable corer
Colander
3-quart saucepan
2-quart shallow ovenproof serving dish
Aluminum foil

Working time: 30 minutes
Cooking and baking time: 1½ hours
Serves: 4 to 6

1. Wash, top, and tail the zucchini and cut into 2-inch lengths. (If you wish to stuff the zucchini whole, soften by salting for 30 minutes and rinsing well before removing the cores.) Peel and cut off a thin slice from the top of 4 of the tomatoes. Scoop out the cores of both vegetables (the pulp can be frozen to be used for soups) and hollow the zucchini to ¼ inch of the skin. Sprinkle both with salt and let drain 30 minutes.

2. Meanwhile, prepare the stuffing. Place the meat, spices, garlic, three-quarters of the herbs, the rice, onion, butter, and 1½ cups water in the saucepan. Bring to a boil, reduce the heat, and simmer, uncovered, 25 minutes, or until the rice is fully cooked and the mixture is thick but still juicy. Stir in the lemon juice and more salt and pepper to taste. Remove the

cinnamon stick and let cool. *Up to this point, the dish can be prepared in advance.*

3. Preheat the oven to 350°.

4. Rinse, drain, and stuff the tomatoes and zucchini loosely. Oil the baking dish with the 2 tablespoons oil and arrange the vegetables attractively. Pile the remaining stuffing over the tomatoes, then cover the stuffing and tomatoes with the tomato tops and the remaining tomato, sliced. Sprinkle with salt and pepper. Cover with aluminum foil, pierced with 2 holes, and bake 30 minutes.

5. Remove the cover and transfer the dish to the upper shelf in the oven. Raise the oven heat to 400° and continue baking 20 minutes.

6. Meanwhile, beat the eggs with remaining herbs, salt and pepper to taste. Pour the egg mixture over the stuffed vegetables and return to the upper shelf in the oven to bake 10 minutes, or until the eggs are firm. Serve hot.

FRAGRANT MEAT TAGINES

◆

These *tagines* of meat and vegetables with preserved lemons and olives are marvelous fragrant dishes, particularly if the vegetables are absolutely fresh and not ripened in crates. If you live near an organic food store I recommend you buy the vegetables there (on their delivery day!)—it can make all the difference.

Though these dishes are extremely good, Moroccans do not normally serve them when they entertain. However. I have found that in Morocco, as in France and Italy, everyday family dishes are sometimes better than the more grandiose fare served to company.

The first recipe, for lamb with carrots and celery, should be treated as a master recipe from which the *tagines* of lamb with fennel bulbs, *fresh* artichokes, cardoons (thistles), fava beans, and baby peas can be made with slight indicated variations. I have also included recipes for lamb *tagines* with three ingredients virtually unknown in the United States, but which hopefully will someday be imported or cultivated. These are wild cardoons whose taste is similar to artichoke hearts; wild artichokes, called *coques*; and Moroccan white truffles (*terfas*), which can be bought canned in America and which are used in a Jewish variation.

Lamb Tagine with Carrots and Celery
(*Tagine Makalli Bil Karfas Bil Kreezoe*)

This fresh-looking *tagine* is best made with tender celery hearts and fresh sweet carrots. However, winter carrots sliced small and stringy celery well scraped will do nicely.

INGREDIENTS

2½ to 3   pounds lamb shoulder, cut into 1½-inch chunks

2   cloves garlic, peeled and crushed
Salt to taste

½   teaspoon freshly ground black pepper

¾   teaspoon ground ginger
Pinch of pulverized saffron

¼   teaspoon turmeric

¼   cup vegetable oil, or less

2   tablespoons freshly chopped green coriander (optional)

½   cup grated onion

2   bunches celery hearts (about 1 pound)

1   pound carrots

1½ to 2   preserved lemons (see page 30), rinsed

½   cup "red" olives, such as Kalamatas or Gaetas (see page 34 for notes on substitutions for Moroccan olives)

¼   cup lemon juice

EQUIPMENT

Paring knife

5½-quart enameled cast-iron or stainless steel casserole with cover

Vegetable peeler

Olive pitter (optional)

Shallow serving dish

Working time: 45 minutes
Cooking time: 2 hours
Serves: 6 (as part of a Moroccan dinner)

1. Trim excess fat from the lamb. In the casserole toss the lamb chunks with the garlic, salt, spices, oil, herbs, and onion. Cover with 1 cup water and bring to a boil. Reduce the heat, cover, and simmer over moderate heat for 1½ hours, turning the pieces of meat often in the sauce and adding water whenever necessary.

2. Separate the celery ribs, cut away the leaves, and wash well. With a sharp knife or vegetable peeler scrape off the strings from the back of each rib. Cut lengthwise down the middle (if uncommonly large), and then crosswise into 2-inch pieces. Set the celery pieces aside.

3. Scrape the carrots and cut into strips the same size as the celery.

4. When the meat is almost tender, add the vegetables and more water, if necessary. Cover and continue cooking until the lamb and vegetables are done. The meat must be butter-soft, nearly falling off the bones.

5. Meanwhile, quarter the preserved lemons and discard the pulp, if desired. (I don't.) Rinse and pit the olives. Add both to the casserole for the last 10 minutes of cooking. Stir in the lemon juice.

6. Place the lamb in the center of the serving dish. Arrange the celery and carrots around the edges of the dish and decorate with lemon quarters and olives. By boiling rapidly, uncovered, reduce the sauce in the pan to a thick gravy, taste for salt, and pour over the lamb and vegetables. Serve at once.

VARIATION:

Lamb Tagine with Fennel (*Tagine el Lahm Besbas*)

In Morocco, wild fennel is sometimes used for this dish; it has a slightly bitter stalk that is removed—it is the inner core that is used. However, they also use sweet fennel bulbs and achieve delicious results.

INGREDIENTS

Same as the preceding recipe, but halve the amounts of garlic, preserved lemon, and lemon juice, and substitute 4 fennel bulbs for the carrots and celery

EQUIPMENT

Same as the preceding recipe

Working time: 30 minutes
Cooking time: 1¾ to 2 hours
Serves: 4 to 6

1. Follow step 1 on opposite page.

2. Quarter the fennel bulbs lengthwise, scrape off the strings, and cut into 2-inch lengths. Split unusually wide strips in half. Add to the casserole after the lamb has cooked 1½ hours. Cover and cook 20 minutes, or until tender.

3. Follow steps 5 and 6 on opposite page.

VARIATION:

Lamb Tagine with Artichokes, Lemon, and Olives

The small artichokes found in Italian markets in the spring are especially good in this *tagine*. Note that canned artichoke bottoms and frozen artichoke hearts will *not* produce a good dish.

INGREDIENTS

Same as for *tagine makalli bil karfas bil kreezoe* (Lamb Tagine with Carrots and Celery, page 255), but halve the amounts of black pepper, preserved lemons, lemon juice, and onions; double the ginger and turmeric; substitute 8 to 10 small artichokes (about 2½ pounds) for the celery and carrots; and leave out the green coriander

EQUIPMENT

Same as for *tagine makalli bil karfas bil kreezoe*

Working time: 30 minutes
Cooking time: 2 hours
Serves: 4 to 6

1. Follow step 1 on page 256.

2. Prepare the artichokes by removing the outside leaves and trimming the bases. Halve each one and remove the hairy choke. Place in acidulated water (water with 2 tablespoonfuls of vinegar added) to keep from blackening while trimming the rest. Rinse and drain before using.

3. Place the artichokes over the pieces of meat after the meat has cooked 1½ hours. Place the rinsed preserved lemon, cut in quarters, on top. Cover tightly and cook 30 minutes. Sprinkle with the lemon juice and olives and cook a few minutes all together.

4. Place the lamb in center of the serving dish. Arrange the artichokes, flat side up, facing in one direction around the rim. By boiling rapidly, uncovered, reduce the sauce to a thick gravy. Readjust the seasoning of the sauce. Swirl the pan once to combine and pour over the meat. Decorate with preserved lemons and olives and serve at once.

Note: An alternative sauce includes a peeled and seeded tomato cooked with the sauce.

Lamb Tagine with Cardoons

Cardoons are domesticated thistles found in the spring (try Italian grocery stores), which have a taste similar to artichokes and an appearance similar to celery when all the stalks are tied together in a bundle. They make marvelous eating and should definitely be searched out and tried. They are not difficult to grow if you have a vegetable garden.

INGREDIENTS

Same as for *tagine makalli bil karfas bil kreezoe* (Lamb Tagine with Carrots and Celery, page 255), but double the amount of lemon juice (cardoons need a great deal of lemon juice); substitute 3 bundles of cardoons, or about 5 cups cleaned stalks, cut into pieces, for the carrots and celery; add ½ cup chopped parsley, and omit the green coriander

EQUIPMENT

Same as for *tagine makalli bil karfas bil kreezoe*

Working time: 40 minutes
Cooking time: 2 hours
Serves: 6

1. Remove the outer stalks and tough parts from the cardoons, separating the stalks, and cutting away the leaves. Wash the inner stem and bleached

inner stalks well. With a paring knife, remove the strings and cut the stalks into 3-inch lengths. Keep the cardoons in acidulated water (vinegar or lemon juice) to avoid blackening them.

2. Follow step 1 on page 256. After the lamb has cooked 1 hour, add the rinsed and drained cardoons, with enough fresh water to cover them in the casserole. (For the first 15 to 20 minutes of cooking, the cardoons must be covered by liquid.) Continue cooking 40 minutes.

3. Follow step 5 on page 256, adding the lemon juice by tablespoons after the first ¼ cup and tasting. Simmer gently, uncovered, to allow the sauce to reduce and flavors to blend.

4. Place the lamb in the shallow serving dish and cover completely with the cardoons. Decorate with the lemon peel and olives. Reduce the sauce, if necessary, over high heat to 1½ cups, and taste again for seasoning—add more lemon juice, if desired. Pour the sauce over and serve at once, or keep warm in a 250° oven until ready to serve.

VARIATION:

Lamb Tagine with Baby Peas

INGREDIENTS

Same as for *tagine makalli bil karfas bil kreezoe* (Lamb Tagine with Carrots and Celery, page 255), but substitute 3 cups shelled peas for the celery and carrots, and omit the lemon juice

EQUIPMENT

Same as for *tagine makalli bil karfas bil kreezoe*

Working time: 20 minutes
Cooking time: 2 hours
Serves: 4 to 6

1. Follow step 1 on page 256, but do not add the coriander at this time.
2. When the meat is almost tender, add the chopped green coriander, shelled peas, and preserved lemon. Cover and cook gently 10 minutes. Serve at once.

Lamb Tagine with Fava Beans

It's a pity fresh fava beans aren't as popular in America as they are in Europe, for they are sweeter and more delicious than many other members of the bean family. During the spring you can find favas in Italian markets.

INGREDIENTS

Same as for *tagine makalli bil karfas bil kreezoe* (Lamb Tagine with Carrots and Celery, page 255), but halve the amounts of the preserved lemons and lemon juice, and substitute 3 to 4 pounds fava beans for the celery and carrots

EQUIPMENT

Same as for *tagine makalli bil karfas bil kreezoe*

Working time: 30 minutes
Cooking time: 2 hours
Serves: 6

1. Follow step 1 on page 256.
2. Shuck the beans. Thirty minutes before serving, add the favas to the casserole with the rinsed preserved lemon. Cover and cook until the meat and the beans are both tender. By boiling rapidly, uncovered, reduce sauce to a thick gravy. After adding 3 or 4 tablespoons lemon juice, taste carefully before adding more.
3. Arrange meat in the center of the serving dish and pour the favas over. Decorate with the preserved lemon and olives. Give a good swirl to the sauce in the pan and pour over. Serve hot.

Lamb Tagine with Wild Cardoons

This is a Tangier specialty. The wild cardoons are gathered by women just outside the city, and sold just outside the cemetery wall leading up from the *socco grande*. Barefoot and garbed in red and white striped cloth and big straw hats with decorative pompons on top, the women are delightful to look at but difficult to bargain with, for they know the value of these bittersweet plants in the kitchen.

One March in New York I found some young and tender wild cardoons (they look like young rhubarb) in an Italian grocery store, but the following year there were none. I asked the owner where I could find some, and he made an interesting, if improbable, suggestion. "Your best bet," he told me, "is to find an old Italian immigrant living in the countryside in New Jersey. If he knows where to find wild cardoons he will sell some to you, but he will never tell you where they are for fear that you will gather them yourself and in the process ruin the root crown so they will never grow there again."

The lesson, I gather, is that if you do find some of these wonderful plants growing wild in nature, as they do in most regions of the United States, you must cut them off carefully at ground level. Gather them only in the early spring.

INGREDIENTS

Same as for *tagine makalli bil karfas bil kreezoe* (Lamb Tagine with Carrots and Celery, page 255), but use half the amount of garlic, and substitute 7 or 8 wild cardoons for the celery and carrots

EQUIPMENT

Same as for *tagine makalli bil karfas bil kreezoe*

Working time: 45 minutes
Cooking time: 2 hours
Serves: 6

Prepare the same as Lamb Tagine with Cardoons (page 258). The cleaning will take a little longer, since there are many prickles to scrape off.

Lamb Tagine with White Truffles

Before you get too excited about the utter decadence and luxury of serving a stew in which the meat is smothered in white truffles, you should know that Moroccan white truffles lack the brilliance of Italian ones, and are not a fraction as expensive. You can buy them in large cans from the Sahadi Importing Company in Brooklyn. (See list of purveyors in the Appendix.) This dish is a typical Moroccan Jewish specialty.

INGREDIENTS

Same as for *tagine makalli bil karfas bil kreezoe* (Lamb Tagine with Carrots and Celery, page 255), but halve the amounts of preserved lemon, lemon juice, and onions; substitute 3 pounds white truffles (Aicha brand) for the carrots and celery; and omit the olives and garlic.

EQUIPMENT

Same as for *tagine makalli bil karfas bil kreezoe*

Working time: 15 minutes
Cooking time: 2 hours
Serves: 6

1. Follow step 1 on page 256.
2. Drain the canned truffles, rinse under running water, and drain again.
3. Follow steps 5 and 6 on page 256, omitting the olives and adding the truffles 5 minutes before serving.

Lamb Tagine with Wild Artichokes

In Morocco this is one of the most popular of the fragrant meat *tagines*; however, as far as I can tell, wild artichokes (*coques**) simply do not exist in the United States. These are the same vegetables used to "turn" milk for *raipe* (see page 40). Possibly it's a blessing since *coques* are very difficult to clean and can ruin a pair of fingernails very fast. They are so well loved in Morocco that 6 pounds is considered usual for this dish.

* *Cynara humilis.*

Tagine of Lamb with Lemon and Olives (*Tagine el Lahm Emshmel*)

Strictly speaking, this excellent dish is not a "fragrant *tagine*," since the sauce is *emshmel* rather than *makalli*. However, it is a *tagine* with lemon and olives, and one of the great classic Moroccan specialties, spicy with a thick lemony sauce and a perfect blending of many flavors. The best olives for an *emshmel* are the green-ripe olives of Morocco, which are flavored with *cedrat*, a kind of thick-skinned and very fragrant lemon that grows throughout the Mediterranean region. However, you can use Greek Royal-Victorias or Kalamatas or Italian Gaetas or even California green-ripe olives marinated in a little lemon juice. (See page 192 for *djej emshmel*, the famous chicken with lemon and olives dish, a variant on the same recipe.)

INGREDIENTS

3 pounds lamb shoulder, cut into 1½-inch chunks
Pinch of pulverized saffron
¼ teaspoon turmeric
1 teaspoon ground ginger
1 teaspoon sharp paprika
½ teaspoon freshly ground black pepper
¼ teaspoon ground cumin
Salt to taste
¼ cup salad oil
½ cup grated onion
¼ cup finely chopped mixed fresh herbs (parsley and green coriander)
2 cups finely minced onion
1 cup green-ripe olives or "red-brown" olives (Greek Victoria—Royals or Kalamatas or Italian Gaetas)
2 preserved lemons (page 30), quartered and rinsed
Juice of 1 lemon

EQUIPMENT

Paring knife
5½-quart flameproof casserole with cover
Olive pitter (optional)
Deep serving dish

Working time: 30 minutes
Cooking time: 2 hours
Serves: 4 to 5

1. Trim the lamb of excess fat and discard. Soak the crushed saffron in a little hot water in the bottom of the casserole. Add the spices, salt, oil, and grated onion, then toss the pieces of lamb in the mixture. Sauté very gently to release spices' aromas and *lightly* sear the meat. Add 1 cup water and bring to a boil. Cover and cook over low heat 1 hour, adding water whenever necessary to avoid scorching the meat.

2. After 1 hour add the herbs and the 2 cups minced onion. Re-cover and simmer until the meat is very tender—that is, almost falling off the bones—and the sauce is thick. (An alternative way to prepare the dish to this point is to cover the meat with 2 cups water and all the herbs and onions and cook 2 hours altogether.)

3. While the lamb is cooking, rinse and pit the olives. Remove and discard the pulp from the preserved lemon, if desired, then rinse and set aside.

4. Add the lemon juice, olives, and lemon peel 10 minutes before serving. Transfer the meat to the deep serving dish and keep warm. By boiling rapidly, uncovered, reduce the sauce to about 1½ cups and taste for seasoning. Spoon the sauce over the lamb, decorate with the lemon peel and olives, and serve at once.

Note: An excellent addition is a tablespoon of tomato sauce.

ROBUST MEAT TAGINES

These robust, highly aromatic *tagines*, flavored with paprika and cumin, are sturdy dishes, nourishing and thick, filling in winter and satisfying to weary travelers and men who have done hard physical work or have just come off the ski slopes that are an hour from Marrakesh. Though they are not among the most elegant of dishes, these hearty stews are absolutely delicious.

Beef Tagine with Cauliflower

Beef *tagines* can be very good indeed. After hours of slow simmering the meat comes out buttery and soft, and the sauce is full of spicy flavor. The spicing in this dish follows the Marrakesh style, while the browning of the meat is Tetuanese.

2½ to 3 pounds beef stew meat, such as shoulder, chuck, or short ribs of beef (with some bone), cut into 1¼-inch chunks

¼ teaspoon turmeric

Salt

¼ teaspoon freshly ground black pepper

¼ cup salad oil

1½ teaspoons sharp paprika (see note)

¼ teaspoon ground ginger

1 teaspoon ground cumin

1 pinch cayenne pepper

1 onion, finely chopped

¼ cup mixed chopped herbs (parsley and green coriander)

2½ pounds cauliflowerets

Juice of 1 lemon

Paring knife

5½-quart flameproof casserole with tight-fitting cover

3½-quart saucepan

Shallow ovenproof serving dish

Aluminum foil

Working time: 20 minutes

Cooking time: 2 hours or more

Serves: 4 to 6

1. Remove and discard the excess fat from the beef. Place the beef in the casserole with the turmeric, salt, pepper, and oil. Fry, turning the meat often to lightly brown all sides. Cover the casserole tightly and cook 15 minutes, *without lifting the cover.* The meat will cook in its own juices, drawn out by the salt over low heat.

2. Stir in the remaining spices, chopped onion, herbs, and very little water. Simmer, covered, 1½ to 2 hours over gentle heat, until the meat is very tender (almost falling off the bones). Add water whenever necessary to keep the meat from scorching.

3. Meanwhile, in a separate saucepan, cook the cauliflower in salted water until nearly tender. Drain and set aside until needed.

4. Preheat the oven to 400°.

5. Transfer the beef and gravy to the serving dish. Place the drained cauliflower over the meat, cover with foil, and bake 15 minutes. Raise the oven heat to the highest setting, remove the covering, and transfer the dish to the

upper shelf in the oven. Bake until the cauliflower is lightly browned. Sprinkle with lemon juice and serve at once.

Note: In Marrakesh *felfla harra* (page 122) is used instead of the paprika.

This recipe and its variation may be prepared with lamb or veal shanks instead of beef.

VARIATION:

Beef Tagine with Sweet Potatoes

INGREDIENTS

Same as the preceding recipe, but decrease the amount of sharp paprika to ½ teaspoon and cumin to just a few *optional* pinches; increase the amount of onions to 1½ medium onions, finely chopped; substitute 2 ripe tomatoes and 1 pound sweet potatoes for the cauliflower; and omit the lemon

EQUIPMENT

Same as the preceding recipe
plus
Vegetable peeler

Working time: 30 minutes
Cooking time: 2 hours 40 minutes
Serves: 4 to 5

1. Follow steps 1 and 2 on page 266.
2. Peel the tomatoes, halve them crosswise and squeeze out the seeds, then cut into chunks. Peel the sweet potatoes and cut them into ½-inch-thick slices.
3. Preheat the oven to 350°. Transfer the meat and gravy to the serving dish. Place the sweet potatoes over the meat and the tomatoes on top of sweet potatoes. Cover with foil and bake 40 minutes, until the meat and potatoes are tender. Remove the foil cover, raise the oven heat to 450°, and transfer the dish to the upper shelf of the oven. Bake until there is a brown spotted crust over the tomatoes. (If there is a great deal of gravy in the pan, pour off into a small saucepan and reduce over high heat to 1 cup before returning it to the dish.) Taste for seasoning and serve at once.

Sefrina (*Beef Stew with Chick-Peas*)

A Jewish specialty of Essaouria, but made similarly in all Moroccan-Jewish communities, *sefrina* is almost the same as *adefina*, said to be the mother of the Spanish *olla podrida*, and first cousin to the European *cholent*.

The name and its cousins aside, the dish is left to cook at a low temperature for a whole night. The original idea was to prepare the dish on Friday, before sundown, and send it out to a community oven, where it would bake all night and be meltingly tender and delicious for Saturday lunch.

This recipe was given to me by a lady from Essaouria, who also had the following instructions, which I find overwhelming but authentic: "Sew a cheesecloth bag large enough to hold 3 cups cooked rice. Boil the raw rice, separately, for 10 minutes and drain. Then mix with oil, salt and pepper, and a little parsley. Spoon into the bag and tie up. Remove the cover, push aside the whole eggs, potatoes, beans, and meat and drop in the bag. When the rice is swollen and tender, remove and serve with the *sefrina*."

In Tangier a variation of this dish, called *orissa*, is made with white beans instead of chick-peas, sweet potatoes instead of regular potatoes, and small white onions browned in oil and honey instead of garlic. The whole is then flavored with cinnamon.

Eggs cooked for so long a time come out creamy and tan-colored. They really are very good.

INGREDIENTS

½ cup dried chick-peas, soaked overnight in plenty of water
4 pounds breast of beef, cut into 8 pieces, plus extra bones
4 potatoes, peeled but left whole
4 raw eggs in their shells, well washed
2 cloves garlic, peeled and roughly chopped
Salt to taste

EQUIPMENT

Water kettle
5½-quart casserole with cover

Working time: 15 minutes
Cooking time: 5 to 6 hours
Serves: 4

¼ teaspoon freshly ground black pepper

¼ teaspoon turmeric or pulverized saffron
     threads or a mixture of both

¼ teaspoon ground ginger

1. Preheat the oven to 375°.

2. Bring 6 cups of water to boil in a kettle. Place the ingredients in casserole in this order: drained chick-peas, meat, bones, potatoes, and raw eggs
(in corners or along the sides). Sprinkle with garlic, salt, and spices. Pour in
the boiling water, cover the casserole tightly, and bake 1 hour.

3. Lower the oven heat to lowest setting and bake 5 hours, or until the
meat is meltingly tender. Serve directly from the casserole.

Lamb Tagine with Fried Eggplant (*Brania*)

I adore this dish, especially the tiny nuggets that are the peeled stems of
small eggplants, and that taste like mushrooms when they are cooked in a
tagine. Note that this dish is for people who don't mind fried foods.

INGREDIENTS

For the lamb and sauce:

   3 pounds rib or shoulder of lamb, cut into
     1½-inch chunks

  ½ cup chopped parsley

  5 cloves garlic, peeled and chopped

1¼ cups grated onion

  ¼ cup salad oil, or less

  1 rounded teaspoon paprika

  ¼ teaspoon ground cumin

  ¼ teaspoon freshly ground black pepper
     Pinch of pulverized saffron
     Salt to taste

2 to 3 tablespoons lemon juice

EQUIPMENT

Paring knife

5½-quart casserole with
  cover

Colander

Paper towels

Skillet

Spatula

Potato masher

Large serving dish

Working time: 1 hour

Cooking time: 2½ hours

Serves: 6

(*continued*)

For the eggplant garnish:

4 pounds small eggplants
Salt
Vegetable oil for frying
4 cloves garlic, peeled and chopped
2 teaspoons sweet paprika
¼ teaspoon ground cumin
⅓ cup lemon juice

1. Trim the lamb of excess fat. Place in the casserole with all the ingredients for the sauce except the lemon juice. Cover with 4 cups water and bring to a boil. Reduce the heat and simmer, covered, 1½ to 2 hours, or until the meat is very tender—that is, falling off the bones—and the sauce has reduced to a thick gravy. Add water, if necessary, during the cooking time. Add the lemon juice and taste for seasoning.

2. Meanwhile, cut off the stems of the small eggplants. Peel the stems and throw these little "nuggets" into the casserole as soon as possible, to cook with the meat. Peel the eggplants in alternating stripes lengthwise. Cut into ¼-inch thick slices, sprinkle heavily with salt, and let drain in a colander 30 minutes to draw off bitterness. Rinse the slices well and pat dry with paper towels.

3. Heat the oil in the skillet and fry the eggplant slices in batches until they are well browned and crisp on both sides. Drain, reserving the oil.

4. Mash the fried eggplant with the garlic, spices, and salt to taste. Reheat the reserved oil and fry the mashed eggplant until crisp and "firm" (about 20 minutes), turning the puree over and over in the oil so that all the water evaporates, and only the oil is left to fry the eggplant, which will become very thick and rich in texture. Drain again and fold in the lemon juice.

5. Arrange the lamb and sauce in the serving dish. Spread the eggplant over the meat and serve hot or warm.

Tagine of Lamb with Green Peppers and Tomatoes
(*Tagine el Lahm Felfla Matisha*)

INGREDIENTS

3 pounds shoulder of lamb, cut into 1½-inch chunks
2 cloves garlic, peeled and chopped
Pinch of pulverized saffron
Salt to taste
1 teaspoon ground ginger
1 tablespoon sweet paprika
¼ cup chopped parsley
¼ cup salad oil or less
2½ pounds fresh, ripe tomatoes, peeled, seeded, and chopped (see page 71)
1 pound sweet green peppers, grilled, peeled, seeded, and chopped (see page 70)
Juice of 1 lemon

EQUIPMENT

Paring knife
5½-quart enameled cast-iron or stainless-steel casserole
Mortar and pestle

Working time: 35 minutes
Cooking time: 2½ hours
Serves: 5 to 6

Trim the lamb of excess fat. Place in the casserole, along with a mixture of garlic, saffron, salt, spices, and parsley pounded to a paste in the mortar. Pour in the oil to make a sauce and toss with the meat. Add 2 cups water, bring to boil, then reduce the heat and simmer 30 minutes. Add the tomatoes and continue simmering for 2 more hours, stirring from time to time while the tomatoes cook down to a thick puree. Add the green peppers 10 minutes before serving. Sprinkle with the lemon juice and serve hot or warm.

Tagine of Lamb with String Beans Smothered in Sweet Tomato Jam

INGREDIENTS

3 pounds lamb shoulder, cut into 1½-inch chunks, with bones

Pinch of pulverized saffron

½ teaspoon freshly ground black pepper

¾ teaspoon ground ginger

Salt to taste

2 cloves garlic, peeled and chopped

2 to 3 tablespoons salad oil

⅔ cup grated onion

12 to 14 red, ripe tomatoes, preferably fresh, peeled, seeded, chopped (see page 71), and drained, 1 cup of the juice reserved

¾ pound fresh string beans

¼ cup chopped fresh green coriander or chopped parsley

1 teaspoon sugar, or to taste

¼ teaspoon ground cinnamon, or to taste

EQUIPMENT

Paring knife

5½-quart casserole with cover

1½-quart saucepan with cover

Large serving dish

Working time: 40 minutes

Cooking time: 2¼ hours

Serves: 4 to 6

1. Trim and discard the excess fat from the lamb. In the casserole, mix the spices, salt, garlic, and oil. Toss with the lamb to coat each piece. Stir in the grated onion and the 1 cup fresh tomato juice. Bring to a boil, reduce the heat, and simmer, covered, 1½ hours. Add water or any leftover tomato juice when necessary to keep the meat moist and avoid scorching.

2. Meanwhile, top and tail the string beans. Transfer 1 cup of the sauce to the saucepan and simmer the beans until tender, along with 1 tablespoon of the herbs. Cover the pan and keep warm.

3. When the meat is very tender—that is, when it falls easily off the bones—remove and keep warm. Add the chopped tomatoes to the sauce in

the casserole and cook down quickly over very high heat, mashing the tomatoes to a puree and constantly turning them so they do not scorch as they reduce. Cook down to about 1½ cups, adding sugar and cinnamon to taste. Return the lamb to the sauce to reheat, and reheat the string beans separately.

4. To serve, arrange the string beans around the rim of the serving dish. Spoon lamb and tomatoes into the center and sprinkle with the remaining chopped coriander or parsley. Serve hot or warm.

Lamb Tagine with Zucchini and Za'atar

The recipe for this delicious *tagine* was collected by a Peace Corps girl, who liked it so much she made up copies and handed them around to all her friends.

INGREDIENTS

3 pounds lamb shoulder, cut into 1½-inch chunks
3 tablespoons salad oil or butter
1 scant cup grated onion
Pinch of pulverized saffron
½ teaspoon turmeric
1 teaspoon freshly ground black pepper
Salt to taste
2 small cloves garlic, peeled and chopped
⅓ cup chopped fresh parsley
2½ pounds zucchini, preferably small ones
1½ to 2 teaspoons *za'atar*, or one or a combination of thyme, marjoram, orégano

EQUIPMENT

Paring knife
5½-quart casserole with cover
Shallow, 2-quart ovenproof serving dish
Aluminum foil

Working time: 30 minutes
Cooking time: 2 hours
Serves: 4 to 5 (or more, if part of a Moroccan dinner)

273

1. Trim and discard the excess fat from the lamb, then gently brown on all sides in oil or butter. Add the grated onion, spices, salt, garlic, and parsley, tossing to coat the meat. Pour in 2 cups water and bring to a boil. Reduce the heat and simmer, covered, 1½ hours, or until the meat is almost falling off the bones. Add small amounts of water whenever necessary.

2. Meanwhile, wash, top, and tail the zucchini and cut into ¾-inch slices. Salt lightly and let drain 20 minutes, then rinse and drain again. Sprinkle with the *za'atar*, finely crushed between the fingertips. Set aside.

3. When the meat is fully cooked, remove it from the casserole, arrange in one layer in the ovenproof serving dish, and cover with foil to keep warm. Add the zucchini to the sauce in the casserole and cook 10 minutes. Remove the partially cooked zucchini slices and, removing the foil, cover the meat attractively with them.

4. Preheat the oven to 350°.

5. By boiling rapidly, uncovered, reduce the sauce to a thick gravy (about 1 cup), pour over meat and zucchini, replace the foil, and bake 20 minutes. Serve at once, with a small sprinkling of extra herbs.

Lamb with Okra, "Roof Tile" Style

This Tetuán dish is called "roof tile" style because the okra is arranged like the green roof tiles of many Moroccan buildings. It steams above a sauce so thick a spoon can stand in it, a prominent feature of Tetuanese cooking.

INGREDIENTS

3½ pounds shoulder of lamb, cut into 1½-inch chunks

3 tablespoons vegetable oil

Salt and freshly ground black pepper to taste

½ teaspoon chopped garlic

1 large onion, finely chopped

¼ teaspoon pulverized saffron, mixed with turmeric

¼ cup chopped parsley

1½ pounds fresh okra (assorted sizes)

EQUIPMENT

Paring knife

5½-quart casserole

Needle and thread

2-quart, shallow ovenproof serving dish

Aluminum foil

Working time: 25 minutes

Cooking time: 2 hours

Serves: 4 to 6

1. Remove the excess fat from the lamb. Brown the meat gently in the oil in the casserole. Sprinkle with salt, pepper, garlic, onion, saffron, half the parsley, and 1 cup water. Cover tightly and cook gently 1½ hours, adding more water when necessary.

2. Meanwhile, wash, top, and tail the okra. Thread them together to form a necklace as described on page 91. Preheat the oven to 350°.

3. Transfer the meat to the serving dish. Add the okra and remaining parsley to the sauce in the casserole. Poach the okra 10 minutes, then remove, discarding the thread. Meanwhile, reduce the sauce over high heat to 1¼ cups and pour over the meat.

4. Arrange the okra in a pyramid fashion over the meat. Make a "tepee" of aluminum foil over the okra, then bake 30 minutes. Serve at once.

Note: Veal or beef could be substituted for the lamb in this dish.

Lamb Tagine Layered with Okra and Tomatoes
(*Tagine Macfool Bil Melokhias*)

Okra is known through the Middle East as *bamia*, but in Morocco it is confusingly called *melokhia*.

Melokhia, elsewhere, is a dark leafy plant (*Cochorus olitorius*), cultivated especially for use in sauces, or for drying and grinding into powder for soups. Fresh, it has a taste somewhere between watercress and sorrel. The only connection I can see between okra and *melokhia* is that they both can be dried in the sun, pulverized, put away for the winter, and then used to make gelatinous soups.

Okra is served often in *tagines* of lamb, where it is a good accompaniment to tomatoes, quinces, small sweet apples, pears, zucchini, and a vegetable very similar to yellow squash called *slaoui*.* One rarely finds okra served alone, though I have heard of a dish prepared in Fez made of pureed okra cooked with onions, green coriander, and parsley.

INGREDIENTS

2½ to 3 pounds lamb shoulder, cut into 1½-inch chunks or 5 or 6 thick chops
2 tablespoons salad oil
2 tablespoons butter
1 large onion, finely chopped
4 cloves garlic, peeled and chopped
Salt to taste
Freshly ground black pepper
2 cinnamon sticks
½ teaspoon turmeric
¼ cup chopped parsley
1 teaspoon chopped fresh green coriander (optional)

EQUIPMENT

5½-quart casserole with cover
1-quart saucepan with cover
Sieve
Shallow ovenproof serving dish, preferably earthenware or stoneware
Aluminum foil

Working time: 20 minutes
Cooking time: 2 hours
Serves: 4 to 6

* A long, smooth-skinned gourd shaped something like a cucumber but usually four times as long, with one end thin and the other bulbous. It is called *poo gwa* in Chinese markets and *doohi* in Pakistani and Indian markets.

1¼ pounds fresh okra or 2 ten-ounce pack-
    ages frozen whole okra
6 red, ripe tomatoes, peeled, seeded and
    chopped (see page 71), or 1 eight-
    ounce can Italian tomatoes, drained,
    seeded, and chopped

1. Lightly brown the lamb on all sides in the oil and butter. Add the onion, garlic, salt, ½ teaspoon pepper, and the other spices. Pour over enough water to almost cover the meat and bring to a boil. Reduce the heat, cover, and simmer 1 hour. Remove the cinnamon sticks.

2. Add the herbs and continue cooking the *tagine* 15 minutes. *Up to this point, the dish can be prepared in advance.*

3. Forty minutes before serving, preheat oven to 350°.

4. Transfer the lamb to the shallow ovenproof dish. By boiling rapidly, uncovered, reduce the sauce to 1 cup in the casserole.

5. Wash, top, and tail the okra. Cut very large okra pods in half. Put them in the saucepan and boil, with a few tablespoons sauce, salt, and ½ cup water, for 5 minutes, covered. Drain.

6. Arrange the okra over the meat and cover with sauce and the chopped tomatoes. Sprinkle with salt and pepper. Cover with foil, piercing once or twice so that steam can escape. Bake in the preheated oven about 40 minutes. Serve at once, with plenty of Moroccan Bread (page 51).

MEAT TAGINES WITH FRUIT

—◆—

No matter what the month, there is a tree somewhere in Morocco bearing fruit for the *tagine* pot. The combinations may seem unlikely at times, but I guarantee you will find them delicious: lamb with quinces, apples, pears, raisins, prunes or dates, with or without honey, with or without a complexity of spices.

In the spring, use greening or winesap apples. In the summer, try fresh apricots, or the type of hard, fuzzy, green crab apples called, in Morocco, *lehmenn.* In winter, I recommend what may be best of all, the heavy and rich *tagines* made with prunes or dates, and, in the autumn, small Seckel pears—and quinces.

Quinces, I think, are a delightful fruit; it seems a pity that these lovely golden "pears" are not well known in America. With honey and lamb, lots of pepper and/or ginger, the quince *tagines* are wonderful.

Quinces can be found in most parts of the United States, and also in cans packed in Japan. There is a rumor that Eve really offered a quince to Adam in the Garden of Eden; it seems unlikely, since quinces shouldn't be eaten unless cooked, but then maybe Adam suffered the additional punishment of a bellyache.

Lamb with Quinces

INGREDIENTS

3 to 3½ pounds lamb shoulder, cut into 1½-inch chunks

Salt to taste

Pinch of pulverized saffron

1 scant teaspoon ground ginger

1 scant teaspoon freshly ground black pepper

1 to 2 pinches cayenne

¼ cup grated onion, drained

2 to 3 tablespoons sweet butter

2 tablespoons chopped fresh herbs (parsley and/or green coriander)

1¼ cups minced onion

1 pound quinces or 1 fifteen-ounce can sliced quinces, drained

1 cinnamon stick (optional)

Granulated sugar

Ground cinnamon

EQUIPMENT

Paring knife

5½-quart casserole with cover

1½-quart enameled or stainless-steel saucepan

Shallow, 2-quart ovenproof serving dish

Working time: 30 minutes

Cooking time: 2½ hours

Serves: 4 to 6

1. Trim and discard the excess fat from the chunks of lamb. Mix the salt, spices, grated onion, butter, and herbs with the lamb in the casserole. Toss together over low heat to release the aromas of the spices, but do not brown the meat. Pour in approximately 2 cups water and bring to a boil. Lower the heat and simmer, covered, 1½ hours, adding water if necessary and turning the meat occasionally in the sauce.

2. After 1 hour, add the minced onions and continue simmering over gentle heat another 45 minutes, or until the meat is very tender and the sauce has become thick.

3. Meanwhile, wash, quarter, and core but do not peel the fresh quinces. As

you work, place pieces in acidulated water to keep them from blackening. Rinse and poach the quinces in mildly sugared water to cover (with the optional cinnamon stick) for 15 minutes, or until barely tender. Remove the quinces and let drain. (If using canned quinces, simply drain.)

4. Preheat the oven to 375°.

5. Transfer the lamb to the serving dish. Arrange the quince pieces attractively among the chunks of lamb, cut side down. (If using canned, sliced quinces, arrange in clusters of slices.) Dust the quinces very lightly with ground cinnamon and sugar. Swirl the sauce in the casserole and taste for seasoning (the taste of ginger and pepper should just peek through). Pour the sauce over and bake 15 minutes on the upper shelf of the preheated oven to glaze. Serve hot, directly from the baking dish.

VARIATION:

Tagine of Lamb with Pears or Green Apples

Follow the directions in the preceding recipe; do not poach apples or pears (except Seckel pears). Instead, gently sauté them in a little sweet butter (with a sprinkling of cinnamon and sugar) until lightly caramelized before placing them among the pieces of meat in the baking dish.

Note: Though it is not traditional, I like to mix apples and quinces (using ¾ pound of each) or pears and quinces with the meat and sauce. Even medlars or crab apples could make a good *tagine,* though I have not experimented as yet.

Tagine of Lamb with Raisins and Almonds, Tiznit Style

Tiznit is a strange, flat city in the southern Souss famous for the silverwork of its jewelers and its red-brown crenellated walls. It was one of the main stopping places for caravans that crossed the Sahara, and its food shows a strong Senegalese and Guinean influence (as does the architecture of its most famous mosque).

This dish is lovingly referred to by Moroccans as "the *tagine* that leaves nothing out." At the end it is sprinkled with a thin film of ground black pepper (a Senegalese touch?), but even without this last fillip it is delicious, and makes a marvelous opening to a dinner with *couscous* of chicken and vegetables.

This *tagine* plays the game of sweet against spicy that I've come to love in southern Moroccan cooking.

INGREDIENTS

3 to 3½ pounds lamb shoulder, cut into 1½-inch chunks

Salad oil

2 tablespoons sweet butter, melted

1½ cups chopped Spanish onions

3 cloves garlic, peeled and finely chopped

Salt to taste

Freshly ground black pepper

1 teaspoon turmeric

¼ teaspoon ground ginger

¼ teaspoon cayenne

½ pound fresh, ripe tomatoes, peeled, seeded, and chopped (see page 71), or 1 cup canned imported Italian tomatoes, drained

EQUIPMENT

Paring knife

5½-quart casserole with cover

Sieve

Shallow ovenproof serving dish

10-inch skillet

Spatula

Paper towels

Working time: 30 minutes
Cooking time: 2 hours
Serves: 5 to 6

(continued)

1 tablespoon mixed fresh herbs (chopped
    parsley and green coriander)
1 cup raisins, soaked in water
    Salad oil for frying
½ cup whole, blanched almonds
    Black pepper (optional—and not recom-
      mended)

1. Remove and discard the excess fat from the lamb. Place in the casserole with 2 tablespoons oil, the butter, chopped onion, garlic, salt, 1 teaspoon pepper, and the other spices. Toss to coat evenly. Add the chopped tomatoes and 1 cup water. Bring to a boil, reduce the heat, cover, and simmer 1 hour, turning the meat often in the sauce.

2. After 1 hour add the herbs and drained raisins. Continue cooking all together another 30 minutes, or until the meat is tender and the sauce has reduced to a thick gravy.

3. Preheat the oven to 350°.

4. Transfer the meat and sauce to the serving dish. Bake, uncovered, until the meat is glazed.

5. Meanwhile, heat salad oil, enough to cover the bottom, in the skillet and fry the almonds on both sides. Drain on paper towels, then sprinkle over the lamb just before serving.

6. The black pepper is traditionally sprinkled over everything at the table— but I don't recommend it.

Tagine of Lamb or Beef with Prunes and Apples (*Tagine Bil Babcock*)

One of the most unusual and luscious Moroccan combinations, this dish is also very good without the apples and with or without the sliced onions. If you leave out the sliced onions and the apples, sprinkle with 1 cup browned almonds just before serving.

INGREDIENTS

3 to 3½ pounds shoulder of lamb or beef chuck
    short ribs, cut into 1½-inch chunks
3 tablespoons sweet butter
2 tablespoons vegetable oil
    Pinch of pulverized saffron
    Salt to taste
½ teaspoon freshly ground pepper
1 scant teaspoon ground ginger
    Ground cinnamon
3 tablespoons grated onion
4 to 5 sprigs green coriander, tied together
    with thread (optional)
1 pound pitted prunes
1 cup finely sliced onion
¼ cup honey or granulated sugar
4 medium tart apples
1 tablespoon toasted sesame seeds, pref-
    erably unhulled

EQUIPMENT

Paring knife
Small and large mixing
    bowls
5½-quart casserole with
    cover
Large skillet
Large serving dish

Working time: 20 minutes
Cooking time: 2 hours
Serves: 6

1. Trim the meat of excess fat. Melt 2 tablespoons of the butter, then mix with the oil, saffron, salt, pepper, ginger, ¼ teaspoon cinnamon, onion, and coriander. Dip each chunk of meat into the mixture and place in the casserole. Over gentle heat turn the pieces of meat, being careful not to burn them, but allowing the aromas of the spices to be released. Add water to

almost cover the meat. Bring to a boil, then lower the heat, cover, and simmer gently for 1 hour.

2. Meanwhile, soak the prunes in 2 cups cold water.

3. After the *tagine* has cooked 1 hour, add the sliced onion to the casserole and cook 30 minutes longer.

4. Drain the prunes and add to the meat. Stir in ¼ teaspoon cinnamon and 3 tablespoons honey or sugar. Simmer, uncovered, until the prunes swell and the sauce has reduced to 1 cup.

5. Meanwhile, quarter and core the apples. Sauté in the skillet, flesh side down, with the remaining tablespoon of honey, a pinch of cinnamon, and the remaining tablespoon of sweet butter until soft and glazed.

6. To serve, arrange the lamb on the serving dish, pour the onion-prune sauce over, decorate with the apples, and sprinkle with the sesame seeds. Serve at once.

VARIATION:

Tagine of Lamb with Apricots and Honey

Follow the directions in the preceding recipe, substituting 2 pounds fresh apricots for the apples and prunes. Don't fry or cook the apricots; just heat them in the sauce at the last minute.

VARIATION:

Tagine of Lamb with Quinces and Honey

Follow the directions in *tagine bil babcock* (Tagine of Lamb with Prunes and Apples, page 283), substituting 1½ pounds fresh quinces (prepared as directed in step 3 on page 284) for the apples and prunes. Poach the quinces in sugared water with 2 cinnamon sticks until tender. For a richer taste, caramelize the drained quinces before adding to the casserole.

Tagine of Lamb with Dates

For this unusual *tagine* use the fleshy Tafilalet dates if in Morocco, or California dates if in the United States. In Morocco no one bothers to pit the dates for date *tagines*; serve pitted or unpitted as you wish.

INGREDIENTS

- 3½ pounds lamb shoulder, cut into 1½-inch chunks
- Salt to taste
- Pinch of pulverized saffron
- 1 teaspoon freshly ground black pepper
- ½ rounded teaspoon ground ginger
- 1 pinch cayenne
- 2 cloves garlic, peeled and chopped
- 2 to 3 tablespoons sweet butter or vegetable oil
- 1 cup minced onion
- 2 tablespoons "coriander water" (see page 28)
- ½ pound dates
- Ground cinnamon

EQUIPMENT

Paring knife
5½-quart casserole
Shallow ovenproof serving dish

Working time: 15 minutes
Cooking time: 2 hours
Serves: 6

1. Trim and discard the excess fat from the meat. In the casserole mix the salt, spices, and garlic. Stir in the butter or oil to make a sauce. Toss with the meat and cook over low heat to release the aroma of the spices. Stir in half the onions, the "coriander water," and 3 cups water. Bring to a boil and simmer 1 hour.

2. After 1 hour, add the remaining onions. Simmer, uncovered, another 45 minutes, or until the meat is very tender and the sauce has reduced to a thick gravy. (You may have to add water during cooking time to avoid scorching the meat.)

3. Preheat the oven to highest setting.

4. Transfer the meat and gravy to the serving dish and place the dates around or among the chunks of meat. Sprinkle each date or cluster of dates with pinches of ground cinnamon. Bake 15 minutes on the upper shelf of the oven, uncovered, until the dates become a little crusty. Serve at once.

Lamb Tagine with Raisins, Almonds, and Honey (*Mrouzia*)

Mrouzia, though it is a combination of lamb and fruits, is different from the preceding *tagines.* It is a special and extremely sweet dish made after the celebration of the Aid el Kebir—the Feast of the Slaughter of the Lamb. On these occasions a family suddenly finds itself in possession of a great amount of meat. Since refrigeration is a luxury, and home freezing virtually unknown, a solution is to preserve the meat in some way—and that is what *mrouzia* is, a form of preserved lamb. If properly done, the meat will keep fresh and edible for as long as a month.

Mrouzia is famous in both Arab and Berber communities throughout North Africa. It is made with the infamous *ras el hanout* spice mixture (see page 24). This same recipe may be followed for rabbit.

Mrouzia is never eaten as a one-dish meal: it is so incredibly rich in sweetness and spices that it can only be consumed in small quantities as part of a large *diffa* of many courses.

This is a shortened version.

INGREDIENTS

3 pounds lamb neck, cut into about 10 pieces, each with some bone left on
Salt to taste
1½ teaspoons *ras el hanout* (page 26)
¼ teaspoon ground ginger
½ teaspoon freshly ground black pepper
Pinch of pulverized saffron
1¾ cups blanched, whole almonds

EQUIPMENT

5½-quart enameled cast-iron casserole with cover
Small mixing bowl

Working time: 15 minutes
Cooking time: 2¼ hours
Serves: 8 (as part of a Moroccan dinner)

2 cloves garlic, peeled and cut up

3 small cinnamon sticks

½ cup sweet butter or salad oil (see note)

1 pound raisins

¾ cup dark, heavy honey, such as Greek Mount
    Hymettus

1 tablespoon ground cinnamon

1. Place the lamb in the casserole. Mix the salt, *ras el hanout*, ginger, pepper, and saffron with 1 cup water and rub into each piece of meat. Add the almonds, garlic, cinnamon sticks, butter or oil, and 2 cups water. Bring to a boil, lower the heat, and simmer 1½ hours. Add more water, when necessary, to avoid burning the meat.

2. Add the raisins, honey, and ground cinnamon and continue cooking 30 minutes.

3. Uncover the casserole and, over high heat, reduce the sauce, turning the meat and fruit often to avoid scorching, until there is only a thick honey glaze, coating the meat, left in the pan. Serve warm or hot.

Note: You may reduce the amount of oil, but if you are planning to keep the dish a long time you will need the full amount.

Tagine of Lamb, Quinces, Amber and Aga Wood*

This extraordinary dish is a specialty of Tetuán, and in fact is made the same way as the chicken with quinces, honey, amber, and aga wood (twenty-ninth of the fifty Tetuanese chicken dishes mentioned in Chapter 9). It is usually made without the aga wood and ambergris unless the dish is to be served for a special occasion, since these two exotic ingredients are considered extremely fine and enormously luxurious. A fingernail scraping of ambergris dissolved in water, then added to the sauce, is credited with aphrodisiacal powers—which might help explain its price of ninety dollars per ounce. An inch-long piece of aga wood, pulverized in a brass mortar with some sugar and then added to the sauce, imparts a rich and musky aroma somewhat reminiscent of the inside of a Gothic church.

INGREDIENTS	EQUIPMENT
3½ to 4 pounds lamb shoulder, cut into 2-inch pieces	6-quart casserole with cover
Salt to taste	4½-quart casserole
Freshly ground black pepper to taste	Mortar and pestle or spice grinder
Pinch pulverized saffron	Warm serving platter
½ teaspoon turmeric	
½ cup salad oil, or less	*Working time:* 30 minutes
¼ cup chopped Spanish or sweet onion	*Cooking time:* 2½ hours
3 pounds quinces, washed, quartered, cored, and skin scored twice	*Serves:* 6 to 8
½ cup orange flower water	
1 teaspoon ground cinnamon	
1/16 teaspoon scraped ambergris (optional)	
1¼-inch piece aga wood (optional)	
2 cups granulated sugar	
2 tablespoons toasted sesame seeds	

* Aga wood can sometimes be found in Middle Eastern grocery stores or, in Morocco, in Tetuánese *parfumeries*. It is called *oud kameria*. Amber, or ambergris, is generally unavailable; a substitute called by the same name can be purchased in Marrakesh spice shops ($1.50 a gram), but it has no potent side effects.

1. In the large casserole mix the lamb, salt, pepper, saffron, turmeric, oil, and onions. Brown the lamb and onions, turning several times, then cook over low heat for 30 minutes. Add 3 cups water, cover, and let simmer 1½ hours, adding water when necessary.

2. After 1½ hours, arrange the quinces, cut side down, in the smaller casserole. Sprinkle the scored skin with orange flower water, ½ cup water, the cinnamon, and 3 cups of the lamb gravy. Bring to a boil and let simmer 30 minutes *without stirring the fruit.* (The quinces will not hold together if they are stirred.)

3. Continue cooking the lamb until soft and almost falling off the bone. Remove to a warmed platter and reduce the gravy until very thick by boiling rapidly, uncovered. Scrape a fingernail-sized piece of ambergris into a small cup. Moisten with 2 tablespoons lamb gravy. Crush with a spoon, then pour into the remaining gravy. Reheat just before serving.

4. Meanwhile, pulverize the aga wood in a mortar or spice grinder with 1 tablespoon of the sugar. Sprinkle the quinces with the aga wood mixture and the remaining sugar. Continue cooking over moderate heat until the liquid begins to evaporate and the sugar begins to caramelize. Swirl the pan (don't stir) to avoid burning the sugar and fruit. When nicely browned, remove from the heat and keep warm.

5. Spoon the lamb gravy over the lamb. Cover with the caramelized quinces and syrup. Sprinkle with the sesame seeds and serve at once.

ELEVEN

———◆———

Desserts

I was staying with the Jaidi family outside of Rabat for the final phase of field work for this book. I had forgotten to bring my alarm clock, which annoyed me, since so much of the important kitchen work is done early in the morning and I didn't want to miss a thing. But I needn't have worried. The first sounds from the kitchen, which was in a separate building in the orange grove that is the Jaidi compound, were loud enough to wake me up, no matter how late I had gone to bed the night before. These were the clinking sounds of brass pestles against brass mortars as various ingredients were steadily, meticulously crushed.

In the courtyard I would find Fatima sitting true Moroccan style, the way many Moroccans seem to do when they are working or relaxing, resting on their heels with their toes as high as two inches off the ground. And usually when I found her she would be pounding the spices for the dishes to be cooked that day, or else almonds for almond paste—the necessary ingredient for several of the greatest Moroccan desserts.

My orange crate was soon set up and covered with Moroccan rugs, and here I would sit with pen and notebook, scales and measuring cups and spoons, for five hours at a time,* noting down all I saw, moving only to look into various pots on various braziers or to practice some piece of kitchen work that I knew I would have to learn.

* This included all work (without benefit of electrical appliances) including the killing, plucking, and purifying of chickens. In an American kitchen the work involved in preparing a series of Moroccan dishes is considerably less.

Madame Jaidi had her crate, too, and would sit there in great regal style (she is a marvelous, masterful woman whose father was the pasha of Mogodor) while huge slabs of meat were brought to her for hacking, or vast pots into which she would throw, always with precision, the various spices that had been ground at dawn.

It went on like this day after day, taking five hours always to prepare the midday meal, which in a traditional Moroccan home is the major meal of the day. I sat on my rug-covered orange crate for weeks, learning and writing and tasting and nibbling, always looking forward to my reward for so much hard work, the midday lunch, at which there were never less than a dozen guests.

It is best to be honest and say that, though this chapter is entitled "desserts," most of the things in it are not actually eaten at the end of a meal. The traditional way to end a Moroccan dinner, and the traditional "dessert" also of most North Africans, is a bowl or platter of fruits and nuts. Usually an enormous platter is offered of carefully arranged plums, apricots, bananas, oranges, and figs, as well as, on a separate platter, cubed melon. In winter a bowl of raisins, dates, dried figs, almonds, and walnuts may replace the fresh fruits. Other fruit dishes, including Orange Salad with Rosewater (page 82) or a dessert of pomegranate seeds mixed with almonds, sugar, and orange flower water, may also be offered—and, of course, there is always the simple but soothing glass of tea.

But the Moroccans are great connoisseurs of sweets, even if they do not usually eat them at the end of their meals. Two of their most famous (and two of my favorites) are the *kab el ghzal* ("Gazelles' Horns," page 296), those divine, sugar-coated crescent-shaped pastries stuffed with almond paste, and *m'hanncha* ("The Snake," page 294), that sublime coil of browned almond-stuffed pastry. These, like the many cakes and cookies and pastries in Moroccan confectionary shops, are usually eaten with tea—which can be at any time. In fact, Moroccans will sometimes fill themselves with sweet cakes *before* sitting down to a special-occasion feast, such as a wedding.

There is another category of sweet dishes that I have included in this chapter: the sweet supper dishes, or prefruit dishes, such things as the sweet dessert *couscous* on page 315, *roz mafooar* (Sweet Steamed Rice, page 317), Moroccan Rice Pudding (page 318), and *keneffa* (Sweet Bisteeya with Milk and Almonds, page 322). All of these are incredible confections that follow a rich and nourishing soup or a series of *tagines*, which in turn are followed by fruit and nuts and sweet mint tea.

But in Moroccan food, as in all Moroccan things, there is always a great exception. There are times when sweet confections are eaten at the important meal of the day, and one of these times occurs during the fasting month of Ramadan, when everything is topsy-turvy, and sweet, fried, honeyed cakes are devoured along with the famous and hunger-quenching hot spicy *harira* soup. But these cakes, called *mahalkra* or *shebbakia* (Free-Form Honey Cake, page 303), are eaten *with* the soup, and not *after* the soup.

ALMOND PASTE CONFECTIONS

———◆———

"The Snake" (*M'hanncha*)

"The Snake" is one of the glories of Moroccan confectionery, a treat not to be missed.

INGREDIENTS

For the almond paste:

    4 tablespoons or more sweet butter, melted and cooled
    ½ pound blanched almonds, finely ground
    ½ teaspoon almond extract
    ⅛ teaspoon gum arabic (optional)
¾ to 1 cup confectioners' sugar, or to taste
    ¼ cup rosewater or orange flower water, or to taste

For the pastry:

    2 ounces phyllo pastry or strudel leaves or 8 large *warka* leaves (page 103)
    5 tablespoons melted sweet butter
    1 egg, beaten
    Confectioners' sugar
    Ground cinnamon

EQUIPMENT

Saucepan
Mixing bowls
Mortar and pestle
Spatula
Pastry brush
9-inch cake pan
Whisk
Baking sheet
Large serving plate

Working time: 20 minutes
Baking time: 40 minutes
Serves: 8

1. Mix the cooled melted butter with the ground blanched almonds and almond flavoring. Pound the gum arabic in a mortar until finely ground and add to the almond mixture. Add the sugar and fragrant water, then mix well and knead to a solid, well-blended mass. Chill.

2. Separate the chilled almond paste into 10 balls and roll each ball into a 5-inch cylinder. Chill.

3. Preheat the oven to 350°.

4. Spread out 1 strudel or phyllo pastry leaf. Brush with some of the melted butter. Cover with a second layer of pastry and brush with butter again. (If using *warka*, spread out 2 warka leaves and overlap them slightly. Do not butter them.)

5. Place 5 cylinders of almond paste along the lower edge, 2 inches from the bottom of each leaf, and roll up the pastry tightly, tucking in the ends. Shape into a loose coil.

6. Brush the cake pan lightly with butter and place the coil in the center. Repeat with the remaining pastry leaves and cylinders of almond paste, extending the coil in the shape of a coiled snake, to fill the pan.

7. Beat the egg and add ½ teaspoon ground cinnamon. Brush the pastry top with the cinnamon-egg mixture and bake 30 minutes, or until golden brown. Invert onto the baking sheet and return to the oven for ten minutes. Invert again, onto the serving plate, and dust with confectioners' sugar. Dribble cinnamon in straight lines to form a lattice pattern. Serve warm.

Note: This cake will keep several days in a cool place. Reheat before serving.

"Gazelles' Horns" (*Kab el Ghzal*)

You will see these pastries everywhere in Morocco, in all sweet shops and bakeries, and they will be of varying quality—sometimes too hard or brittle, sometimes too thick. My suggestion is to try one first before buying a whole bag; the best are those made from the thinnest pastry—they break in half practically at a touch.

INGREDIENTS

For the almond paste:

    Same as the previous recipe, but omit gum arabic and rosewater (see note below)

For the pastry:

2¼ cups unbleached all-purpose flour
  3 tablespoons sweet butter, melted
    Pinch of salt
    Orange flower water (optional)
    Confectioners' sugar (optional)

EQUIPMENT

Mixing bowls
Electric mixer with dough hook (optional)
Damp cloth
Rolling pin
Serrated pastry wheel
Needle
2 baking sheets
Serving plate

Working time: 1 hour 15 minutes
Baking time: 10 to 15 minutes
Makes: 3 to 4 dozen

1. Prepare the almond paste as described in step 1 on page 294, but divide into 4 equal parts before chilling.

2. Make a firm dough with the flour, 2 tablespoons melted butter, and about 1 cup lukewarm water. (In very rich Moroccan homes orange flower water is used.) Add a pinch of salt. Knead at least 20 minutes, until silky and elastic. (If you have a mixing machine with a dough hook attachment, knead on slow speed 12 minutes.)

3. Preheat the oven to 325°.

4. Separate the dough into 4 equal parts. Grease 3 of the parts with a little melted butter and cover with a slightly damp cloth. Roll out the remaining dough, on a lightly buttered surface with a lightly buttered rolling pin, into a long strip, pushing with the rolling pin to stretch the dough. Make half turns with the dough, rolling in both directions. Dust with flour if the dough seems *too* sticky, but only very lightly. As you roll, wrap the dough around the wooden rolling pin to help stretching, being very careful not to break the dough. Roll and stretch until you have the thinness of cardboard.

5. Place the long strip horizontally in front of you. Using one part of the chilled almond paste, roll 1¼ teaspoons of it at a time between your palms to make sausage shapes 1¾ inches long—thicker in the center and tapered at the ends. Place the almond paste cylinders in a row, 1 inch up from the lower edge of the dough and about 2 inches apart. *Stretch* the sheet of dough below the almond paste as thin as possible and fold over the paste to cover it completely. Press the dough together to seal. Cut with the pastry wheel around each mold to form a crescent horn shape. Repeat with the remaining dough.

6. Pick up each "horn," and, pressing lightly with the second and third finger and thumb of each hand, shape it into a crescent. Prick each horn with a needle twice, to prevent puffing and splitting. Place them on a baking sheet, and bake 10 to 15 minutes, or until only very pale gold in color. Do not allow the crescents to brown or they will harden. The crusts should be rather soft but will crisp slightly upon cooling. Sprinkle at once with orange flower water and roll in confectioners' sugar if desired. Serve piled high on a serving plate.

Note: Another excellent almond paste, more work but much lighter in texture, can be made with 10 ounces *freshly* blanched and peeled almonds *pounded in a mortar*. These are then mixed with ¾ cup granulated sugar, orange flower water, and ¼ teaspoon almond extract.

Shredded Pastry with Almonds (*Ktaif*)

This Tetuanese pastry dessert was no doubt adapted from the Turkish *cadaif* (a honey-walnut pastry made with a type of pastry similar to *warka* but differently prepared) learned when the Turks occupied Algeria in the sixteenth century. This recipe is adapted from Lord Bute's *Moorish Recipes*.

Ktaif is indeed very similar to *cadaif*. In the Middle East the dough is pushed through a sieve onto a hot pan and then removed before it is fully cooked. In Tetuán there is a special instrument for making *ktaif*, a tin cup with two fine, protruding, open nozzles. The soft pastry dough is pushed through this gadget into a lattice pattern on a flat metal tray. The lattice is then removed and another made until all the batter is used up. The "lattices," which look like shredded wheat, are piled on top of each other and moistened with melted butter. In the Middle East the "lattices" are baked in even layers and look very attractive, while in Tetuán they are, in the words of Lord Bute, "by no means the most attractive to the eye."

You can buy the dough already prepared in Middle Eastern pastry shops, where it's called "*cadaif* pastry." (If frozen, defrost thoroughly before use.)

This pastry will keep about four days, and, if broken up and piled onto a serving dish, it will look *somewhat* attractive.

INGREDIENTS	EQUIPMENT
5½ cups confectioners' sugar	1½ quart stainless steel or enameled saucepan
1 cinnamon stick	
1 tablespoon lemon juice	Candy thermometer (optional)
¾ cup orange flower water	
¾ pound whole, blanched almonds	Skillet
Butter for frying	Paper towels
2 to 3 teaspoons ground cinnamon	Electric blender
1 pound "*cadaif* pastry" threads	Mixing bowl
1 cup sweet butter, melted	Large skillet or casserole with shallow sides

Large spoon
2 spatulas
Serving dish

Working and cooking time:
1 hour
Serves: 8

1. Prepare a syrup by boiling 4 cups of the sugar with 2 cups water, the cinnamon stick, and lemon juice, uncovered, until it thickens (about 220° on a candy thermometer). Stir in ¼ cup of the orange flower water and continue cooking a few minutes longer. Set aside to cool.

2. Meanwhile, prepare the filling. Fry the almonds in butter until lightly browned. Drain on paper towels. Pulverize in the blender, then mix with the cinnamon, remaining confectioners' sugar, and enough orange flower water (½ cup or less) to moisten to a paste.

3. Place half the pastry strands in the large skillet and pour over half the melted butter. Cook together *without browning,* by regulating the heat. After 10 minutes there should only be a light golden crust on the bottom of the pastry. Turn the pastry over and gently fry the other side very lightly. (The strands will tend to stick together in one or two big pieces.) Transfer the strands to a plate and, using the remaining butter, repeat with the second batch of pastry. Pour off any excess butter and spread the almond mixture over the pastry in the skillet. Cover with the first batch of pastry. Pour the syrup over and cook the whole thing together about 15 minutes, basting the pastry with the syrup until well absorbed, and turning the pastry from the bottom to the top as it crisps. Continue until all the strands are crisp and well moistened, and the "whole is one shapeless mass." Leave in the pan to cool. Break up into 1½-inch nuggets and serve at room temperature.

Pastry Stuffed with Almond Paste and Dipped in Honey (*Braewats*)

These are extremely rich pastries, and no more than one or two are likely to be consumed by each person. It's not that they're not delicious; they are incredibly sweet. Happily these sweet *braewats* keep a long time when put up in airtight containers.

This is the traditional recipe as prepared in Fez, but you can make them a number of different ways—that is, you can use plain almond paste, made according to the directions in the *m'hanncha* recipe ("The Snake," page 294), or you can blend ¼ pound almond paste with ½ pound dried, stoned dates that have been pounded and mixed with a little orange flower water and butter. I have heard that some people make the filling with dried figs, too.

INGREDIENTS	EQUIPMENT
½ pound blanched whole almonds	Skillet
Salad oil for frying	Spatula
Sweet butter, melted and cooled (optional)	Paper towels
	Electric blender
1½ teaspoons ground cinnamon	Mixing bowl
Scant ½ teaspoon almond extract	Damp towel
2 to 3 tablespoons confectioners' sugar	Pastry brush
Orange flower water	Small saucepan
¼ pound phyllo pastry or strudel leaves or 24 small (8-inch) *warka* leaves (page 103)	Baking sheet (optional)
	Flat dish
2 cups dark, heavy honey, such as Greek Mount Hymettus	*Working time:* 45 minutes
	Baking time: 30 minutes
	or
	Frying time: 8–10 minutes
	Makes: 2 dozen pastries

1. Fry the almonds in the oil until golden. Drain on paper towels and grind in blender until smooth and pasty—if you have drained them too well you will

need to add a few tablespoons cooled melted butter. Transfer to the mixing bowl and flavor with the cinnamon, almond extract, sugar, and 1½ tablespoons orange flower water. Knead to a solid mass.

2. If using phyllo or strudel pastry leaves, unroll one sheet at a time, keeping the others under a damp towel. Brush the entire sheet sparingly with melted butter (you will need about ½ cup altogether). Cut lengthwise into 3 equal parts and place a nugget of almond paste at the bottom of each strip. Fold according to Klandt directions on page 118, or into triangles, as explained on page 123. (If using *warka* leaves there is no need to brush with butter; otherwise follow the procedure for strudel or phyllo dough.)

3. Preheat the oven to 350°.

4. Heat the honey with 2 or 3 tablespoons orange flower water. (Avoid burning by continually controlling the heat.)

5. Bake the rolls in a 350° oven for 30 minutes, or until puffed and golden brown on both sides, or fry in not-too-hot oil until golden, turning once. Transfer at once to the simmering honey, allowing the hot honey to penetrate the pastries for 2 to 3 minutes. Remove to a flat dish to dry. Store when cool.

Sesame Seed, Almond, and Honey Cone (*Sfuf*)

A charming Tetuanese confection considered a great fortifier—to be served at weddings.

INGREDIENTS	EQUIPMENT
1 pound all-purpose flour	Large skillet, such as a paella pan
½ cup sesame seeds	
2 tablespoons butter, softened to room temperature	Mortar and pestle or electric blender
¼ cup granulated sugar	Large mixing bowl
½ cup almonds, blanched and ground fine in a blender	Serving plate

(*continued*)

1 teaspoon ground cinnamon	*Working time:* 30 minutes
Pinch grated nutmeg	*Makes:* 3 cups
1 to 2 tablespoons liquid honey	
Confectioners' sugar	

1. Toast the flour in the skillet, turning it constantly until it turns a lovely light brown. Add the sesame seeds and butter and continue stirring over moderate heat until the sesame seeds turn golden and are well mixed with the flour. Then add the sugar, almonds, and spices and cook together for 2 or 3 minutes, stirring all the while.

2. Put the honey in the mixing bowl and gradually, with the aid of a wooden spatula, beat in the almond–sesame seed–flour mixture. Place on a serving plate, form into a cone, decorate with crisscrossing lines of powdered sugar (or coat completely with sugar), and serve with Moroccan tea.

Note: Sfuf is eaten communally with small demitasse spoons.

VARIATION:
Zomita

Substitute ginger for the cinnamon and nutmeg, toast the almonds before grinding, and mix the butter when hot with 1 cup honey. Combine the mixture of almonds, sesame seeds, spices, and flour with the butter and honey, then roll into fingers and serve as a candy.

Note: In some parts of the north barley flour is used in place of ordinary white flour.

FRIED CAKES

———◆———

Free-Form Honey Cake (*Mahalkra or Shebbakia*)

This is one of the famous honey cakes served with spicy *harira* soup for Ramadan, but it is also good on the dessert tray with other cookies for afternoon tea. These cakes are very sweet—when you bite into *mahalkra* you are biting into pure honey.

This somewhat difficult recipe has been vastly scaled down in consideration of American tastes. In a Moroccan home it wouldn't make sense to make less than five hundred cakes. Friends and neighbors help, and then everyone goes home with a large batch. Ramadan lasts a whole month, and the culinary frenzy at sundown is truly incredible.

INGREDIENTS

1½ cups plus 1 tablespoon sweet butter
1 package active dry yeast or ½ package baker's yeast
3 large eggs
¾ teaspoon salt
½ teaspoon double-acting baking powder
2 to 3 tablespoons orange flower water
1 teaspoon vanilla extract
2½ tablespoons white vinegar
2 pounds all-purpose flour
Pinch of pulverized saffron
Salad oil for deep frying
5 cups dark honey
⅓ cup sesame seeds, oven toasted

EQUIPMENT

Small and large saucepans
Large and small bowls
Whisk
Rolling pin
Serrated pastry wheel
2 baking sheets
Large, deep saucepan
Tongs
Colander

Working and frying time:
2 hours
Makes: 35 cakes, approximately

1. Melt and cool the 1½ cups butter. Sprinkle the yeast over ¼ cup luke-warm water, stir to dissolve, and set in a warm place until bubbly.

2. In a mixing bowl beat the eggs with the salt, baking powder, orange flower water, and vanilla. Then add the vinegar and melted butter.

3. Place the flour in large mixing bowl and make a well in the center. Slowly pour the egg mixture into the flour, stirring constantly with a wooden spoon until well combined. Then add the bubbling yeast. Work into a stiff dough, adding only as much water as you need. Knead well by pressing down and pushing forward with the heel of your hand and folding the dough over onto itself. Knead until smooth and elastic.

4. Blend 1 tablespoon butter with the pulverized saffron until bright yellow. Then blend into the dough. Separate the dough into 4 equal parts. Cover and let stand 10 minutes.

5. Take one ball of dough and slap it around to flatten it out. Butter the rolling pin and start rolling the dough out until it is as thin as thick cardboard, about 10 inches round. Trim all around with the pastry wheel and cut into pieces approximately 5 x 3 inches. Make 5 parallel incisions to form 6 strips *within* each piece. Loop every other strip in your fingers and then bring the lower opposite points together so that a pretzel shape is formed. Place them on a buttered baking sheet covered while preparing the others. (The shape is really unimportant as long as they look more or less like pretzels.)

6. Heat the honey in a large, deep saucepan. (Honey tends to boil up rather high.) Heat the oil in the skillet to a depth of at least 1¼ inches. Fry 6 or 7 cakes on both sides until brown (not light but not too dark). Immedi-ately drop the cakes into the hot honey. As soon as the honey boils up, re-move the cakes to the colander to drain. Sprinkle at once with sesame seeds. Serve cool.

Note: Another type, also called shebbakia, is made by pressing leavened batter through a pastry tube (or flower pot), in the shape of rosettes, into boiling oil.

Fried Pastry from Sefrou

Sefrou is a charming town near Fez with a large Sephardic community. These cakes no doubt come from Spain, brought by the Jews in 1492.

INGREDIENTS

3 cups all-purpose flour
Confectioners' sugar
⅛ teaspoon salt
2 whole eggs, plus 1 egg yolk
2 tablespoons orange flower water
Salad oil
2 cups honey

EQUIPMENT

Mixing bowls
Deep-sided 14-inch skillet or
    deep fryer
Rolling pin
Long, pronged fork
Colander or rack for drain-
    ing

Working and cooking time:
1½ hours
Makes: 2½ dozen pastries

1. Mix the flour, ¼ cup sugar, and salt in a bowl. Add the eggs, egg yolk, and enough orange flour water to make a rather soft dough. Turn out onto a board and knead well until both smooth and elastic. Separate into 6 equal balls, coat with oil, and let stand 30 minutes.

2. Heat oil in the skillet or deep fryer to a depth of 2 inches. Have a colander or draining rack ready.

3. Roll out one ball of dough by first flattening with oiled hands and then rolling to stretch into a large rectangle. Repeat with a second ball, place the rectangles on top of one another, and roll them together. Cut into 2-inch strips lengthwise.

4. Place one end of the strip in the oil, and as it swells and fries *slowly* start to wrap the *fried end* around the long, pronged fork, while at the same time feeding more of the uncooked strip into the oil. Keep on turning and folding the strip until the strip is finished. The oil should be maintained at a constant

temperature so that the pastry does not brown too much, but comes out a pale beige. Remove to drain and continue until all pastries have been rolled, fried, and drained well.

5. Dribble the honey over the pastries and sprinkle with confectioners' sugar. Serve at room temperature.

Note: These pastries will keep a few days in a cool place.

Sponge Doughnuts (*Sfinges*)

Sfinges are commonly eaten in the morning, along with a glass of mint tea or a cup of coffee. Their name derives from the Greek σπογγος, which is the word for "sponge."

Just outside Tangier, in the village of Hayani, there are some light-blue colored stalls (light blue being a symbol of good luck in Morocco) where *sfinges* are prepared. I would often stop by these stalls to fetch some for my children. I used to watch, fascinated, as the *sfinge* maker squeezed dough in his oiled hand, and then allowed a round "crown" the size of a plum to emerge from between his forefinger and thumb. He would pierce a hole through the center, twirl the dough into a ring, and then toss it into boiling oil, where it immediately puffed up into a large, crisp, golden crown. He then fished it out with an iron hook and strung it with others on a wire coat hanger to drain. I would choose a particularly well-formed lot, pay for them by weight, and rush home while they were warm, to sprinkle them with confectioners' sugar and serve them to my children along with hot chocolate.

INGREDIENTS	EQUIPMENT
1 package active dry yeast	Small and medium-sized
½ teaspoon granulated sugar	bowls
4 cups all-purpose flour	Formica or marble work-
1 teaspoon salt	space, *gsaa*, or large basin
Salad oil for frying	Clean towel

Confectioners' sugar (optional)

Deep-sided skillet or deep
   fryer
Tongs, skewers, and slotted
   spoon
Fat thermometer (optional)
Paper towels

Working time: 40 minutes
Frying time: 20 minutes
Makes: 2 to 2½ dozen

1. Sprinkle the yeast and sugar over ¼ cup lukewarm water. Stir to dissolve, cover, and set in a warm place until the yeast is bubbling and has doubled in volume.

2. Combine the flour and salt. Make a well in the center and pour in yeast and enough lukewarm water to make a stiff dough. Knead well by vigorously pushing parts of the dough outwards and folding it back onto itself until it is smooth and elastic.

3. Place a bowl of lukewarm water by your side. Gradually add water to the dough by sprinkling 2 to 3 tablespoons water on the work surface and covering it with dough. Punch down with your fists, making squishy noises as you work the dough, until it absorbs the water. Turn the dough over and repeat. Wet your hands as you work and continue adding water in this fashion until the dough looks spongy and is very sticky. Pick the dough up and begin to slap it down many times to loosen it up. Continue adding water by tablespoons at intervals, until the dough is so elastic that it moves with the movement of your hand en masse as you raise it and slap it down again. Place the dough to rest in a bowl that has been rinsed out with warm water, then cover with a clean towel and leave to rise in a warm place for 1 hour, or until it has doubled in volume. To test the dough, twist off a piece and flip it in your hands; it should become a smooth ball. If it is not ready, leave it for another 10 minutes before forming rings.

4. Pour oil into the skillet or deep fryer to a depth of 2½ inches. Heat to 400°.

5. Oil your hands lightly and squeeze out a small amount of dough between thumb and forefinger to form a small ball. Break it off with your other hand and punch a hole in the center with your thumb. Let it fall loose to form a "bracelet," and then slip it into the hot oil. Repeat with the remaining dough. Fry 4 or 5 doughnuts at a time until golden, swollen, and crisp, turning them over once with a skewer. Drain on paper towels. Serve with a sprinkling of confectioners' sugar if desired, though in Morocco they are usually eaten plain to be dunked in coffee.

VARIATION:

Pancakes

This dough used for *sfinges* can be thinned to make a pancake batter. These pancakes are best cooked on a flat earthenware pan or on a soapstone griddle. In Morocco soft soap or beaten egg yolk is first rubbed on the surface of the pan to make it smooth. When it is well heated a spoonful of batter is dropped on and cooked on both sides until lightly browned. These pancakes, a type of *rghaif,* puff up considerably, and go well with butter and honey.

Note: Another pancake popular in Morocco is the *beghrir,* which is a pale yellow yeast-semolina pancake cooked only on one side. It looks like a honey-comb with many little holes. To be good it must be very light; unfortunately this isn't always the case in Moroccan homes.

Stamp Pastries (*Taba*)

This Tetuanese dessert is made with eggs, flour or cornstarch, and a special iron usually patterned in the form of an eight-petaled rose.* The iron is first heated up by being dipped in fat, then slid over the batter and returned to the fat, where the picked-up batter cooks. The resulting pastry, light and golden

* Available in Scandinavian, German, and Italian stores.

yellow, is then immediately dipped into an orange flower water syrup called *knelba*. Piled high and decorated with almonds, *tabas* are a lovely sight.

INGREDIENTS

1 cup plus 1 teaspoon granulated sugar
1 tablespoon lemon juice
2 tablespoons orange flower water
2 eggs, plus 1 egg yolk
  Pinch of salt
1 cup all-purpose flour
1 cup milk, approximately
  Salad oil for frying
  Handful of slivered almonds, previously toasted
    in the oven

EQUIPMENT

2-quart stainless steel sauce-
  pan
Mixing bowl
Whisk
Deep fat fryer or deep-sided
  skillet
"Sockerstuvor rosette" iron
  at least 1 inch thick (with
  an eight-petaled flower de-
  sign)
Perforated spoon
Paper towels
Serving dish

Working time: 20 minutes
Waiting time: 2 hours
Cooking time: 20 minutes
Makes: 18 *tabas*

1. Make a syrup by boiling 1 cup sugar with 1¼ cups water and the lemon juice 5 minutes, or until it has thickened. Add the orange flower water and set aside to cool.

2. Beat the eggs and extra egg yolk, with a pinch of salt and the teaspoon of sugar, until creamy. Stir in the flour and enough milk to form a smooth batter. Let stand 2 hours, covered.

3. Pour oil to a depth of 2½ inches into the skillet or deep fryer. Heat to 375°.

4. Plunge the iron into the fat and immediately lift, drain, and dip into the batter. (Do not let batter run over top of rim; it will be difficult to remove from the rosette iron.) Immediately dip the batter-coated iron into the hot

fat and fry until the batter turns golden. (When cooked the *taba* will just start to slip off the iron.) Spoon out, drain on paper towels, dip into the cooled syrup, and place on the serving dish. Reheat the iron in the fat and repeat until all the batter is used.

5. Sprinkle the pastry with the slivered almonds and serve at room temperature.

MOROCCAN COOKIES

————◆————

Though the Moroccans make many types of cookies, only the *ghoribas* and *fekkas* seem unusual *and good* to me. However, to make up for the brevity of this section, I have included a recipe for the legendary *majoun*.

Semolina Cookies (*Ghoriba*)

These cookies are somewhat different from the traditional Middle Eastern and North African *ghoriba* in that they are based on semolina flour (hard wheat), which has its own marvelous taste and texture. These are lovely light cookies, sugar-dipped, the size of half-dollars.

When I was learning to make these cookies I was a good student, following the lead of all the ladies in the kitchen. Whatever they did I followed, but when it came time to making *ghoriba* mounds, with their perfectly shaped domes, I couldn't seem to get them right. No matter what I did I couldn't achieve the domes because the dough kept sticking to my palms. The other ladies, however, used a complicated rolling, clutching, squeezing, and back-and-forth motion that produced perfectly smooth balls and left their hands clean of dough. They then transferred the dough to their other palm, tapped the balls lightly, and produced one-inch discs with slightly raised domes that were smoother and much more celestial than mine.

I was glad, however, that when it finally came time to eat them our cookies tasted the same.

INGREDIENTS	EQUIPMENT
Sweet butter	Saucepan
¼ cup salad oil	Electric beater
2 large eggs	Mixing bowl
2 cups confectioners' sugar	Rubber spatula
2⅔ cups semolina flour	2 baking sheets
1 teaspoon double-acting baking powder	Flat plate
⅛ teaspoon salt	
½ teaspoon vanilla extract	*Working time:* 20 minutes
	Baking time: 15 to 18 minutes
	Makes: 3½ dozen cookies

1. Heat ¼ cup of butter in the oil. When melted, remove from the heat and set aside.

2. Use an electric beater to beat the eggs and 1⅔ cups of the confectioners' sugar together until soft and fluffy. Add the butter-oil mixture and beat a few seconds longer. Using the spatula, fold in the semolina flour, baking powder, salt, and vanilla. Blend well.

3. Preheat the oven to 350°.

4. Prepare the baking sheets by smearing with dabs of sweet butter. Place the remaining ⅓ cup confectioners' sugar in a flat dish. Form the cookies by pinching off walnut-sized balls of dough and rolling between your palms until a perfect sphere is formed. (Since the dough is very sticky, it's a good idea to moisten your hands from time to time.) Flatten the sphere slightly, dip one side into powdered sugar, and arrange on a buttered baking sheet.

5. Bake on the middle shelf of the preheated oven for 15 to 18 minutes. When they are done, the cookies will have expanded and crisscross breaks will appear on their tops. Allow to cool and crisp before storing.

Note: They will keep at least a month in an airtight tin container.

Anise-Flavored Melba Toast Rounds (*Fekkas*)

These little cookies must get their name from the "runner" chickens also called *fekkas*, for they are tough little things with a good taste. They are very popular for tea dunking, doubtless because they can stand the heat!

There are two ways to make them, the traditional way and the way that produces *krislettes*. *Krislettes* are not as popular as *fekkas*, possibly because it's hard to dunk diced cookies into tea, but they are good for exercising the teeth.

The traditional *fekkas* require two bakings, which in Morocco means sending trays of cookies twice to the community ovens. If you live far away, this can make life difficult. In fact, when I made these cookies I had to cross town to the house of a friend who had an oven nearby. The dough is rolled into foot-long cylinders and left to rise for an hour or two. These cylinders are then pricked all over and sent at once to the oven to be only partially baked. They are next returned to the house and left to harden all night. By the following morning they are very heavy. A thin-bladed knife is used to cut very fine slices, which are then sent back to the oven for a final baking. When the cookies are cool they are packed in tin boxes to be brought out for days afterwards for afternoon tea.

INGREDIENTS	EQUIPMENT
1 package active dry yeast	Small and large mixing bowls
3 to 3¼ cups pastry flour	Formica or marble work-
¼ teaspoon salt	space
Confectioners' sugar	2 baking sheets
½ cup sweet butter, melted and cooled	Towels
1 scant tablespoon aniseed	2 cake racks
1 scant tablespoon sesame seeds (toasted, optional)	
¼ cup orange flower water	

Working time: **40 minutes**
Rising time: **1½ to 2 hours**
Baking time: **30 minutes (approximately)**
Makes: **Enough cookies to fill a 1½-quart container**

1. The day before, soak the yeast in ¼ cup lukewarm water until bubbly.

2. Combine the flour, salt, 1¼ cups sugar, the bubbling yeast, cooled melted butter and spices in the large mixing bowl. Stir in the orange flower water and then enough lukewarm water to form a firm dough. Knead well until smooth, then turn out onto a board dusted with more confectioners' sugar. Break into 4 portions. Roll each into a ball and cover.

3. Take one of the balls and shape the dough into a 1-inch-thick cylinder by rolling back and forth with some force. The dough will be sticky at first, but after some strong, firm rolling with palms down it will start to stretch as you slide your palms toward the ends to lengthen the mass. Stretch and roll the dough until you have a 10- to 12-inch cylinder of even thickness. Repeat with the remaining balls. Place on the baking sheets, cover with towels, and let rise in a warm place until doubled in volume. When doubled, prick each tube with a fork to deflate.

4. Preheat the oven to 375°.

5. Bake the tubes 20 minutes, or until barely golden. (They should not be cooked through.) Remove from the oven and let cool on racks overnight.

6. The following day, slice the cylinders crosswise into very thin cookies and arrange flat on ungreased baking sheets. Bake in a 350° oven until pale golden brown and dry, about 10 minutes. When cool, store in airtight tins.

Kif Candy (*Majoun*)

This innocent-looking candy was once made in my presence in Morocco; but at the time I did not write down exactly what my friend Mohammed did. A disapproving Moroccan cook kept muttering to me, while Mohammed stirred and tasted the mixture. Needless to say he took quite a bit and spun around a frog pond four times before disappearing down the road at very high speed.

In searching out the proportions I came upon *The Hashish Cookbook* written by "Panama Rose" and published in New York. A little bit of detective work among the "Tangier Mafia" in New York revealed the identity of "Panama Rose," and from deduction I figured out she most likely learned to make *majoun* from Mohammed. Her recipe is very similar, except in the method of adding the *kif* (*cannabis*).

I deny, absolutely, that I have ever tested this recipe; on the other hand, let me tell you how Mohammed made *majoun:*

He placed about one pound of *smen* (Cooked and Salted Butter, page 39) in a casserole with plenty of water and about 3 cups stalks, seeds, and leaves of *kif*. After bringing it to a boil he let it simmer 2 hours, then carefully strained it into a large, deep roasting pan. He then threw away the stalks, seeds, and leaves and let the butter cool and rise to the top in the refrigerator overnight.

He then placed the butter in the casserole with 1 pound chopped dates, 1 pound chopped figs, ½ pound raisins, 1 teaspoon ground ginger, some ground cinnamon, 1 tablespoon aniseed, ½ cup dark, heavy honey, and ½ cup each ground almonds and walnuts (these proportions are from *The Hashish Cookbook*). He then cooked all this together until it became very thick and brown. He added some orange flower water and *ras el hanout* to taste, and packed the *majoun* in clean jars.

My suggestion: Eat with care—never more than one tablespoon at a time.

Note: This recipe should not be confused with the kifless but still potent *majoun* of Tetuán—a marmalade laced with aga wood and ambergris.

SWEET SUPPER DISHES or PREDESSERTS

I would love to say something romantic about these sweet supper dishes, often served after a rich and nourishing soup or a succession of meat or chicken *tagines*, though not strictly speaking as desserts. However, good-tasting and substantial as they are, I cannot think of them without beginning to laugh, recalling some experiences in Moroccan homes when there were no guests for dinner and the evenings were devoted to watching TV.

It seemed almost absurd to me to sit at a table with a Moroccan family, devouring these sublime sweet dishes with large tablespoons from a communal platter while we watched the tube, where third-rate Saudi Arabian love stories were being enacted with much feverish movements of the eyes. However, since centuries of invasions, the rise and fall of mighty dynasties, and forty-three years of being a "protectorate" of France have not destroyed this culture, it will probably survive the horrors of the television age.

Sweet Dessert Couscous

A palace dish—very rich and good, though its sweetness can be overwhelming, even when followed by ice-cold milk. A good after-theater dish to be served following the scrambled eggs described on page 58 and *harira* (page 59).

Correctly this should be made with *seffa*, a type of *couscous* that is finely rolled semolina and water with other flour omitted. As I've noted, this finer form of *couscous* is not yet available in the United States, but you can simulate its lightness and texture by steaming ordinary *couscous* an extra time.

INGREDIENTS	EQUIPMENT
2 pounds *couscous* or *seffa*	Large, shallow pan
11 tablespoons sweet butter	Sieve
1 cup whole, blanched almonds	Small saucepan
1 cup shelled and peeled walnuts	Chopping knife
5 tablespoons granulated sugar	Electric blender
Salt	Mixing bowl
½ pound dates, pitted and chopped	*Couscousiere*
Ground cinnamon	Cheesecloth
Confectioners' sugar	Large serving platter

Working time: 30 minutes
Total steaming time: 1 hour
Serves: 12 (as part of a Moroccan dinner)

1. Follow step 1 (first washing and drying of *couscous*) in the master instructions, page 136). (If for some reason you are able to obtain real *smeeda*, used to make *seffa*, ignore this step. Simply dampen before steaming.)

2. Melt 5 tablespoons of the butter. Chop the nuts coarsely, then pulverize them with the granulated sugar in the blender. Knead with 3 tablespoons of the melted butter to make a paste.

3. Fill the bottom of the *couscousiere* with plenty of water and bring to a boil. Then rub inside of the top container with butter. Follow steps 2 and 3 (first steaming and second drying of the *couscous*) in the master instructions (page 136). Steam the *couscous* 30 minutes.

4. Toss the drying *couscous* with the remaining 2 tablespoons butter.

5. Return the grain to top container and continue steaming 20 minutes, fastening the top to the bottom as instructed on page 136. Dump out again and slowly work in about 2 cups water and 1 tablespoon salt. (If you continuously work the grains and *then* add 3 or 4 tablespoons of water at a time, the *couscous* will easily absorb the 2 cups. If, on the other hand, you add water too quickly and the grains do not absorb it, simply spread them out and let them dry for a while.) Rub the nut paste between your fingers and toss with the dried *couscous* grains.

6. Steam the dates alone 15 minutes in the top part of the *couscousiere*. Remove the dates and pile the *couscous* back for a final steaming of 10 minutes. Mix with the dates and remaining butter. Arrange in an elongated mound and decorate with lines of cinnamon shooting from the top like rays of sunlight. Serve with spoons and ice-cold milk, and with confectioners' sugar separately in a bowl.

Note: A handful of raisins or fried almonds can be substituted for the nut paste and dates. In this case the dish is called *msfouf*.

Sweet Steamed Rice (*Roz Mafooar*)

Rice can be steamed like *couscous*, decorated with cinnamon and sugar, and served with a cold glass of milk as an evening dish. It is delicious when preceded by a bowl of soup or a *tagine kebab meghdor* (Seared Lamb Kebabs Cooked in Butter, page 238).

Of course you can prepare steamed rice the French way, which is easier and will give you an excellent result, but if you handle rice just as you do *couscous* you will get absolutely separate grains, and that is a fine point that can *make* this dish. It will come out light and airy and will look splendid piled high on a silver dish streaked with confectioners' sugar and ground cinnamon.

INGREDIENTS

Vegetable oil
3 cups raw rice, preferably long grain
¼ cup sweet butter
Salt to taste
Confectioners' sugar
Ground cinnamon

EQUIPMENT

Couscousiere with cover
Cheesecloth
Large, shallow pan or basin
Wooden spoon
Large serving plate

Working time: 15 minutes
Steaming time: 1 hour approximately
Serves: 12

1. Toss the dry rice with oiled fingers until all the grains are lightly coated. Bring plenty of water to a boil in the bottom of a *couscousiere*. Pile the rice into the lightly oiled top container. Fit top onto bottom as for making *couscous* (page 136), *cover* the top container tightly, and steam 20 minutes.

2. Dump the rice into the shallow pan and sprinkle with water. Press the rice down with the spoon to break up lumps and enable the rice to absorb the water, then stir up and smooth out again. Sprinkle with a little more water and let stand 5 minutes. Pile back into the top part of the *couscousiere*.

3. Steam 20 minutes, *tightly* covered, being certain no steam escapes from the sides.

4. Dump out again and sprinkle with salted water, working it in as you would with *couscous* and raking it to keep it fluffy. Spread out to dry for 5 to 10 minutes, then pile back into the top container.

5. Steam again 10 minutes, then turn out and break up the lumps. Stir in the butter and some salt to taste. Form a huge mound on a serving plate and dust with confectioners' sugar and streaks of cinnamon, as described in step 6 on page 317.

Moroccan Rice Pudding (*Roz Bil Hleeb*)

In Morocco, where the electric blender is virtually unknown, the execution of this recipe is a long and arduous task. The pounding of the almonds alone is a labor of love, and they are only used as a base for milk, orange flower water, and other ingredients that will overwhelm them. It also takes a long time to knead the almond paste in water and then extract all the resulting juices. The cooking is long, but requires little attention if the burners of your stove can be set at a very low heat; otherwise you will have to stir often to avoid burning the rice.

The decoration of this dish is very simple: the rice is presented in an enormous bowl spotted with 4 dabs of sweet butter just on the verge of melting. Each guest is given a large spoon and the pudding is eaten in communal style.

Roz bil hleeb is good cold and will keep a few days in the refrigerator.

⅓ cup whole, blanched almonds

2¼ cups medium- or small-grain rice

½ cup confectioners' sugar

2 three-inch cinnamon sticks

½ cup butter

½ teaspoon salt

½ teaspoon almond extract

2 quarts milk (approximately) (may be half fresh and half condensed milk)

⅓ cup orange flower water

Chopping knife

Electric blender

Sieve

Heavy-bottomed 4-quart saucepan with cover

Very large serving bowl

Working time: 10 minutes

Cooking time: 1 hour 20 minutes

Serves: 12

1. Chop the almonds coarsely, then liquefy in the blender with ½ cup very hot water. Press through the sieve into the saucepan. Return the almond pulp to the blender and add another ½ cup hot water. Whirl in the blender again, then sieve into the saucepan once more.

2. Add 2 cups water to the almond milk and bring to a boil. Sprinkle in the rice, sugar, and cinnamon, then add half the butter, ½ teaspoon salt, the almond extract, and 1 quart milk. Bring to a boil, then reduce the heat, cover, and simmer 30 minutes, adding more milk if necessary.

3. Continue cooking the rice, adding more milk and stirring often until the whole is thick and velvety, but loose. As the milk becomes absorbed add more; in all you will need about 2 quarts milk. Add the orange flower water and taste for sweetness. (The dish should be barely sweet; add more sugar if desired.)

4. Continue cooking for 15 to 20 minutes, stirring continuously to prevent the rice from burning.

5. Pour into the serving bowl and decorate with the remaining butter, in 4 dabs.

Pudding (*Mulhalabya*)

This Tetuanese dish comes from the Middle East. The recipe was given to me by a young Tetuanese girl who told me the modern way to serve *mulhalabya* is with a fruit cocktail underneath. However, I prefer it "straight" and find its slightly shimmery, not-quite-firm texture soothing.

INGREDIENTS

5 tablespoons cornstarch
3 cups cold milk
½ cup granulated sugar (or to taste)
2 tablespoons orange flower water
½ teaspoon grated lemon peel (optional)
½ cup whole, blanched almonds
   Salad oil for frying
½ teaspoon ground cinnamon

EQUIPMENT

Small mixing bowl
3-quart stainless-steel or enameled cast-iron saucepan
Individual serving dishes
Skillet
Spatula
Paper towels
Nut grinder or chopping knife

Working time: 10 minutes
Cooking time: 5 minutes
Serves: 6

1. Mix the cornstarch with ½ cup of the cold milk to a smooth paste. Heat the remaining milk to a boil, then lower the heat and mix in cornstarch mixture, all but 2 tablespoons of the sugar, and stir constantly with a wooden spoon until thickened—that is, when a thick coating appears on the back of the spoon. Stir in the orange flower water and optional lemon peel. Remove from the heat, and pour into individual serving dishes.

2. Brown the almonds in the oil, drain on paper towels, and crush well. Mix with the remaining 2 tablespoons sugar and the cinnamon. When a skin

begins to appear on the surface of the pudding—and *not* before—sprinkle with the almond mixture. Chill.

Moroccan Cream of Wheat (*Herbel*)

This is a favorite dish of Berbers, and, by custom, is eaten on New Year's day.

The new wheat is soaked in hot water for over 24 hours and then drained and pounded in a wooden mortar, after which it is sieved, to remove the husks, and cooked a long time (5 to 6 hours) over a charcoal brazier. It is then seasoned with salt and made creamy with fresh milk and butter.

To make it, simmer 1 cup whole wheat grains in 4 cups water for 3 hours, adding a little sugar and milk at the end. Dab with butter.

Cornmeal Porridge (*Asidah*)

Someone called this dish "the hamburger of the Souss." *Asidah* is made from white corn (hominy grits), boiled in water to cover for hours until it is like a creamy pudding, thick and pale yellow, salty and buttery from the addition of a good dollop of *smen*. The first three fingers of the right hand are used to pluck some *asidah* from the communal plate, dip it into liquid *smen* and then convey it to the mouth. The men of the Souss say that *asidah* makes them virile and strong.

Sweet Bisteeya with Milk and Almonds (*Keneffa*)

This specialty of Marrakesh is considered a regal ending to an important meal, when you feel fruit would not be enough. Actually, it is and it isn't, depending on how you feel about watching a delicate creation destroyed before your eyes. The *warka* leaves (you can substitute phyllo or strudel dough) are fried, two at a time, until golden crisp, then drained and piled high (sometimes as high as 16 inches) with browned almonds and thickened almond-milk sauce spooned between layers. It looks splendid, until you are forced to serve it by cutting it with a knife. Immediately the frail tender leaves break into a million pieces, become soggy in the sauce, and 5 minutes later you are facing a decimated and badly crumbled mass.

There is however another way: you can put just a tiny bit of milk sauce between the layers and serve the major part in small bowls as "dips" for each guest. By this method *keneffa* more or less maintains its dignity while being consumed.

INGREDIENTS

- 5 phyllo or strudel leaves or 20 eight-inch *warka* leaves (page 103)
- Salad oil for frying
- 1 cup whole, blanched almonds
- 2 tablespoons confectioners' sugar
- Ground cinnamon
- 3½ tablespoons cornstarch
- 1 quart plus ⅓ cup milk
- ½ cup superfine granulated sugar
- Pinch of salt
- 2 to 4 tablespoons ground blanched almonds
- 2 tablespoons rosewater or orange flower water

EQUIPMENT

Scissors
Large skillet
Paper towels
Chopping knife or rolling pin
Small mixing bowl
3½-quart stainless steel or enameled cast-iron casserole
Large chop plate

Working time: 30 minutes
Cooking time: 15 minutes
Serves: 6

1. Early in the day, separate the leaves of pastry and cut into uniform 8-inch circles. (When working with phyllo or strudel dough remember to keep the leaves you are not actually handling under a towel so they do not dry out.)

2. Put the oil in the skillet to a depth of ½ inch and heat. Fry the pastry leaves (2 pressed together at a time) on both sides until pale golden and crisp, adjusting the heat to avoid browning. Drain on paper towels. Make 10 sets. (Fry the *warka* the same way.) Leave the oil in the skillet.

3. Brown the whole almonds in the oil. Drain and, when cool, chop coarsely or crush with a rolling pin. Mix with confectioners' sugar and cinnamon to taste.

4. Blend the cornstarch in the ⅓ cup cold milk to a paste. Heat the remaining milk to boiling with the superfine sugar and pinch of salt. Stirring constantly with a wooden spoon, add the paste and cook until thick or until the sauce coats the back of the spoon. Add the ground almonds and perfumed water. Whisk until very smooth and continue cooking 1 minute. Remove from the heat and let cool in the pan. Chill, if desired.

5. Later in the day, just before serving, assemble the *bisteeya*, or *keneffa*. Place 2 sets of leaves on the chop plate and sprinkle with half the chopped browned almonds. Cover with 3 sets of leaves and spoon over 2 spoonfuls of milk sauce. Cover with another 2 sets of leaves and sprinkle with the remaining almonds. Cover with the remaining leaves and spoon over 1 or 2 spoonfuls of sauce. Serve the remaining milk sauce as described in the introduction or pour around the *keneffa*.

TWELVE

———◆———

Beverages

You will see water sellers in *souks* throughout Morocco, portioning out their penny's worth of liquid after elaborate exercises designed to convince the buyer that his cup has been hygienically rinsed. While the poor buy water by the cup, however, the rich drink water that has been perfumed with gum arabic or the essence of orange blossoms. In Fez I once had a deliciously refreshing drink served between the spicy courses of a lengthy meal. I was told the method for making the perfumed water: some grains of gum arabic are thrown into a charcoal brazier and then an empty water jug is inverted over the fumes. Afterwards the jug is filled with water, which catches the aromatic scent.

Fruit juices are popular in this country, where Islam forbids the consumption of alcohol. One often drinks orange juice and lemonade flavored with orange flower water, and sometimes, too, concoctions of pomegranate and lemon juice, and grape juice flavored with cinnamon.

Sharbat (a fruit or nut milk drink) is particularly rich, cool, and satisfying served in the late afternoon on hot days when dinner will be late and members of the household need sustenance.

Apple Milk Drink (*Sharbat*)

INGREDIENTS

2 red eating apples
2 tablespoons granulated sugar
2 scant teaspoons rosewater or orange flower
   water
2 cups cold milk
   Shaved ice (optional)

EQUIPMENT

Vegetable peeler
Paring knife
Electric blender
Small glasses

Working time: 5 minutes
Serves: 2 to 4

Peel and cube the apples. Place in the blender jar with the sugar, perfumed water, and milk. Whirl at high speed 15 seconds. Serve, with shaved ice, if desired, in small glasses.

Almond Milk Drink (*Sharbat Bil Looz*)

INGREDIENTS

½ pound whole blanched almonds
½ cup granulated sugar
   Orange blossom water or rosewater
1 cup milk

EQUIPMENT

Electric blender
Strainer
Mixing bowl
Small glasses

Working time: 10 minutes
Serves: 4

Blend the almonds with the sugar, a dash of perfumed water, and 1 cup water until smooth. Pour through a strainer, pressing down hard with the back of a wooden spoon to extract as much liquid as possible. Stir in 1 more cup water and the milk. Chill and serve in small glasses.

Note: If the flavor is bland, add a dash of almond extract.

Coffee Ras el Hanout (*Maure Kaoua*)

For those who love to play with spices, coffee with *ras el hanout* has got to be some kind of *ne plus ultra*. The mixture of peppery and sweet spices give it a flavor that is both sweet and warm, mysterious and indefinable.

I have met Moroccans who dismiss this kind of coffee as "low class," but I also know others who drink it regularly, and even one family from Rabat whose members add grilled ground chick-peas to give the coffee an additionally strange and smoky flavor.

INGREDIENTS

2 whole nutmegs (about 4 teaspoons ground nutmeg)
4 blades cinnamon (about 1 teaspoon ground cinnamon)
6 to 8 dried rosebuds
12 whole cloves (about ½ teaspoon ground cloves)
⅛ teaspoon gum arabic
1 tablespoon ground ginger
2 pieces of galingale* (about ½ teaspoon ground galingale)
2 allspice berries (about ⅛ teaspoon ground allspice)
¾ teaspoon ground white pepper
3 blades mace (about ½ teaspoon ground mace)
15 white or green cardamom pods
1 teaspoon fennel seeds
1 teaspoon aniseed
1 tablespoon sesame seeds

EQUIPMENT

Electric blender
Fine-wired strainer
Small container with screw-on top

Makes: ⅓ cup (approximately)

* Known also as *laos;* available at H. Roth & Sons (see Appendix A).

1. Combine the spices in an electric spice grinder or blender. Sieve and bottle carefully to preserve the freshness.

2. When making coffee, add ¼ teaspoon to every ½ cup ground coffee before making coffee in your usual fashion. (It makes no difference whether you are using black Turkish-style coffee or American roast.)

MOROCCAN TEA

———◆———

Moroccans, along with the Chinese, the Japanese, and the British, are a people who make an enormous fuss over tea. Tea is often served before and always after every meal, is sipped for endless hours in Moorish cafés, and is prepared at any hour of the day or night that a friend or stranger enters a Moroccan home.

One of the most interesting articles I have ever read about Morocco was published several years ago by Paul Bowles. He wrote of the ambience and meaning of Moorish cafés, and in so doing explored much of the meaning of Moroccan life in sensual terms.

Tea first came to Morocco in the 1800s, brought from the Far East by British traders who quickly found a limitless market. It is always served in small glasses decorated with colored rings, arranged on a tray (usually silver) etched in elaborate concentric circles. It is poured from a high-held, silver-plated pot of the so-called "Manchester" shape.

I loved Moroccan tea from the first moment I drank it—loved its excessive sweetness and its strong minty taste. (Spearmint is considered the best for tea, but other kinds of mint will do.) The seasonal addition of fresh white orange blossoms will perfume tea even further, and I have been informed that some Moroccans also add scraped ambergris.

There is something sublime about sitting in a familiar Moorish café. My favorite is perched high on rocks in the Marshan of Tangier, overlooking the Straits of Gibraltar, where hawks hang in mid-air and then drop suddenly down. I've spent hours there holding a glass, thumb on its bottom and fore-finger on its rim, inhaling its sweet essence, then slowly sipping.

Everyone, of course, makes tea his own way, but there is a basic formula. First you should use green tea, preferably the type known as Gunpowder or Chun Mee. Secondly, the spearmint should be fresh—dried mint from bottles simply won't do. Thirdly, and very important, the pot should be absolutely clean.

To make a 3-cup pot (enough for 6 small glasses) rinse the pot with boiling water and then throw this water away. Put in 1 tablespoon tea, ⅓ cup sugar, and a handful of fresh spearmint. Cover with boiling water and allow the tea to "steep" for *at least* 3 minutes, stirring a little at the end, but not too much. Then pour out a glass, look at it, taste it, and correct the sweetness if necessary before serving.

Traditionally you drink three glasses (whether at a reception, at teatime, or after dinner) before taking your leave. Today this rule is rarely observed, and in a Moorish café all rules are meaningless; you sip for hours, you talk, you read, and you enjoy.

WINES AND LIQUEURS

◆

The Koran, of course, forbids the use of alcohol, but Moroccan Jews have for many years distilled liqueurs from such things as pomegranates, grapes, raisins, dates, and honeycombs. There is a famous colorless aniseed-flavored fig brandy called *mahya* that is brewed by the Jews of Telouet in the High Atlas Mountains.

When the French took over Morocco they immediately planted vineyards, just as they had in Algeria and Tunisia. Today the three countries of the Maghreb produce nearly 10 percent of the world's wine, some of it very good and very inexpensive. The principal Moroccan vineyards are around Rabat and between Meknes and Fez, but to me the most interesting Moroccan wine, and one that is quite good and unique, is the Gris de Boulaouane—the so-called "gray" rosé made from grapes grown south of Casablanca.

Red wines of note are Cabernet, Vieux Papes and Sidi Larbi. The white wines are Chaudsoleil, l'Oustalet, and Valpierre.

Appendixes

A: *Suppliers and Sources for Mail Order*

Dean & DeLuca, Inc.
121 Prince Street
New York, N.Y. 10012
(Almonds, assorted flours, honey, chick peas, shallow porcelain dishes, roasted pimientos from Spain, French orange flower water, *couscousieres*, *couscous* by weight, spices)

Peloponnese Products
Aegean Trader
P.O. Box 1015
Point Reyes Station, Calif. 94956
(Quality olives, including Napfplion, Kalamatas and cracked-green; extra-virgin olive oil, fragrant dried thyme and oregano)

Sahadi Importing Company, Inc.
187 Atlantic Avenue
Brooklyn, N.Y. 11201
(Olives, spices, *za'atar*-plain, black cardamon, white truffles)

Karnig Tashjian
Middle East & Oriental Foods
380 Third Avenue
New York, N.Y. 10016
(*Kadaif* pastry, phyllo pastry, olives, spices)

Fred Bridge and Company
212 East 52nd Street
New York, N.Y. 10022
(12–, 13–, and 14–inch *bisteeya* pans, large shallow porcelain baking pans)

Casa Moneo
210 West 10th Street
New York, N.Y. 10011
(Shallow earthenware *cazuelas* to be used in place of *tagine* pans)

Aphrodisia Products, Inc.
28 Carmine Street
New York, N.Y. 10014
(Spices)

Williams-Sonoma
P.O. Box 7456
San Francisco, Calif. 94120-7456
   (*Couscousieres*)

Frieda's Finest Produce Specialties, Inc.
P.O. Box 58488
Los Angeles, Calif.
   (Unusual fresh vegetables: write to locate a
   nearby store)

D'Artagnan
399–419 St. Paul Avenue
Jersey City, N.J. 07306
   (Fresh free-range chickens)

Summerfield Farm
Route 1
Box 43
Boyce, Va. 22620
   (Quality lamb and baby lambs for
   mechoui)

Glen Echo Farms
Wendell, N.H. 03783
   (Quality lamb and baby lambs for
   mechoui)

Almond Growers Exchange
1802 C Street
Sacramento, Calif. 95814
   (Fresh whole almonds)

B: *Weights and Measures*

Pinch	⅛ teaspoon	7 drops
1 teaspoon	⅓ tablespoon	60 drops (⅙ fluid ounce)
3 teaspoons	1 tablespoon	½ ounce
4 tablespoons	¼ cup	2 ounces
5⅓ tablespoons	⅓ cup	2⅔ ounces
8 tablespoons	½ cup	4 ounces
12 tablespoons	¾ cup	6 ounces
16 tablespoons	1 cup	8 ounces
2 cups	1 pint	16 ounces
4 cups	2 pints	1 liquid quart

A *Table of Equivalents for This Book*

INGREDIENT	AMOUNT	EQUIVALENT
Almonds		
unshelled, whole	1 pound	1½ cup nutmeats
shelled, whole or slivered	5½ ounces	1 cup nutmeats
	½ pound	1½ cups nutmeats
shelled, grated by nut grinder	5½ ounces	2 cups grated nutmeats
shelled, grated by electric blender	5½ ounces	1½ cups nutmeats
Butter		
¼ stick	1 ounce	2 tablespoons
½ stick	2 ounces	¼ cup
1 stick	4 ounces	½ cup
1½ sticks	6 ounces	¾ cup
2 sticks	½ pound	1 cup (16 tablespoons)
4 sticks	1 pound	2 cups
Chick-peas		
	½ cup dried	½ can or 1 cup cooked
	1 cup dried (½ pound)	1 can or 2 cups cooked
Couscous		
	1½ pounds	4 cups
Dates		
	1 pound	2 cups pitted

Flour
all-purpose	1	pound	4½ cups
cake flour	1	pound	5 cups
semolina flour	1	pound	2⅔ cups

Garlic

⅛ teaspoon   1 medium clove

Green coriander

1 cup leaves   ½ cup chopped

Lemon

2 large   ½ cup juice (approx.)

Onions

3 oz.	1 medium onion
4 oz.	1 cup diced
5 oz.	½ cup grated
1 pound	1½ cups grated or 3½ to 4 cups sliced
12 oz.	1 cup grated

Phyllo pastry leaves

1 pound   25 sheets (approx.)

Prunes

1 pound	2½ cups dried
1 pound	4 cups cooked

Rice

½ pound	1 cup raw
1 cup raw	3 cups cooked

Sugar
Confectioners'

1 pound	4½ cups
2¾ ounces	1 cup

Granulated and superfine

1 pound	2½ cups
6½ ounces	1 cup

Tomatoes

1 pound	3 medium
1 pound	1¼ cups pulp

C: *Suggested Menus*

DINNER FOR 8 (I)

Bisteeya (page 108)
Chicken with Lemon and Olives (pages 189–196)
Omar's Couscous (page 142)
Moroccan Bread (page 51)
Fruit

DINNER FOR 8 (II)

Five Salads:
Orange, Lettuce, and Walnut Salad (page 81)
A Tomato and Green Pepper Salad (pages 69–74)
Carrot Salad (page 75)
Zeilook (page 67)
Mohk (Brain Salad I or II, pages 86, 87)
Djej Mechoui (Roasted Chicken, page 212)
Seksu dar Marhzin (Pumpkin Couscous, page 140)
Moroccan Bread (page 51)
Fruit

DINNER FOR 8 (III)

Fish (Shad) Baked with Stuffed Fruit (page 169)
Lamb Tagine with Zucchini and Za'atar (page 273)
Seksu Tanjaoui (Tangier Couscous, page 153)
Moroccan Bread (page 51)
Fruit

BERBER DINNER FOR 8 TO 10

Kouah (Skewered and Grilled Liver, page 237)
Byesar (Puree of Fava Beans, page 92)
Mechoui (Roasted Lamb, page 234), Served on Lemon Leaves
Cheesha Belboula (Berber Couscous with Barley Grits, page 158)
Hot Miklee (page 127), with Butter and Honey
Moroccan Bread (page 51)

TETUÁN DINNER FOR 8 TO 10

Balakia (Bisteeya, Tetuán Style, page 114)
Marak Silk (Tagine of Swiss Chard, page 90)
Lamb with Okra, "Roof Tile" Style (page 275)
Moroccan Bread (page 51)
Mulhalabya (Pudding, page 320)

FEZ DINNER FOR 8 TO 10

Four Assorted Salads (pages 66–88)
Djej bil Hamus (Chicken with Chick Peas, page 203)
Tagine bil Babcock (Tagine of Lamb with Prunes and Apples, page 283)
Moroccan Bread (page 51)
Melon

MARRAKESH DINNER FOR 8

Kefta (pages 247–254)
Djej Emshmel (Chicken with Lemons and Olives Emshmel, page 192)
Tagine Kebab Meghdor (Seared Lamb Kebabs Cooked in Butter, page 238)
Moroccan Bread (page 51)
Keneffa (Sweet Bisteeya with Milk and Almonds, page 322)

RAMADAN DINNER FOR 8

Harira I or II (pages 58, 60)
Scrambled Eggs
Dates
Shebbakia (Free-Form Honey Cake, page 303)
A Fragrant Lamb Tagine (pages 254 to 264)
Moroccan Bread (page 51)

FAMILY DINNER FOR 6

Kefta Mkaouara (Meatball, Tomato, and Egg Tagine, page 250)
Djej Mafooar (Steamed Chicken, page 216)
Moroccan Bread (page 51)
Fruit

FAMILY DINNER FOR 6

Marak Matisha bil Melokhias (Tagine of Okra and Tomatoes, page 91)
Beef Tagine with Cauliflower (page 265)
Couscous with Seven Vegetables in the Fez Manner (page 145)
Moroccan Bread (page 51)
Fruit

D: *Glossary*

Agadir   A Southern port town on the Atlantic coast, in the heart of the Souss.

Aid el Kebir   The Festival of the Sacrifice of the Lamb, occurring on the tenth day of the twelfth month of the Muslim calendar and commemorating the sacrifice of Abraham.

Atlas   Any one of three mountain ranges (the Middle Atlas, the High Atlas, or the Anti-Atlas) that run roughly east to west across Morocco.

Baqqula   A wild Moroccan herb combining the tastes of watercress, arugula, and sorrel.

Baraka   A special kind of God-given luck, often associated with leadership.

Berber   The original inhabitants of North Africa, now constituting about 80 percent of the Moroccan population. By religion they are Muslim, but their ethnic origin is not Arab.

Bled   The countryside.

Bisteeya   Perhaps the greatest of all Moroccan dishes, a pie of fine pastry stuffed with chicken, eggs, almonds, spices, and covered with cinnamon and sugar. Also, the generic term for a variety of pastry dishes.

Caid   A governor or chief. Usually appointed.

Casablanca   The largest city in Morocco, as well as the principal port and center of business and commerce. Not especially known for its cuisine.

Casbah   A fort or fortified castle.

Charmoula   Marinade for fish.

Coque   A small wild artichoke.

Couscous   Two meanings: (1) the national dish of Morocco, prepared in numerous variations; (2) the tiny balls of rolled semolina flour with which the dish is made.

Couscousiere   The utensil in which *couscous* is cooked.

Dar Mahkzen   Palace.

Diffa   Moroccan banquet.

Djej   Chicken.

Djemaa el Fna   The great square of Marrakesh.

Erfoud   An oasis famous for its many varieties of dates.

Essaouira   A port town on the Atlantic coast, due west of Marrakesh. Essaouira had a large Jewish population, and is something of a gastronomic center.

Fassi	A person from Fez. Sometimes used to refer to the powerful and wealthy elite of that city.
Fez	A great inland city, the oldest of the four royal capitals. One of the three great gastronomic centers of Morocco.
Gdra del Trid	An enameled earthenware dome used for stretching the dough for the classic Arab dish, *trid*.
Gsaa	A large, shallow wooden or clay basin used for kneading dough.
Imilchil	A tiny town in the Middle Atlas, the site of the famous Berber *moussem* called The Festival of the Betrothed.
Istiqlal	Name of the Independence party, whose original members were instrumental in ending the French Protectorate.
Kefta	Ground meat.
Kif	Marijuana.
Kimia	A kind of magic that gives its possessor the power to multiply food.
Kissaria	The portion of a *medina* devoted to commerce.
Kliir	A kind of preserved meat, similar to *basturma*.
Koutoubia Mosque	The largest and most famous building in Marrakesh.
Ksra	Moroccan bread from the *bled* (countryside).
Maghreb	That portion of North Africa encompassing Morocco, Algeria, and Tunisia.
Marrakesh	A great city in southern Morocco, one of the four royal capitals and one of the three gastronomic centers.
Mechoui	Berber-style spit-roasted lamb. Can also be used to describe a form of roasting chicken.
Medina	The old quarter of a Moroccan city, usually a place of closely built homes with few windows, and narrow, mazelike streets.
Meknes	Somewhat west of Fez, one of the four royal capitals and a city of gastronomic importance. Built, like Versailles, as a royal enclave.
Mhamnsa	Large semolina pellets.
Moussem	A Berber festival, usually with some religious significance, at which Berber folk-dancing and singing may be observed and Berber food tasted.
Nasrani	Literally, a Nazarene—that is, a Christian. Used by Moroccans to describe non-Muslim foreigners such as Europeans and Americans.
Pasha	Similar to the mayor of a large city.
Ramadan	The Muslim month of fasting.
Rif	The most northern range of mountains in Morocco, running parallel to the Mediterranean.
Safi	An important city, south of Casablanca and north of Essaouira on the Atlantic coast, known for certain fish and seafood specialties.
Sebou	An important river that runs from the Middle Atlas, through Fez, to the Atlantic. Famous for its delicious trout and shad.

Sefrou	A town south of Fez with a large Jewish population. Known for some delicacies.
Seffa	Fine rolled semolina flour containing no additions of other flours.
Shaban	Total satisfaction, as at the end of a Moroccan *diffa*.
Smeeda	Semolina flour.
Smen	Preserved butter.
Souk	Shop, store, or stall where things are bought and sold.
Souss	Southwest region of Morocco.
Sultan	The king of Morocco.
Tagine	A slowly simmered Moroccan stew, the basic Moroccan dish—there are literally hundreds of recipes for *tagines*.
Tagine slaoui	The shallow earthenware pot in which a *tagine* is cooked and also served. Has a high conical top.
Tangier	Important Moroccan city, situated on the Straits of Gilbraltar, known for its cosmopolitan atmosphere. Perhaps the most Europeanized Moroccan town.
Tetuán	One of the three great gastronomic cities of Morocco, where the cuisine shows a strong Andalusian influence.
Tobsil del bisteeya	The pan in which *bisteeya* is cooked.
Tobsil del warka	The pan upon which *warka* leaves are cooked.
Warka	Fine pastry leaves, used in *bisteeya* and other dishes.
Za'atar	An herb, close to orégano, marjoram, and thyme, found only in the Mediterranean region.

Bibliography

Some Books on Morocco and Moroccan cookery

Barbour, Nevill. *Morocco*. London, 1965.

Bowles, Paul. *Their Heads Are Green and Their Hands Are Blue*. New York, 1963.

Bute, John. Fourth Marquis of. *Moorish Recipes*. London, 1954.

Cowan, George D., and Johnston, L. N. *Moorish Lotus Leaves*. London, 1883.

Field, Michael and Frances. *A Quintet of Cuisines*. New York, 1970.

Guinaudeau, Z. *Fes vu par sa cuisine*. Rabat, 1958.

Harris, Walter. *The Land of an African Sultan*. New York, 1889.

Landry, Robert. *Les soleils de la cuisine*. Paris, 1966.

Laoust, E. *Mots et choses berbères dialetes de Maroc*. Paris, 1920.

Legey, Françoise. *The Folklore of Morocco*. London, 1935.

Maxwell, Gavin. *Lords of the Atlas*. London, 1966.

Meakin, Budgett. *The Moors*. London, 1902.

Oppenheim, Monah. *Contributions to the Culinary Art: A Collection of Family Recipes and Cookery Clues*. New York, 1961.

Perrier, Amelia. *A Winter in Morocco*. London, 1873.

Roden, Claudia, *A Book of Middle Eastern Food*. New York, 1972.

Sefroui, Ahmed. *The Moussem at Imilchil*. Rabat, 1967.

Smires, Latifa Bennani. *La cuisine marocaine*. Paris, 1971.

Westermarch, Edward. *Wit and Wisdom of Morocco*. New York, 1931.

Index